MASTERY THROUGH ACCOMPLISHMENT

Developing Inner Strength for Life's Challenges

Mastery Through Accomplishment

Developing Inner Strength for Life's Challenges

Hazrat Inayat Khan

OMEGA PRESS

1985

For information on the Sufi Order in the West
founded by Hazrat Inayat Khan write to Sufi Order,
P.O. Box 574, Lebanon Springs, N.Y. 12114, in the
United States, or l'Ordre Soufi, 23 Rue de la
Tuilerie, 92150 Suresnes, France, in Europe.

Mastery Through Accomplishment
© 1978 by Sufi Order. All rights reserved.
Revised printing 1985

OMEGA PRESS
P.O. BOX 574
LEBANON SPRINGS, N.Y. 12114

Printed in the United States of America
ISBN 0-930872-07-X (paper)
Library of Congress # 79-101639

EDITOR'S NOTE

The material in this book was gathered from transcripts of talks given on the subject of attainment by Hazrat Inayat Khan. The lectures in this book cover the whole period of Hazrat Inayat Khan's teaching, from 1917 to 1926. Because attainment was a central theme of his teaching, he returned to the subject again and again. Thus, inevitably, there was a repetition of certain material, which the reader will notice in this volume. Rather than edit out the repetitions, we have left the lectures essentially as Hazrat Inayat Khan spoke them in order to retain as far as possible the flavor of the original teaching. These teachings include previously unpublished material, such as The Githas on Sadhana, as well as material culled from various volumes of the Sufi Message series: "The Purpose of Life" from Volume I, and chapters from other volumes, particularly Volumes VI, VII and VIII. The original selection of material was done by Taj Inayat.

—Munir Graham

DEDICATION

This new edition of *Mastery Through Accomplishment* was made possible through an anonymous donation given in remembrance of a beautiful and courageous singer who died in December 1984 at the young age of 56. Although she never read this book, her life exemplified the teachings of Hazrat Inayat Khan in this important volume and it seems fitting that its republication has been dedicated to her.

Judith Raskin was internationally recognized in her early 30's for her angelic quality of voice and great poetry and musicianship. After an operation for breast cancer, she began trusting herself to life on a deeper level and so overcoming her fear of dying. To her surprise, she remained alive. She also discovered the depths of her willpower as she regained use of an arm that doctors predicted would be permanently paralyzed.

Her musical career and inner growth continued for the rest of her life and increasingly she also experienced great satisfaction in training young singers and developing public interest in the performing arts. She shared with students, colleagues and her own family and friends the secret of discovering and manifesting their unique gifts by patiently trusting their inner selves rather than weighing outer probabilities.

Her presence was like a chalice of some inspired or magical substance. She did not encourage imitation but that one should aim for the target of one's own being and that mastery—in music or life —came when the arrow has lost itself in the goal.

All profits from the sale of this book will go to The Judith Raskin Publishing Fund to continue publication of this and other works of Hazrat Inayat Khan.

Introduction

"The Sufi chooses a life in the world with renunciation."

In order to become what you are, it is helpful to see yourself in another yourself who is better able to manifest potentialities dormant within yourself than you have managed so far.

We are used to thinking of meditation as an exercise conducted in seclusion. But is there such a thing as meditation in action? In most spiritually oriented people one may uncover both the ascetic and the knight. If life in the world is to be renounced, what was the purpose of creation?

In Hazrat Inayat Khan's teachings to his pupils on this subject, part of which is herewith released to the public, the master shows how stimulating it would be to introduce the kind of mastery mustered by the recluse into the hustle-bustle of active life. The result: crystal-clear insight, better programming and motivation, and ultimately freedom.

The master stresses achievement as being essential to the growth of individual potential, since situations and problems challenge one into consolidating latent attributes into tangible qualities in our personalities, for "the human personality is the end-product of the life process."

Hazrat Inayat Khan does not teach desirelessness, since he sees in every human striving a divine impulse that may have become deviated: "It is the interest of the Creator that has made this creation; every achievement increases one's power to attain a still greater achievement."

Yet, curiously enough, renunciation which seems diametrically opposite to interest may at times prove beneficial to achievement. Giving up the fruits of action opens the door to a still greater achievement. "When a person has in view an object he wants to attain, he is smaller than the object; but when the person has attained the object, he is greater than the object; and as he holds the object which he has attained, so he diminishes his strength; but when he renounces the object he has attained, he rises above the object . . . . Every gain that a person has in view limits him to a certain extent to that gain, directs his activities in a certain channel, and forms the line of his fate. At the same time it deprives him of a still better gain and of the freedom of activity which might perhaps accomplish something still better . . . . All the world that man has made has come from the power of interest, but at the same time the power of indifference is greater still, because, although motive has power, yet at the same time motive limits power. Yet it is mastery that gives man the power to accomplish things. Without a motive the power of the soul is like an ocean, but at the same time that ocean-like power cannot be used without a motive."

The art of the Yogis and dervishes consists in harnessing all nascent impulses, even as the yacht's master turns the power of the wind to his purpose, instead of drifting where it lists. For the master, the purpose of life is mastery. Here lies the secret of the foreboding power of the ascetic and his uncanny intuition. "In him is awakened that spirit by which the whole universe was created . . . . Every impulse is a power in itself, and every time when the will withdraws an impulse, the will is charged with a new strength of life."

This seems particularly pertinent at a time when uninhibiting techniques in popular psychology are letting the "Jack out of the box" of the psyche, with little hope of ever recovering the upper hand. "Master is he who controls things, and he becomes a slave who is controlled by circumstances . . . . If your horse does not obey you, it is because your fingers do not obey you." Once you have mastery over yourself, everything will go right.

Pir Vilayat Inayat Khan

Contents

MASTERY AND ACCOMPLISHMENT, continued

THE PURPOSE OF LIFE

The Path
of Attainment

Attainment

The secret of life is the desire to attain something; the absence of this makes life useless. Hope is the sustenance of life; hope comes from the desire of attaining something. Therefore this desire is in itself a very great power. The object which a person wishes to attain may be small compared with the power he develops in the process of attainment. The Hindus call attainment *Sadhana*; the power gained through attainment is called in Sanskrit *Siddhi*, and it is this which is the sign of spiritual mastership.

By learning the mystery of attainment one learns the divine mastery which is suggested in that phrase of the Bible, "Thy will be done on earth as it is in heaven." This phrase is a veil which covers the mystery of attainment. On coming to earth, man, who is the instrument of God, loses connection with that divine power whose instrument he is, thus keeping not only himself but even God from helping His will to be done. When man, who is born to be the instrument of God, does not perform his mission properly, he naturally feels dissatisfied. It does not mean that he does not accomplish what he desires, but it is the reason he is unhappy. This condition is like a hand out of joint: it is not only the hand that suffers, but the person whose hand it is, not being able to use it, suffers also. Therefore in accomplishing the work he undertakes, in attaining to the aim he has in life, man not only helps himself but he also serves God.

The way in which spiritual attainment is reached must be considered from quite another point of view. It cannot be done in the same way as material attainment. And it is discouraging when after striving perhaps for many years one does not seem to have arrived anywhere. The one who strives to attain the things of this world finds the proof of having attained them by holding them. He says, "This is mine," because he possesses it. Spiritual attainment on the contrary wants to take possessions away; it does not even allow one to possess oneself. This can be a great disappointment for a person whose only realization of having attained something is in possessing it. Spiritual attainment, however, comes by not attaining.

Then there is the question of the difference between a spiritual person and a person who possesses nothing. The difference is indeed great, for the spiritual person without any possessions is still rich. Why? Because the one who does not possess anything is conscious of limitation, but the spiritual person who does not even possess himself is conscious of perfection. But how, one asks, can a limited man be conscious of perfection? The answer is that the limited man has limited himself; he is limited because he is conscious of his limitation. It is not his true self which is limited; what is limited is what he holds, not himself. That is why Christ said, "Be ye perfect even as your Father which is in heaven is perfect."

Spiritual knowledge does not lie in learning something, but in discovering something, in breaking the fetters of the false consciousness and in allowing the soul to unfold itself with light and power. What does the word 'spiritual' really mean? Spiritual means spirit-conscious. When a person is conscious of his body, he cannot be spiritual. It is like a king who does not know his kingship. The moment he is conscious of being a king, he is a king. Every soul is born a king; it is only afterwards that he becomes a slave. Every soul is born with kingly possibilities, but they are taken away from him by this wicked world. This is told in many symbolical stories, as in the story of Rama from whom the beloved Sita was taken away. Every soul has to fight for this kingdom and to conquer. It is through that fight that the spiritual kingdom is attained. No one will fight for one, neither one's teacher nor anybody else. While those who are more evolved can help one, each man has to fight his own battle, and find his own way to that spiritual goal.

An intellectual thinks that by adding to his knowledge he may attain spiritual knowledge. This is not so. The secret of life is boundless but knowledge is limited. Eyes see only a very short distance, and the human mind is just as limited. Those who see can see by not seeing, learn by not learning.

The way of spiritual attainment is contrary to the way of all material attainment. For material attainment one must take; for spiritual attainment one must give. In material attainment one must learn; in spiritual attainment one must unlearn. If a person is conscious of his body and thinks it is all that can be known of him, his spirit is covered up. In English one says he has lost his soul; but it is only covered, for how can anything that is possessed be lost? If a man thinks so he is limited. Neither objects nor beings are lost; they may be temporarily covered up, but they are still there. Nothing made can ever by destroyed; it is only a covering and an uncovering. No relations and connections are ever separable. The separation is outward; inwardly there is never separation. They are separated from one's consciousness, but when the consciousness accommodates them, then nothing in the world can separate them. What does one learn by this? That spiritual attainment is to be reached by the raising of the consciousness from limitation to perfection.

There is another side to this question. There is no one, wise or foolish, who is not progressing slowly or quickly towards the spiritual goal. The only difference is that the one is attracted by it, and faces his goal, making his way towards it, while the other has his back turned to it and is drawn towards the goal without being conscious of it. Poor man, he does not know where he is being taken, but he goes just the same; his punishment is that he does not see the glory he is approaching, and his torture is that he is being drawn towards the opposite pole to that which he desires. His punishment is not different from that of the infant who walks into the water of the lake and whose mother pulls it back by its shirt; but it is looking all the time at the lake.

From a religious point of view it seems very unjust of the divine Judge that one should be deprived of that perfect bliss which is spiritual attainment. But from the point of view of metaphysics no soul will be deprived of this knowledge at any time in eternity.

What does Sufism teach on this subject? Sufism avoids words, words from which differences and distinctions arise. Words can never express the truth fully. Words promote argument. All the differences between religions are differences of words; in sense they do not differ, for they have all come from one source and to the same source they return. This very source is a store for them, it is their life, light, and power. Therefore the way of the Sufi is that if he does not agree with somebody in a particular idea, he takes a step higher instead of differing on the lower plane. For the wise person there is no difference. The main thing that Sufism teaches is to dive deep within oneself, and to prepare mind and body by contemplation so as to make one's being a shrine of God, which is the purpose for which it was created.

What is needed first, both for worldly and spiritual attainment, is self-discipline. Many experience, and a few know, that things go wrong when one's self is not disciplined. Those who give way to anger, passion. or emotions easily may seem for the moment successful, but they cannot continually succeed in life. Very often misfortunes follow an illness or a failure; the reason is that one weakness gives way to another, and so the person who goes down continues to go down and down. It is natural sometimes to take a step downward, for the path of life is not even. But the wise way is that if one has gone down one step, the next step may be taken upward. No doubt it means resisting the force that pulls one downward, but that resistance only secures the path of one's life.

What generally happens is that man does not mind a little mistake. He does not take notice of a small weakness. He underestimates a little failure, and in this way in the long run he meets with a great failure. It is wise, therefore, no matter how deep one has fallen, to fix one's eyes upward, to try to rise instead of falling. It is very interesting to observe that when one points towards God in heaven it is always upward, although in reality God is everywhere and so is heaven. What makes one think that God or heaven is upward is a natural impulse in man, a divine impulse which gives an inclination to rise above. This shows that success, its attainment, is divine pleasure; failure and its experience are divine disappointment.

People who blame destiny for their failure take the path of least resistance, but there are more difficulties in the path that appears to be of least resistance. Difficulties will become less for the man who struggles with life as he goes forward. The man who takes his path easily finds that the difficulties become more numerous as he goes on. This does not mean that one should choose in life a path of more difficulties; it only means that on the path of attainment difficulties must not be counted. Difficulties rise over the head of him who looks at them with awe; but the same difficulties fall at the feet of him who takes no notice of them. The man who fails in the world fails to attain spiritual bliss also.

Man is the king of his domain; his coming on earth takes away his kingdom bit by bit. During that trial he is tested to see if he uses that human virtue which helps him to attain mastery over his kingdom. Whatever a man's life, he will not be satisfied, for his soul's satisfaction is in fulfilling its purpose. The day when he arrives at that mastery, the day when he has regained the kingdom he had lost, he can say, "Thy will be done on earth as it is in heaven." And in this is accomplished the fulfillment of his being born on this earth.

What is it to have self-discipline? It is to be able to say "I can" and not "I cannot." Of course the words "I cannot" are often used when a person does not think it would be wise or just to do a certain thing. In that case it is different. But when there is something he believes to be just, to be good, to be right and he still says "I cannot," it is then that self-discipline is lacking. When a person says "I cannot tolerate, I cannot endure, I cannot bear, I cannot forgive," these are all signs of lack of self-discipline.

Some people say "I cannot rise above my faults." The only way to overcome one's faults is by struggle, struggle in the spiritual path. Such a struggle is faced for instance by a person who during a disagreeable conversation has an inclination to retort; he does so, but at the same time the power to fight, to give back, has left him. By dispersing his force in returning insult for insult he has lost his power. By controlling this inclination his power would have been a thousandfold greater, although at the moment when something like this happens, and one humiliates oneself and crushes one's pride and one's self, one feels crushed both ways: by not answering and then by the crushing of one's self. And to be able to say "I have answered him back!" gives one a certain pride, a certain satisfaction.

In order to see this question more clearly one must picture oneself as two beings, one the king and the other the servant.

When one of them expresses a wish, it is the king who wishes; and the part that says "I cannot" is the servant. If the servant has his way, then the king is in the place of the servant. And the more the servant has his way, the more the servant rules and the king obeys. In this way naturally conflict arises inwardly and that reflects upon the outer life, making the whole life misery. One may be pious or good or religious, it makes no difference. If man does not realize the kingdom of God within himself, nor realize his spirit to be a king, he does not accomplish the purpose of life.

Knowledge and Power

The secret of the working of the whole universe is in the duality of nature. In all aspects of nature two forces are working, and it is their action which balances life. Therefore in the path of attainment the power which manifests as enthusiasm or action is not sufficient; knowledge and the capacity for work are also necessary. Very often a person fails to succeed with all his enthusiasm and power of will, and the reason is that either by the power he has he pushes his object along like a ball, or with his strength he hammers the rock, which he really needs whole, and not in pieces. Power is no doubt most necessary in attainment, but in the absence of knowledge power may prove helpless.

By power I mean power in all its aspects, the power that one possesses in outer life, and the power of mind and body. It is the power of mind which is called will power. No doubt many with knowledge will fail through the lack of power.

If an object is pulled from both sides, by power and knowledge, then also there will be no success. It is the cooperation of these two powers which is the secret of all success. Success, be it of a material character or of some other nature, is always success. Success, however small, is a step forward to somethng great; and failure, however small, is a failure and it will lead to something still worse.

Success should not be valued according to its outer value. It must be valued according to what it prepares in oneself. And failure, however small, makes an undesirable impression upon oneself. This shows how very necessary it is to keep the balance between power and knowledge. It is of great value to try to develop power and knowledge in attaining one's object.

There are two kinds of people who become tired of life in the world: the one who has risen above the world, and the one who has fallen beneath it. The former has attained his object, but the latter, even if he left the world, would not be satisfied by any other life. His renunciation of worldly things means nothing. It only means incapacity. It is the conqueror of the life of the world who has the right to give up the struggle of the world if he wishes to. But he from whose hands the life of the world is snatched away by his fellow men and who is incapable of holding it, who cannot progress, who cannot attain in life what he wishes to attain, if he left the world it would not be renunciation, it would simply be poverty.

It is not by any means selfish or covetous to want to succeed in life. By success man is inclined upwards. Only when, intoxicated by worldly success, he closes his eyes to what lies beyond on his path, he stands still, and that standing still is death. When the many successful people whom we see in this world do not progress spiritually, it means that they did not continue in the path of success. In reality all roads lead to the same goal: business, profession, science, art, religion, or philosophy. When people do not seem to have arrived at their proper destination it is not because they have preferred one path to another, it is because they have not continued on their path.

Very often people who lack knowledge and have more strength than is necessary destroy their own purpose. While wanting to construct they cause destruction. The greatest fault of human nature is that every man thinks that he knows best. When he speaks to another he thinks that the latter knows but half; and when he is speaking about a third person he thinks that that person knows only a quarter. Some few who do not rely upon their knowledge are then dependent upon the advice of others; therefore their success or failure depend upon the advice of others.

It is most difficult in life to have power and possess knowledge, and together with these to have clear vision. And if there is any way of keeping the vision clear, it is by retaining the balance between power and knowledge. Man generally gets unbalanced, for when there is power he wants to exert it. Also, man is always involved in reasoning; in that way he easily loses his balance. Then one must try to judge whether he attaches too much importance to power, not cultivating knowledge enough.

Take for instance a man who is perhaps very enthusiastic in a certain business; just with his will power he wants to get as much money as he can, without any thought of how it will be used. He has only the strength of the purpose "I must succeed," and he gives all his energy to it without thinking about it. In that way he might achieve success, but still there is always a danger. And then there is another man who is thinking out a thousand things before taking a step in an affair, contradicting everything with his own knowledge. What one should do is this: if one takes one step in power, one should take another step in knowledge, and then there will be balance, then one's life becomes rhythmic. Just like the accent in musical two-four time: there is the strong accent, and then comes a weak accent. Now there is power, then there is thinking.

There are many in this world who from enthusiasm push away the object of their attainment like a football. They mean to grasp it, but unintentionally they push it on, and this happens when a man is too enthusiastic to attain a certain thing for which he has not made himself ready. One should remember that in the path of attainment one must first feel strong enough to bear the burden of what one wishes to lift. The wisdom one sees working behind nature has intended and arranged that every being and every thing shall bear the weight that it is intended to bear. Very often man's ambition outruns his power of bearing. Before thinking whether he is entitled to a certain thing or not, he strives to attain it; and it is this which very often causes failure. Man must first become entitled to have what he wishes to have; this makes it easy for him to gain what he he wishes to gain, and it easily attracts to him what he wishes to attain.

Desiring is one thing, and imagining is another. Lying in a grass hut one might desire a solid wall around one's hut, but one can imagine a palace standing before one; however, it is not imagination which helps in the attainment, it is the earnest desire.

There are things which are within one's reach and there are things which are beyond it. One must first prove to one's own self one's capability of attaining what is within one's reach. This gives one sufficient self-confidence to attain that which is beyond one's reach.

In the path of attainment one must keep the eye of justice open. One must be able to know what is right for one to attain, and which attainment one does not deserve. There is no soul in this world who is not striving after something. To one the object of his striving is distinct, to another perhaps it is perplexing. Yet there is no one alive who is not striving after something. According to the extent that the object is clear to one, it is easy to attain.

In the process of attainment there are four stages. In the first place, the object one wishes to attain must be concrete in one's mind. Next it must be reasoned out how the desire can be materialized. Third, what material is to be obtained and used for it. The fourth stage is the composing, forming, or building of that object.

The central theme of the whole of creation is attainment. In the striving of all souls in the world there is only one impulse, and that is the divine impulse. Yet for the man who strives ignorantly after something and goes about it wrongly, it ends in disappointment; and disappointment not only to himself but even to God. The one who knows his affairs, and who accomplishes them rightly, fulfills the mission of his life and the wish of God. No matter what man accomplishes, it is only a step towards something else. As a man goes on accomplishing in the path of attainment, in the end he arrives at the purpose of his life. In the end, attainment is the aim of all souls, although in the beginning they may seem different.

The secret of all attainment is in the realization of the self. Both the impulse to attain a thing and the control of that impulse are necessary. Very often a man loses the chance of attaining something through his overenthusiasm which puts his life out of balance. At the same time the power of impulse is a great power and the person who has no strength in his impulse must certainly lose. One should strike a balance between impulse and control. There must be an impulse, but it must be under control. A person who is overjoyous at having riches must realize that he may very soon lose them; and it is the same with everything.

The balance is kept by knowing that nothing which the earth can offer is more precious than one's soul. The one who runs after things, those things run away from him, frightened of his continual pursuit. But the one who does not go in pursuit of objects will find that they inevitably become his own. When God becomes one's own, what will not become one's own?

For the very reason that God is divided on earth into different beings, and reunites Himself in one Being, His power is unlimited. The real object of all people on earth is the same as the object of God in heaven; but this object can only be attained if man will yield up his desire to the desire of God, if man will give himself up to the Self of God. That is the meaning of the sacrifice of Abraham; that is the real meaning of the crucifixion: to crucify the lower self.

In the path of attainment confidence is necessary. It is according to one's confidence that the object of attainment is drawn closer. It is not by overenthusiasm, for overenthusiasm is intoxication. A person intoxicated by enthusiasm is liable to do the wrong thing instead of the right one. It is always the inner power which is the secret of attainment, and the less it is expressed, the better. A person who allows his power an outlet only wastes it. It is the conserving of this power which makes man a reservoir of power with which all things can be accomplished. For the person who has attained to the mystery of Sadhana, there is nothing in this world which cannot be attained; all is within his reach, his power, his grasp. As high as one's object of attainment is, so high one rises; and as low as the object of attainment is, so low is the person. If the object is honor-giving, one will be honorable; if the object is painful, one will be sad; if the object is pleasant, one will be joyous; if the object is exalting, one will be holy. Therefore, a person must know what object to keep before his view, what object he should pursue in life.

There are many childlike people who do not know what is their object in life. One minute they think it is one thing, another minute they think it is another thing. In the end they arrive at nothing because they have no object set before their view. No one can depend upon a person like this. Even the birds are frightened to sit upon a moving branch. The person whose object is set is the one whose life is settled, whom one can call serious, on whom others can depend. The person who does not know his own mind cannot help his fellow men; he will only upset them. He can neither attain for himself nor can he help another. One should therefore remember continually to keep one's mind so clear that one can see one's object before one: its character, its nature, its value; and then to set forth every effort to pursue that object patiently till one has attained it. No matter how small the object, the attainment of it builds a step towards the final goal.

Concentration

Concentration is the chief means of attainment. Concentration does not mean sitting and thinking of a certain thing, but it means holding a certain idea or object in the mind at all times. The result of concentration depends upon how much one loves the object of attainment. However great a person may be in holding the thought firmly in mind, he cannot bring about as great results as a person who loves the object he holds in concentration. Love is all powerful, and it naturally gives power in one's concentration, be it for a person, for wealth, for position, for knowledge, or for God. Whatever one loves one gets, small things or great things.

It is better to get a small thing than nothing, because it thus gives a mastery. In every gain through life a person takes a step forward. Every object has a separate path for its achievement, but in the end all must come to the same goal. Do not, therefore, look with contempt upon someone if he is in pursuit of something that you consider inferior to your ideal. Know rather that it is his path, though perhaps not yours.

Mostly, by the continual changing of the object and by indecision in regard to an object, one produces weakness, which will produce inferior results. It is often better to accomplish a certain thing by external means, if it can be so accomplished, than by a forced mental effort, which should, however, be used when it is necessary. One should look at it with an economical point of view; and if the power of the battery is all exhausted, then one will feel the lack of it. Therefore a mental effort for the accomplishment of small things is an unnecessary outlay of force. In other words, the mind must be allowed to work normally with every action.

When a person works mentally and does not act outwardly, this may produce a lack of balance, for action must balance thought and thought balance action. This danger always stands before the mental worker. An object in life, however, must be accomplished, sometimes even at a cost greater than the value of the object itself when attained, because it is the effort and the success which make one capable and it is failure that drags one to a still greater fall. Therefore the price one pays, or the effort one makes, is greater than the object, because it opens a further way for future success; and a loss may be a small loss in itself and yet it may be a greater loss in reality. It is for this reason that people who are successful continually succeed, and with failure a person tends towards failure.

In order to keep the concentration on the right path one must keep the object always before one. Surroundings, environment, atmosphere, everything helps to bring about the desired attainment. The environment helps towards the accomplishment of the desired object. Things that are around you in the house, the clothes you wear, the food you eat, the people you meet, all these things have an effect upon your life. Do not, even in jest, think, speak or act against the object you have in view, because it will have a wrong and depreciating psychological effect.

One should constantly think of the object he desires with hope and trust, and even dream of it. And, truly, no dream will be lost if it is expressive of the desired object. Because it is, first of all, the desire that brings about the dream, and every desire, if held in the mind, must someday, somehow, be realized. Constancy in holding one object to its fulfillment is most necessary.

But after the accomplishment one must not cling to the habit thus formed. He must be able to turn from one object to another after his desire has been accomplished. A person who desires an object is smaller than the object. But when he attains the object, he and the object are equal. When he clings to the attained object, he is beneath the object. But when he renounces the acquired object, he rises above it. It is then that he can be called the master of his object.

Common sense is necessary in the path of attainment, but not to such an extent that the reason should dominate and lead the will. The will, in action, must lead the reason. If the reason is allowed to lead the will, the will many times becomes paralyzed; but when in cooperation the will leads the reason, then the path of attainment becomes illuminated. The work of common sense in the way of attainment is really to make one understand and comprehend the real meaning and object of the desire: "Am I really worthy to receive this? Do I in truth deserve it? Can I sustain the purpose of the object when I have acquired it? Can the object become worthy of my pursuit? Shall I prove worthy of the test which the attainment of the object would require?"

In the path of attainment, many lose their way and go astray, especially those who are regardless of consideration. There are objects which cannot bring anything but harm, and there are many in this world who would never stop to think of the harm to another as long as they think that they are safe. But since the very nature of the world is give and take, and as every action has its reaction, and as every cause has its own similar effect, how can one really think that he can be safe by causing harm to another?

Often, in many attainments through life, there is found a benefit for one by the loss of another. And thus we see it go up and down, through life, like a scale. This is a matter of time and experience, and often one finds that a momentary gain is more disastrous than the loss would have been. Therefore, the wise have a greater gain as their object through life than the objects of sense of the average man, who is ever in pursuit of transitory gain, and in success and in failure both he is at a loss because in the end he gets little. The wise, therefore, fix their eyes on that divine attainment, that divine ideal, which is the best object possible, and by the attainment of that object they enjoy eternal bliss.

One must not talk much, nor indiscriminately, about one's attainment, for it is a great waste of power. A person who tells all his friends and everyone whom he meets, "I am going to build up that business," has, at the start, already a lesser chance of success than the one who thinks and ponders upon the subject and keeps quiet, says nothing to anyone, or at least tells only those who he thinks may be helpful to him.

The secret of all attainment, spiritual or material, is centered in reserve. When a person has told his plans to others, he has let out the energy that he should have kept as a reservoir of power for the accomplishment of his object. A thing unspoken is alive in the mind; and when spoken, it is as dead.

The more valuable your object, the more it must be guarded, as all precious things need strong guarding. When a person tells others of his plan, each one looks at it from his point of view. Some understand, some do not understand; some have a sympathetic view, and some take an unfavorable attitude toward it. And every person's attitude has something to do with your life and with your affairs. If you have wholeheartedly engaged yourself in the accomplishment of a plan, many outside influences can hinder it.

The teaching, "Be wise as a serpent," may be interpreted, "Be quiet as a serpent." It is quietude that gives wisdom and power. The thought held in mind speaks to the mind of another, but the thought spoken out most often only reaches the ears of a person. Every plan has a period of development; and if man has power over his impulse, by retaining the thought silently in mind he allows the plan to develop and to take all necessary changes that it may take for its culmination. But when the impulse expresses the thought, it, so to speak, puts out the flame, thus hindering the development of the plan. The wise speak with their mind many times before they speak about it to anybody.

One must put aside a certain time of the day or night to devote entirely to the concentration of one's attainment; and by being faithful in this practice one gains his object in the end, and thus he learns the only way of mastery.

The attitude of mind is the most important thing in attainment. The person who attains success by injustice and oppression and by wronging others will meet with failure when he does right, and the one who achieves his success by his goodness, mercy and right doing will fail when he changes his method and looks for success by doing wrong. This proves that success, as generally so termed, depends upon the fixed attitude; thus the change of attitude mars it. If by thought success is brought to one, one must then continue his method of thinking. If by action it is brought, one must continue the action. If both thought and action are used, both must be continued. For it is the attitude which is the most important part in attainment.

Be obstinate in the path of success. Nothing should keep you back from your effort when your resolution is once taken. Renounce your object of attainment only when you have reached it and you have a better one in view. But when you have attained the object and you cling to it, then you hinder your own progress, for the object is greater than yourself. You are greater than the object when you are able to renounce it after attaining it.

There are two kinds of renunciation: renunciation by mastery and renunciation by weakness. When you could not reach the apple and then said, "Oh, I would not eat that apple, I am sure it is sour, and it is no use bothering myself about it," then that renunciation is through weakness. But renunciation in the sense of right and justice is better than attainment. When you wish to pick the apple and you renounce the desire by thinking, "I have no right to eat this apple, as it belongs to another person's garden, not mine," then you rise to a higher development than in accomplishing your object.

Every step one takes in evolution changes one's ideal. In your stage if you love a jasmine today, it is possible that in your next step in evolution you may have grown above it and you love a rose. And it is not necessary that you should keep to the jasmine when your evolution brings you to the love for the rose; thus one is kept back from progressing. Contentment is a great virtue, but it is a virtue only when you have mastered the thing and risen above it. But if you are contented before you have mastered, then contentment, in that case, is a weakness. Things in themselves are not merits, neither are they faults, but they become so by their proper or improper use. Thus merits may become faults and faults become merits. Therefore let the wise choose the path of wisdom, and by that torch they may journey through life.

One great moral point must be understood: one must never desire any attainment which blinds one to what is right and just, and which destroys kindliness in the heart, which is the essence of God in man.

Hope

We live by the hope of attainment—without this one cannot exist—be it spiritual or material, of a selfish nature or of an unselfish one. It is not necessary that all should have one and the same object for their attainment, nor is it possible. It is, however, desirable that we should hold in our thought the best and highest attainment possible for us. It is not necessary for us to force ourselves to have a much higher object of attainment, which we are incapable of holding. The object, however, must surely be high, but within the possibility of our own reach. We must not select our object of attainment by noticing that others have the same aim and are in pursuit of the same object; but we must feel and realize that our heart yearns for it.

It is not necessary that we should kill our desire for lack of the presence of the object we desire, but it is wise always to realize the value of the object and its real nature. Things that pass from one hand to the other are but changing things, and be sure that when you gain a thing from another you may have to pass it on to another also when the time comes, willingly or unwillingly. Therefore be always in search of things that will endure, that will last long, and adopt ways of attaining them by right and just means. It is far better to renounce a thing which can only be procured through the sacrifice of right and justice, than to go in pursuit of things which will bring in the end disappointment and disaster, as they are the natural results of the lack of right and justice.

Your object of attainment should be decided and settled in your own mind, and there should be no change. Any difficulty in obtaining it must not frighten you. With patience, faith, and trust you must pursue your object. Do not for one moment think how small you are before your object of attainment, or how incapable you are of achieving it, or how long it must take to reach it, or where or how the means can be provided to get it. Before you think of all these things, think of one thing: "The object is there and it belongs to me; it is my birthright, it is my natural right, it is my divine right that it should be mine." Then turn to other things, think of things which will help you to procure it. If the rein or the rope of hope is let loose or loosened, then no effort will be of any use. If patience fails you, then there is no sustenance. If your mind changes, then your self is the cause of your failure. Then you want a rose and after attaining the rose you wish you had chosen a jasmine, after attaining the jasmine, you cry, "Oh, why did I choose this flower? Why not the other?" and when they are both before you, you have lost the power to choose either the one or the other.

When your object is, or seems to be, in a mist, do not cover yourself with clouds because your object seems far off. If you do, everything will become dark before you; but if you keep your light clear, then the ray shooting from your own soul will in time clear the mist. But if you yourself are in confusion whether to have this object or that object or no object, then there is no hope for you. For you must ever bear in mind that the light and life that goes out from you to the object are quite as important as that light which comes to you from the object. Therein lies the great mystery of the trinity in all things: the knower, the thing to be known, and the power or light or knowledge which connects them. If the way seems closed, it will be opened; if the means are lacking, they will be given, they will be attained; if the object is far off and beyond your reach, it will be drawn to you, if only you can hold fast to the rein, the rope of hope, with complete faith and trust in God, the Giver of all things, the Possessor of all things.

There is a belief, and many have this belief, that external help can be had to further one's attainment: help from saints, sages, masters, spirits, or angels. No doubt there is a great deal of truth in all this, and help comes as you ask for it and need it, and all kinds of helpers will help you as you call upon them. But at the same time self-help must not be neglected or ignored, for after all is said, self-help is the best of all help, and all will strive to help the one who tries to help himself.

To what extent one should expect external help can be best explained by the fact that to the extent of our wish and our will-power we attract help and power of accomplishment. In our desire for the accomplishment of good and helpful things we attract good helpers, and in the evil things one desires one attracts evil helpers. The Satanic side of life is ever ready to help man, as is God. As soon as a person has a determined evil thought all the means of help about one begin to manifest themselves. The help in good thoughts comes more slowly upon the physical plane, whereas with a bad thing it comes more quickly. Pebbles, like the line of least resistance, are found everywhere, but diamonds are so rare! Evil motives and deeds take much less time to accomplish their purpose and less trouble, while good things are accomplished with great patience and perserverance. And the difference can only be realized in their results.

It is, in truth, in the end that man knows what he has striven after. Evil has ever in the end a weakening power, while virtue is a strengthening power. A disappointment or a failure in the path of virtue will give more happiness in the end than success and accomplishment of desire in the path of evil. The loss which one has experienced along the path of virtue is far preferable to gain in the pathway of evil.

There are three stages in every wish: inclination, pursuit, attainment. It is after these three stages that the result of man's wish is manifest and not until then that man realizes his wish in its fullness. In the first stage the wish is apt to be in confusion; in the second stage there is an absorption in the idea and action; in the third stage there is the joy of fulfillment or a sorrow at the loss.

But a result, later, may prove that one would even prefer the sorrow to the joy and its consequences. For even a joy may prove to be the cause of a greater sorrow. It is so easy to wish for a thing! But it is difficult to know if it will prove good for one or not. For what one loves today he may hate tomorrow; and if the wish today be fulfilled tomorrow, when the time of love has expired and the time of hatred approaches, then it would have been far better had one forgotten the wish as soon as it was born.

To want a thing is an easy matter, but to want it continually is a difficult thing. And how much time man wastes on wanting things and then not wanting them! This wanting faculty works also in childhood. Therefore the great task in life is to watch our desires, to know, to understand, and to analyze: What I want, why I want it, and how I can get it, and what result will it be likely to bring about? It is the part of wisdom, when once you have studied and understood this question, to continue going forward intelligently, courageously and steadily along the path of attainment and to pursue until the end.

When talking about optimism and pessimism, I should say that there are times when the conditions do not allow man to be hopeful, even if by nature he is optimistic. The one who is placed in a situation where everything seems to stand against his prospect in life, cannot keep his eyes open, see the condition, and at the same time have an optimistic view. When the conditions in life go against and everything stands in opposition, it is most difficult for one to have a hopeful attitude in life. Outwardly, the conditions stand against belief; inwardly, the reason supports the conditions, for reason is a slave to all that stands before it. Therefore, if under such circumstances an optimistic person shows no longer optimism, he is not to be blamed.

No doubt, the one who in spite of all conditions against and in spite of his reason, helpless to find a way, still strikes the path of hope, is much more advanced than the pessimistic soul, for he, whether he knows or does not know, is holding the rope which is attached to Heaven and which is the only source of safety. This rope is the faith and trust in the greatness and power of God which is within; and however much things may seem to be against, yet his faith in God can turn all things in time in his favor. It is denying what one does not wish to happen, even to the moment that the happening is knocking at the door, and still denying. That person will turn that happening into something that he desired. Misfortune will turn into good fortune, disease will turn into health, and death will turn into life.

There is no such thing as impossibility. All is possible. Impossibility is made by the limitation of our capacity of understanding. Man, blinded by the law of nature's working, by the law of consequences which he has known through his few years of life on earth, begins to say, "This is possible and that is impossible." If he were to rise beyond limitations, his soul would see nothing but possibility. And when the soul has risen high enough to see all possibility, that soul certainly has caught a glimpse of God.

They say, God is almighty; and I say, God is all-possible. Possibility is the nature of God, and impossibility is the art of man. Man goes so far, and cannot go any further. Man makes a flower out of paper, giving it as natural a color as possible; yet he says it is not possible to make it fragrant, for he has his limitations. But God, Who is the maker of the flower and Who is the Giver of the fragrance, has all power; and man, who is wakened to his limitation, becomes more and more limited the more he thinks of it. In this is created the spirit of pessimism. The man who is conscious of God Almighty, and who in the contemplation of God loses the consciousness of his own self, inherits the power of God, and it is in this power and belief that the spirit of optimism is born.

Patience

The greater the object of your pursuit, the greater patience it requires. There is a side in human nature which keeps one impatient and which makes one feel that he should mount to the top immediately; however, when one rushes impatiently toward the accomplishment of one's object, one often fails. In climbing there are steps, and one should gradually climb. One must hold before one's mind the object, but one must see at the same time the steps that one has to climb. If patience will not help in climbing the steps and in journeying the necessary distance, there will come a fall. This shows that there are three chief things in the path of attainment: steadiness of concentration in holding the object of concentration firmly before oneself; at the same time, noticing with open eyes the many steps that one must climb to reach the object; and the third thing is patient perseverance.

Patience is the most difficult thing in life; and once this is mastered, man will become the master of all difficulties. Patience in other words may be called the power of endurance during the absence of the desired things or conditions. They say death is the worst thing in life, but, in point of fact, patience is often worse than death. One would prefer death to patience, when patience is severely tried.

Patience is a life power, it is a spiritual power and the greatest virtue that one can have. For it is a cross, and on this the patient one is crucified. And as resurrection follows crucifixion, so all success and happiness must follow the trying moments of patience. Noticing the steps toward the goal is the work of intelligence, and this helps to make the work of patience fruitful. But patience and intelligence both become wings to the power of concentration. This is a power to hold the desired thought firmly, so that it may not change.

You must pity the man who cannot decide between two things. He lacks concentration. Single-mindedness is the chief secret of concentration. One must keep one's object steady in the mind, and must not allow anything to change the mind from the object. Even things more useful, precious, and better must be considered as temptation. The object that once man has and once he has embarked upon its attainment, he must accomplish it to its very end, or else not have any object in life.

What one values in life is worth striving for, whether material or spiritual gain. Those who weigh the object that they wish to attain with the difficulty or the cost that is required for its attainment neither know the full value of the object nor do they know the way of attainment. The first principle that one must learn in the path is to esteem the object of attainment more than the cost one has to pay for it. Even if the object be not of the value of its cost, still the law of attainment is to attain a desired object at every cost.

The great ones who have achieved great things in life have achieved in this way. Nothing in the world could take them away from what they wished to achieve. Even a life's cost they considered too small a price for the object of attainment. When this spirit directs the spiritual path man arrives at having God-communion, for the true pursuer will never go halfway. Either he gains, or he loses himself. The words "Hatha Yoga" mean abstinence, or sternness, to want what one wants, and nothing else in its place will satisfy one. Those who are discouraged and come back from half the way will never arrive at a destination. Especially in the path of God a person who takes one step forward with hope and two steps backward in doubt will go back or will linger on in the same place. By the sincere pursuit of the object, be it heavenly or earthly, with a willingness for all sacrifice, one attains to what the soul longs for: perfection, the only satisfaction in life.

Progress in the path of attainment sometimes produces too much self-confidence in success, and if it comes untimely, it produces a sort of negligence and often it weakens enthusiasm. For instance, one may build a house very carefully and attentively, particular about every detail; and when it has come closer to the finish, one might think that as it came right so far, it must of necessity be finished rightly. Then one may neglect, and may lose some of the enthusiasm and attention to every detail, which may result in disappointment. Therefore self-confidence and enthusiasm and attentiveness are forces which must be economically used, not with extravagance.

The force which is given at the commencement of the work must last till it is finished; if it breaks in the middle, often the whole effort is broken. Pride is a great enemy of man. Sometimes man is proud of the great object he has before him to accomplish. The man who has finished a part of his work often becomes proud with the hope that he will be able to finish the whole. But pride in all its forms is blinding; a proud man cannot see his path clearly. Even after the attainment of a certain object in life, it is wise not to attribute the credit of it to oneself but to see that power and wisdom in the Almighty God.

After one has accomplished something in life, it often happens that one becomes a captive of his accomplishment, as a spider becomes captive in his web. As the nature of life is freedom, no attainment is valuable, however great, if it masters the freedom of the soul. And therefore man must always take care that he stands above things he has attained instead of standing below. Master is he who controls things and affairs of life, and he becomes a slave who is controlled by the things of this earth.

Life's greatest secret is the continuity of progress. When progress stops, it is as death, and as long as man is progressing, mortality cannot touch him. Attainment or no attainment, pursuit after something man's soul cares to reach must be continued, and by single-mindedness one must build a path from earth to Heaven and from man to God.

Motive

An important rule of psychology is that every motive that takes its root in the mind must be watered and reared until its full development. And if one neglects this duty, one does not only harm the motive, but by this the will power becomes less and the working of the mind becomes disorderly. Even if the motive be small and unimportant, yet a steady pursuit after its attainment trains the mind, strengthens the will and keeps the inner mechanism in order.

For instance, when a person tries to unravel a knot, and then he thinks, "No use giving time to it," he loses an opportunity of strengthening the will and attaining the object desired. However small a thing may appear to be, when once handled one must accomplish it, not for the thing itself, but for what benefit it gives. Yes, thought must be given as to its importance and value in the beginning, when the motive begins to take root in the mind, and one must avoid an undesirable and unimportant motive taking place.

When the motive does not receive a direction, it does not necessarily die away, it takes its own path and culminates in some shape and form quite different from what you had desired. All ugliness, crookedness, and defect in nature and art is mostly caused by this.

The success of the motive depends entirely upon the concentration, for mind is productive and creative. It produces and creates all that it forms in itself first as a thought. This concentration must not necessarily be practiced for some time during the day or night, but the motive must cover all things of life and make the whole life as one single vision of the object of concentration. The object of concentration must cover, above all things in life, one's personality. In other words it may be said that either the motive should live or the personality. In order to make a motive successful, the personality should be covered entirely by the motive.

Life is one, singly and collectively, according to both these points of view. And you cannot live yourself, separate from the motive; either the motive should live or you, either the motive must become you or you become the motive. Which means one thing should be sacrificed for the other, either personality sacrificed for the motive or motive sacrificed for personality. It is the greatest truth in the world that it is one that lives and it is two that die. And Rumi has said it beautifully in his verse where he says:

The Beloved is all in all, the lover only veils Him,
The Beloved is all that lives, the lover a dead thing.

Whatever your pursuit in life, whatever your aim, whatever be your motive, for a real success in a motive you must offer yourself first as a sacrifice for it. The great ones and small ones, all who have accomplished something in their lives, whether an earthly gain or a heavenly bliss, they have sacrificed a part of themselves, or their whole being, even to such an extent that some have arrived at the point where they no more exist for themselves, but for the motive. It is they who know what is success, and it is they who can teach the path of accomplishment.

Mastery and Accomplishment

Destiny

It is said in the *Gayan*,[1] "The present is the reflection of the past, and the future is the re-echo of the present." Destiny is not what is already made; destiny is what we are making. Very often fatalists think that we are in the hands of destiny, driven in whatever direction in life destiny wills; but in point of fact we are the masters of our destiny, especially from the moment we begin to realize this fact. Among Hindus there is a well-known saying that the creation is Brahma's dream; in other words, all manifestation is the dream of the Creator. I would wish to add to this that destiny means the materialization of man's own thought. Man is responsible for his success and failure, for his rise and fall; and it is man who brings these about either knowingly or unknowingly.

There is a hint of this in the Bible, in the principal prayer taught by Christ, in which it is said, "Thy will be done on earth as it is in heaven." It is a psychological suggestion to mankind to make it possible that the will of God, which is easily done in heaven, should also be done on earth. And the English saying that man proposes and God disposes supports this; it suggests the other side of the same truth. These seem to be two contrary ideas, yet they explain the same theory: that what is meant by destiny is changed by man, but that destiny also changes man's plans.

[1]See Gayan, Vadan, Nirtan

The more we study life the more we understand that it is not only qualifications, enthusiasm, and energy that count, but also the design, the plan already made. And according to that plan man has to go through his destiny. No doubt one should not use this to support the argument of some fatalists who think that they can sit back comfortably and wait for better times to come. They may wait for the rest of their lives and not accomplish anything.

The question of destiny can be better explained by the picture of an artist meditating on a certain design he has in his mind. The first stage is to create the design in his mind. The second is to bring it onto the canvas; and when he draws this picture on the canvas, it may suggest something to him that he had not thought of when he made the design in his mind. And when the artist has finished his picture, he will see that it is quite different from what he had originally thought of.

This shows that our life stands before us like a picture; when all that has been designed beforehand begins to happen, our soul will receive a totally different suggestion from the picture. Something that was lacking may have been put in, and in this way the picture is improved. For there are two kinds of artists: one who paints the plan which has been made in his mind on the canvas, and the other who takes suggestions from the picture itself as he goes on painting. The difference is that the one is merely an artist and the other is a master. The latter is not bound to the plan; the former has designed something and is bound to what he has designed; he is limited.

One sees the same thing with a composer of music. He composes a certain melody in his mind; he ponders over it and wishes to put it on paper. But when he plays his composition on the piano, the music suggests improvements to him. He plays the same musical idea that he first had, but he is able to perfect and complete it when he has heard it with his own ears.

That is a picture of our life. There is one man who is driven by the hand of destiny: he does not know where he comes from; he does not know where he is going. He is placed in certain conditions in life. He is busy with something, occupied with something, and he cannot see any other way of getting on; he may desire something quite different, he may have difficulty in putting his mind to what he is doing, but he still thinks he must go on. That is the man who has not yet understood the meaning of this secret. But there is another man who even after a hundred failures is still determined that he will succeed at the next attempt. That man is the master of his success

There are two parts in man. One part is his external self which the soul has borrowed from the earth; and the other part is his real self which belongs to his source. In other words an individual is a combination of spirit and matter, a current which runs from above and attracts to it the earth from below, shaping it in order to make it a vehicle. The human body is nothing but a vehicle of the soul which has come from above and has taken the human body as its abode; thus an individual has two aspects of being: one is the soul, the other is the body. It is the meeting of the soul and the body which makes the mind, and these three together make an individual.

The external part of an individual can be likened to the outer form of a globe, while the mind takes the place of the finer inner machinery. This is the mechanical part of being. There remains the soul which is the divine heritage, a spiritual current shooting forth from that Spirit which is the source of all things. Therefore the soul has in it a potentiality, a creative power as its divine heritage. On the one side man is limited and imperfect; on the other side he represents the unlimited and perfect. That is why Christ has said, "Be ye perfect even as your Father which is in heaven is perfect." It means: one not only inherits from one's earthly parents, but one also inherits that creative power which makes one's life from the Father in heaven.

A soul is born with a mechanism which one calls mind and body. From infancy a soul naturally finds itself limited in captivity. All the tragedy of life comes from limitation. If you ask a hundred people what is the difficulty in their life, each one will name a different struggle that he is facing at the time; but in reality it will be the limitation of life which has caused the tragedies in every form. Man grows up in limitation, and this limitation suggests to him at every step that he is imperfect, handicapped, weak, captive, incapable; and it is because of this constant suggestion of imperfection that he begins to say, "I cannot endure it, I cannot stand it, I cannot bear it, I cannot forget it, I cannot forgive." A man begins to think all these things because he is imperfect, because of all the continual suggestions which arise in life and convince him that he is limited. Naturally, therefore, as the man goes on, whether he is successful or unsuccessful, whether he is more qualified or less, whatever his condition may be, his mind holds the thought that his power and inspiration, his knowledge and capability are limited. He cannot understand anything else but that, and he remains totally unaware of that spark which continually shines in his heart and which may be called his divine inheritance.

Is there a possibiltiy of changing or of improving our destiny? We in our material life become so rigid in our thinking that we cannot imagine something existing and at the same time improving and changing. We are only capable of recognizing change as far as we can see it, and the moment we cannot see that change any more we call it destruction or death. In other words what we call destruction or death is only a change. We cannot follow, we cannot see the link; it is not visible to us, we cannot fathom it, and therefore we say that it is the end. But is there anything that ends, that is destroyed, or anything that has ceased? Nothing. All these words are our own illusion, our own conception, a conception which is only true as long as we have not seen the continuity. As soon as we understand this mystery, we no longer continue to have that conception. When we see life end suddenly, we call it death. We say a word, in this case 'death,' and once that word is spoken it is the end of the matter for us. But the word is never silent, it continues, if not in this then in another sphere.

So it is with thought. We have a thought and then we say, "I have forgotten." Yes, the mind has forgotten, but the thought is not dead. It is going on; it never ends. Is there anything that ends? Nothing. such words as 'beginning' and 'end' are our conceptions, and the further we go in studying life the higher the realization we get of those conceptions. It is this principle which is called unlearning. People are proud and satisfied with what they have learned; but the further one goes, the more one finds that learning ends in unlearning.

Then another learning begins. It is like turning life inside out. We are walking on the same earth under the same sun, but we are looking at a different world with different eyes. Life is a different life to us then and the meaning of every word is different. Those who have realized in themselves the possibility of improving their lives, do improve them. But the one who thinks, "I cannot help it; I am what I am; I get angry, I cannot help it; I get annoyed, I cannot help it; I cannot understand, I cannot bear it": that person comes under his own suggestion and he naturally becomes weaker every day and cannot accomplish things. But the one who realizes that life begins with spirit, says, "What does it matter; if I fail today I will succeed tomorrow. The present limitation does not discourage me."

It is never too late in life to improve; there is always scope for the man who wants to improve himself. But the man who is content with himself, or so discouraged that he does not want to improve, falls flat. There is no way for him to accomplish anything in life.

The spirit of those who went to mountain caves or lived in the forests was a meditative one; one might think it was an undesirable life. Yes, perhaps undesirable to follow, but in relation to what they reached the experience they gained was most desirable. There is much that could be exchanged between East and West. The West has improved and cultivated and invented many things which should go to the East. And the experience of those in the East who went to the forests and sat in meditation under the shade of trees should be taken to the West. It is this that will bring East and West closer, to the best advantage of the whole of humanity.

There is a story of Timurlenk, the great Moghul emperor, a man whom destiny had intended to be great. Yet he was not awakened to that greatness. One day, tired of the strife of daily life and overwhelmed by his worldly duties, he was lying on the ground in a forest waiting for death to come and take him. A dervish passed by and saw him asleep and recognized in him the man that destiny had intended to become a great personality. The dervish struck him with his stick and Timurlenk woke up and asked, "Why have you come to trouble me here? I have left the world and have come to the forest. Why do you come to trouble me?" The dervish said, "What gain is there in the forest? You have the whole world before you; it is there that you will find what you have to accomplish, if only you realize the power that is within you." He said, "No, I am too disappointed, too pessimistic for any good to come to me. The world has wounded me; I am sore, my heart is broken. I will no longer stay in this world." The dervish said, "What is the use of having come to this earth if you have not accomplished something, if you have not experienced something? If you are not happy, you do not know how to live!" Timurlenk said to the dervish, "Do you think that I shall ever accomplish anything?" The dervish answered, "That is why I have come to awaken you. Wake up and pursue your duty with courage. You will be successful; there is no doubt about it." This impression awakened in Timurlenk the spirit with which he had come into the world. And with every step that he took forward, he saw that conditions changed and all the influences and forces that he needed for success came to him as if life, which before had closed its doors, now opened all to him. And he reached the stage where he became the famous Timurlenk of history.

The Spirit of Mastery

In all walks of life it will be proved to the seeker after truth that there is a key to success, a key to happiness, a key to advancement and evolution in life; and this key is the attainment of mastery. The question is, how does one attain mastery? There are three stages. The first stage of mastery is the attaining of self-control. And when once self-control is gained, then the second stage is to control all the influences that pull one away from the path which one wishes to take. And when one has been victorious in this second stage, then there is a third stage which is the control of conditions, of situations. The man who is responsible, the man who has control over conditions and situations, is greater than a thousand men who may be otherwise well qualified but do not have this. The one who is able to control them may sit in his chair appearing to do nothing, but he will accomplish more than one who is doing things all day long. Very few can imagine to what an extent a man can gain power, especially as life today is a continual strife for nothing, a busy life without much accomplishment. We cannot imagine to what an extent the power of the mastermind can accomplish things. But it is done behind the scenes. Those who do little come forward and say they can do so much, but those who really do something say little.

There are three aspects of the mastermind or Sahib-e Dil as he is called in Persian. These three aspects are connected with three different temperaments. One is the saintly temperament, another is that of the master, and the third is the temperament of the prophet.

When a person has attained mastery, it may be called an inner initiation. From that time he is consciously used to fulfill a certain purpose. Every soul is here on earth in order to fulfill a certain purpose in the scheme of life; but when one has reached mastery, from that moment one is chosen by Providence to be used as a tool, an instrument, to accomplish a certain purpose. Humanity, every single human being, is a kind of raw material which destiny uses. The mastermind, however, is a finished instrument which destiny handles to accomplish its purpose.

The saintly temperament is the negative temperament, resigned, perfectly resigned, to the will of God. The saint has learned patience, confidence, endurance, tolerance. He has carried the cross, he is crucified a thousand times in his life. He knows what love means. He has taken a path of devotion; he leads a life of service; he has effaced himself; he has crushed his personality. He has dissolved the rock out of which he was made into water. His way is not the way of the hammer but of the water. The hammer breaks a rock but the water surrounds it and makes its way. That is why the saintly personality gives peace and harmony and comfort to those who come in contact with it. It is such a personality which heals and lifts up those who are groping in darkness, who are touching the depths of the earth. He has developed the love that one sees in a mother and father but he has that love for every person, for every soul. It is not just a fable that the trees and plants and rocks spoke to the saints. It is the truth. When a person has developed that sympathy, he is sympathetic to rock and plant and tree; everything in nature opens up before him. It is through that at-one-ment that he is able to communicate with every form of life, whatever it is. Therefore, it is not necessary that he should leave the world; whether he is in the forest or amidst the world's strife, the soul of man is always capable of rising to the greatest heights, if only he wishes to attain to them.

The other aspect is the aspect of the master. Resistance against all that increases his weakness, that appeals to his weakness, the tendency of continual perseverance, courage and boldness, firmness and steadiness, all such qualities manifest in the master. That is the difference between saint and master. One is active, the other passive; one is resigned, the other persistent. But at the same time both are going forward. Only their ways are different; one is the positive way, the other the negative way; one is the way of power, the other of gentleness. Nevertheless, both have their purpose to accomplish in the scheme of nature.

In the master's path the will is used mostly in regard to outer things; in the saintly path the will is used to control one's own self; in other words it is used for the time being against one's own self. The saint is resigned to Kaza, and the master has regard for Kadr. But in order to know the will of God it is wise first to take one's own will in hand and use it in the knowledge that it is given for some great purpose in life.

And the third aspect is the aspect of the prophet in whom these two qualities are balanced. On one hand the prophet is power, on the other hand gentleness itself. On the one hand the prophet is courage, on the other he is the personification of divine sympathy. On the one hand the prophet is enthusiastic in his desire to change the condition of humanity, on the other hand the prophet has retired from all things of life. All these opposite qualities are balanced in the spirit of the prophet.

The work of the prophet is a greater work than that of the master or saint. They can remain behind the scenes, but the prophet is before the world to awaken humanity, to raise mankind to a higher consciousness, to inspire it, and to voice the truth so that it may have its echo on the earth, in the sky, everywhere. Do not be surprised, therefore, when you hear that the words of Buddha or Muhammad are still being cherished after so many years, or that the personality of Christ still has power after two thousand years. They have won humanity; they were prophets because that part of their experience which we know in history was real and will always remain real. Mastery is not only a means of accomplishing the things of the world, but it is that by which a person fulfills the purpose of his life.

Everything to be found on earth, such as gold and silver, gems and jewels, is all for mankind. And all that gives happiness, such as power, intelligence, harmony, peace, inspiration, ecstasy, joy, also belongs to man. Man can make a heavenly experience his treasure, just as well as an earthly possession. It is not necessary for man to leave all the things of the world and go into retreat. He can attend to his business, to his profession, to his duties in life and yet at the same time develop this spirit in himself which is the spirit of mastery. The spirit of mastery is like a spark; by blowing continually upon it it will grow into a blaze, and out of it a flame will rise.

Man does not need to trouble about what is lacking outside, for in reality all is within himself. And if he will keep this idea before him and blow on the spark of mastery by constant contemplation, then one day that flame will rise and his life will become clear and his power will indeed be great.

Free Will

There are two opposite opinions existing in the world: one belongs to those who are called fatalists, those who believe in fate, and the other is the opinion of those who believe in free will. And if we look at life from both these points of view we shall find reasons for and against each. There are many instances in life where there are qualifications, conditions, inclinations and every possibility of progress; yet at the same time there is some unknown hindrance and one cannot find out what it is. A man may work for years and years and not succeed. There are also many who hope and believe that all good things will come of themselves, but just by hoping and believing good things do not come; it takes an effort and persistence, it needs patience to accomplish things. This shows that there is truth in both possibilities; but at the same time the middle way is the best, the way of understanding how far free will works and also where free will is hindered.

Life according to the mystic's point of view can be divided into two aspects. One is the preparatory aspect, and the other is that of action. The preparatory aspect is the time before a person is born and the other aspect is the time after his birth. A person may be born into a certain condition which becomes the foundation of his life's course; for instance among people who are addicted to drink or in a rich family. The credit for what he does, considering that condition, belongs to him, but that condition is something he has not made; from it he has to develop and evolve through life. And the question is how this condition is brought about.

Eastern philosophers have had different ideas about this matter. The way that the wise and the mystics look at it is that man is a ray of the spirit, like a ray shooting forth from the sun. Therefore the origin of all souls is one and the same, just as the origin of the various rays is in the one sun. But as these rays shoot forth they pass through three different phases; in other words, they penetrate through three different spheres. When the ray shoots forth, the first sphere it passes is the angelic sphere, the next is the sphere of genius or jinn, and the third is the physical sphere. These spheres are recognized in the metaphysics of the East.

Now the nature of each sphere is such that the ray or soul when it penetrates through a certain sphere must clothe itself in the garb of that sphere. Just as a person from a tropical country going to a cold climate must adopt the clothes of that climate, so the soul, which by origin is intelligence and a ray of that Sun which is the source and goal of all beings, adopts a certain garb with which it is able to enter, to stay, and to pass through that particular sphere. Therefore, according to the metaphysics of the East, man is an angel, a jinn, and is also man. In these three conditions the soul is the same, though the garb it has taken makes it seem different. Passing through the angelic sphere the soul is angel, passing through the sphere of the genius the soul is jinn, passing through the physical sphere the soul is man. The soul's condition in the preparatory stages of angel and jinn in the end makes it man.

What about the animals, and about many other beings and objects which show some part of life in them, such as trees and plants and rocks? All these are preparatory coverings which make the clothes, the garb, for the soul. There is a saying of a great sage of Persia who lived 500 years before Darwin and who gave his ideas on biology: he said that God slept in the rocks, God dreamed in the plant, God awoke in the animal, and God realized Himself in man. It tells that this process, from the vegetable to the animal, from the animal to man, is really the progress of the garb. For instance the first clothes were made of the bark of a tree. Then as people went on making clothes they found better materials and finally came to the finest. Man is the finest material: his garb, not his soul. His soul is the same as that of the man of a thousand years ago. The material has changed and has progressed with the evolution of the soul which has adorned itself with it. In this way the vanity of creatures has been made manifest. And as the matter of our bodies changes every few years, we attract a finer and finer quality of matter as we grow spiritually. Spiritual advancement has an influence upon the body.

There is also another outlook on this subject: that although the soul, as a ray, goes forward to the physical sphere, yet its nature is to go backward, because it follows the law of gravitation. Just as the body which is made of clay is drawn to the earth, so the soul which belongs to the spirit is drawn to the spirit. "But," one may say, "we can see the body drawn to the earth, we can see all things of the earth drawn to the earth, but we do not see the law of gravitation working in the soul." Actually we do see it, but we deny it, because we do not look at it that way. For there is a dissatisfaction, a discontent, in every soul. A man may be in a palace or in a cottage, but no matter what condition he lives in there is an innate yearning and longing which even he himself does not recognize. One thinks today that one longs for money, tomorrow for a position, for fame or name; one goes from one thing to another. It just goes on, and when in the end one has reached one's object one wants something else. It is the law of gravitation, that yearning towards the Spirit, the Sun, which is at the back of it. That is why in ancient times people worshipped the sun god as a symbol of the sun within us, the sun which cannot be seen by our eyes, but which is the source and goal of all beings, from which we have come and to which we are drawn. As it is said in the Qur'an, "From God we all come and to Him we have to return." That means: there is a spirit, the spirit of all things, the essence of life from which we come and towards which we are drawn.

These three spheres can only be entered on one condition, and that condition is that the soul must clothe itself in the garb belonging to that particular sphere. It is that garb which makes an entity of the soul which hitherto was without any distinction or attribute; as soon as it has adopted this garb it becomes an entity. Before it was only a divine ray. The first garb makes the soul an entity known as an angel; the next garb makes it a mind; and the third garb makes it a body.

Is the mind within the body, and is the soul within the mind? As according to science the brain is within the body, one could think that the mind too is within the body, but it is not so. It is as much within as without. It is vaster and wider than the physical body. A jug cannot contain the water of a lake, and so the body cannot contain in itself the mind; yet the jug can contain some water from the lake, and the body can contain some of the mind within itself.

But the word 'within' has a quite different meaning from that which we attach to it in everyday language. When we speak of the mind being within it means a different dimension; it does not mean in the head or in the breast. It means within each atom of the body, and within every nerve and every bloodcell. And at the same time it means within, it means behind or beneath or under or nearest to the soul, nearest to our being. That is the meaning of within. The mind is both within and without the body; and so in the same way the soul is both within the mind and without the mind.

One might ask to what extent the jinn world and the angelic world occupy space in our world and pervade it. But what is space? Space is that which accommodates. The mind is a space also, a space which is wider than the world. Our eye is a space too; and as the mind does not mean the brain, so the space in the eyes of our body is not the only space; behind it is another space which is connected with it. And when this idea becomes clear to man, that there is another space, different from this outer space which already accommodates so much, then the vision of the heavens is opened before him. When a Chinese philosopher was asked what the soul is like, he answered that it is like the pupil of the eye. He meant to say that the soul is an accommodation, like the pupil of the eye, which is so small and yet accommodates so much.

And think of the heart. If there were a thousand universes it would accommodate them all, it is so large. As the former Nizam of Hyderabad, who was a mystic, said, "What is the universe and the entire cosmos? If the doors of the heart are open, the heart proves to be larger than the whole cosmos." What little one can understand of this is shown by the sign of the cross: there is a horizontal space and there is another kind of space which can be pictured as a perpendicular line. It is to explain the latter space that the mystics and seers have used the word 'within', and to explain the space of the world, they have used the word 'without'.

The entities or souls which shoot forth from the Spirit into these three spheres have in each of them the experience of meeting those souls which are returning from manifestation. It is just like a person going from the United States to the Far East and another going from the Far East to the United States, and both meeting in Europe. They give each other whatever they have. The one coming from the Spirit gives magnetism, electricity, intelligence, freedom and freshness, love and life; and the one returning gives experience, knowledge, impression, expression, desires, wishes, thoughts of the wickedness and goodness of the earth, all that he has learned and earned and done and wants to accomplish. All these things are exchanged. It is like the way in which one man may come from Europe with an introduction to the United States which would take him into the best society, and another one who has not received any introduction might go to quite the wrong people.

Thus the soul comes on earth already prepared during the journey through these two spheres. Now supposing for instance the returning soul of Shakespeare met in the world of the jinn another soul coming from the inner Spirit and gave all its experience and qualities and attainments to this soul which was coming to the earth, then this soul would be born with the same qualities as Shakespeare: with the tendency to write poetry, and with much of the knowledge which Shakespeare expressed in his works. According to the Hindus this person may be called the reincarnation of Shakespeare. But one might think, "What has happened to Shakespeare himself; is it not Shakespeare who has come again in this person?" Yes, but what we know of Shakespeare is of his mind and his body. Shakespeare's soul was a divine ray; it had no peculiarity that might serve as a proof of his being Shakespeare. The Shakespeare in him was outwardly his physical body, and inwardly his mind. That mind was impressed on a soul who came forth onto the earth with the heritage already received from Shakespeare. And for Shakespeare to continue further toward the inner Spirit it was necessary to throw away that garment. Therefore the mind of Shakespeare was a garment borrowed from the jinn plane. That garment he may have given to another one. So if you say, "What about Shakespeare?" the first question really is: who was Shakespeare? Because it is not the soul, it is the garment which has come again, renewed. The difference is only in words; in its deeper sense there is no difference.

There seems to be a great dissimilarity between the ideas of Buddhism and those of Christianity about reincarnation. The reason is that the message of Jesus Christ was given to the children of Beni Israel, to those prepared to understand God as the King, as the Master of the Day of Judgement, as the One who is all justice and all power; while the message which Buddha gave was to the people of India, who were more metaphysical and scientific. The simple people of India had their gods and goddesses, and they were satisfied with their religion; but the intellectual class was not satisfied with the gods and goddesses alone and with a religion of devotion. They were scientific and logical; they had their own philosophies. Buddha's mission therefore was to give the people of India an understanding beyond what religious devotion can teach. That is why he did not give the essential wisdom in the form of religion, but in the form of philosophy. The common belief was in reincarnation; and it was much easier for the Master not to attack that particular belief but to build on that belief a wonderful structure.

Some Buddhists today whose insight is great wonder why Buddha gave his theory, and why he did not give a reason for it. I was very much interested once in San Francisco where a Buddhist came to see me. He was a well-known preacher of Buddhism in Japan. There was another man present who had read many Buddhist books. I was eagerly waiting to hear what this Buddhist priest had to say, but he did not think it necessary to say anything. In order to make him speak I said I would so much like to know the Buddhist teaching about reincarnation. But the other man, the one who had ready many books, said, ''Reincarnation is the principal idea in the Buddhist religion; that one is born again and again; and that is what constitutes Karma.'' But I was eager to hear something from the priest! After the other had finished his explanation, I asked the Buddhist preacher if this was right.

And in his simple way of speaking, he said, "What this gentleman has said is his belief." He said no more.

If one should ask if there is such a thing as reincarnation the answer is both yes and no. Why? Because in both answers there is sense and both answers are true. When you look at life as one life then you do not look upon people as separate entities. Then you cannot say that this person has reincarnated as another. It is the One who is all, and each one is nothing. Either you look at life in that way or you look at life by seeing each person as a separate entity. Naturally, as everything has to go on being something, it must still exist after it is destroyed, it must have an existence in some form. But the destruction or death is only a change. Something cannot be nothing. If it is nothing to our eyes, it is because we do not see. Everything must exist in some form or other. Thus the theory of reincarnation teaches that there is nothing which will be nothing, that everything will be something, must be something.

The other conception is this: if the source is one, the goal is one, then all that we see is phenomena as long as we do not look deeply. When once we look deeply we shall no longer distinguish separate entities; then we shall see one life, one Being; and then there is no reason to think about reincarnation. The thought of Buddha was the same as the teaching of Jesus Christ, only given to Hindus in another form. The religion of the Master was the same whether he was called Buddha or Christ. The more we think of this subject, the more we shall find that a preparation is made for man before he is born on earth; and it is that preparation which makes him able to live the life on earth.

What is this life on earth? Is this a life which is fixed and designed, or is there free will? Very often people do not understand the meaning of the term free will, and specially those who claim most to have free will have the least of it. They are so conscious of their free will and yet they do not know where it comes from. When they have an inclination to laugh or cry, to sit or move, they believe that it is because they want to do it; but they do not know where the thought came from. Do we not feel everyday at some time an oppression, seemingly without reason, or a feeling of hilarity or of despair, or a desire for action and at other times a feeling of lethargy? We think that whatever comes into one's mind is free will. But free will is quite different from that. We each have our free will, and that free will gives us the power to work to some extent within the activity of the whole. But both that which we decide and that which conditions create can all be summed up in the Will of God. We have our individual part to perform, and we must do what we feel is right.

How can there be free will, one might ask, if all is God? The power of water is different from the power of fire; the power of fire is different from the power of earth. So the action of each individual is different, although in the soul of each there is God. According to conditions and education temperaments differ; yet God is in all.

There are many things one has to overcome before one sets forth upon the journey to higher realization; but at each step one takes towards the realization of truth one will feel more self-confident. And the more one overcomes all doubts and the more one's self-confidence grows, the greater will be one's will; and the closer to truth one reaches, the more light one will see. And what is that light? It is the light of Self-realization.

Action

To say that results are according to deeds sounds simple, for almost everyone knows it. But not everyone always follows it; and the reason is that knowing a law does not necessarily enable man to observe that law. Besides the nature of life is so intoxicating that, absorbed in the activity of life, one mostly forgets this rule. It is natural, however, that this most simple thing should be very difficult to practice, because one generally neglects to think seriously about it. In order to prove this theory, that the results of a deed are similar to the deed, one need not go far; one can see numberless examples in one's own life and in the lives of others. For it is like an echo; what one does has an echo, and in that echo is the result.

Zarathushtra says that actions may be divided into three kinds: deed, speech, and thought. One may not do wrong, but one may speak wrongly. One may not speak wrongly, but one may think wrongly, and the wrong is done just the same. And how many people excuse themselves by saying, "I only said it, but I did not do it!" A person can even excuse himself by saying, "I did not say it, I only thought it."

According to the ideas of the mystics, the world in which we make our life is an Akasha, and Akasha means capacity. It is pictured by them as a dome, and whatever is spoken in it has its echo; therefore, no one can do, say, or think anything for one moment which will become nonexistent. It is recorded, and that record is creative. It is not only what one does, says, or thinks that is recorded in the memory or in the atmosphere, but that record also creates at every moment, so that every line and letter of it becomes the seed or the germ that produces a similar effect.

I once heard a sculptor say that every man is the sculptor of his own image. Not only is this true, but every man is also the creator of his own conditions, favorable or unfavorable. The difficulty is that man never has the patience to wait till he see the result, for the result takes some time to manifest, and before that he may meet with contrary effects. For instance a man who has just robbed another person may have the good luck to find in the street a purse full of gold coins. Naturally he will think, ''What a good result after good work! Now that it is shown that I have done good work, I must continue it! It is the simple ones who say things against it, but I have seen the good results in my own experience.'' Life is so intoxicating that it gives man no time to think that the result of one's deed is perhaps waiting, that what happens today may be the result of something else further back.

When we consider the law of action we see that it can be divided into five different aspects. One aspect is the law of the community; this law is made for the comfort and convenience of the members of that community. Another aspect can be called the law of the state; it is the law by which different classes of people and different communities are governed as one whole. No doubt this aspect of the law is as limited as the mind of man. Naturally, therefore, many laws are rejected, and many new laws are made and brought into practice. And as time goes on people will see that the members of the community or the state will always wish for changes to be made in the law. This has always been and will always be.

The third aspect of the law is the law of a Church, which perhaps comes from a tradition; a law that people accept, not only because it is a law by which they are governed, but because it is a law that is concerned with their faith, with their belief, which is sacred to them. It is this law which builds a conscience, more than any other aspect of the law.

But then there is another aspect and that is the law brought by the prophets from time to time. And what is this law? It comes as an interpretation of the hidden law which a prophet has been able to see; but a law given by a prophet is also related to the period in which he lived, to the people of that period and their particular evolution. Thus this law is brought about by two actions. One action is the condition of humanity at that specific time, reflected in the heart of the prophet; and the other is the light of God, shining from above to make that condition so clear that a solution can be found for it. It is this solution which can be called the divine law, given by the prophet.

When we study the religions given by various prophets to different people in this world in different periods of the world's history, we shall find that the truth which is behind all the religions is the same; if the teaching differs it differs only in the law they have given. People have always disputed in vain over this difference in the laws that the different teachers have given to their people, not realizing how much that law depended on the people who received it and on the time when it was given.

But these four laws mentioned above: the law of the community, of the state, of the Church, and of the prophet, all have their limitations. There is, however, one law which leads man towards the unlimited, and this law can never be taught and can never be explained. At the same time this law is rooted in the nature of man, and there is no person, however unjust and wicked he may seem, who has not got this faculty in his innermost being. It may be called a faculty, for it is the faculty of discerning between right and wrong.

But what determines that something should be called right or wrong? Four things: the motive behind the action, the result of the action, the time, and the place. Wrong action with the right motive may be right; and a right action with wrong motive may be wrong. We are always ready to judge an action, and we hardly think of the motive. That is why we readily accuse a person for his wrong, and excuse ourselves readily for our wrong, because we know our motive best. We would perhaps excuse another person as we excuse ourselves if we tried to know the motive behind his action too. A thought, a word, or an action in the wrong place turns into a wrong, even if it was right in itself. A thought or word or action at a wrong time may be wrong although it may seem right. And when we analyze this more and more we shall say, as a Hindu poet has said, "There is no use in feeling bad about the wrong deed of another person. We should content ourselves with the thought that he could not do better." To look at everything, trying to see what is behind it, to see it in its right light, requires divine illumination, a spiritual outlook on life. And this outlook is attained by the increase of compassion. The more compassion one has in one's heart, the more the world will begin to look different.

There is another side to this question. Things seem to us according to how we look at them. To a wrong person everything looks wrong, and to a right person everything looks right; for a right person turns wrong into right, and a wrong person turns right into wrong. The sin of the virtuous is a virtue, and the virtue of a sinner is a sin. Things depend very much upon our interpretation, as there is no seal on any action, word, or thought which determines it to be wrong or right.

There is still another side to it: how much our favor and disfavor play their part in discerning right and wrong. In someone whom we love and like and admire, we wish to see everything wrong in the right light. Our reason readily comes to the rescue of the loved one. It always brings an argument as to what is right and what excuses his wrong. And how readily do we see the faults and errors of the one whom we disfavor; and how difficult it is for us to find a fault, even if we wanted to, in someone we love! Therefore, if in the life of Christ we read how he forgave those who were accused of great faults or great sins, we can now see that it was natural that the one who was the lover of mankind could not see faults; the only thing he could see was forgiveness. A stupid or simple person is always ready to see the wrong in another and ready to form an opinion and to judge. But you will find a wise person expressing his opinion of others quite differently, always trying to tolerate and always trying to forgive still more. The present is the reflection of the past, and the future will be the echo of the present; this saying will always prove true.

The Sufis of Persia have classified the evolution of personality in five different grades. The first is the person who errs at every step in his life and who finds fault with others at every moment of his life. One can picture this person as someone who is always likely to fall, who is on the point of tumbling down; and when he falls, he at once catches someone else and pulls him down with him. This is not rare if we study the psychology of man. The one who finds fault with another is very often the one who has the most faults himself. The right person first finds fault with himself; the wrong person finds faults with himself last; only after having found fault with the whole world does he find fault with himself. And then everything is wrong, then the whole world is wrong.

The next grade of personality is that of the one who begins to see the wrong in himself and the right in the other. Naturally he has the opportunity in his life to correct himself because he finds time to discover all his own faults. The one who finds fault with others has no time to find fault with himself. Besides he cannot be just; the faculty of justice cannot be awakened unless one begins to practice that justice by finding the faults in oneself.

The third person is the one who says, "What does it matter if you did wrong or if I did wrong? What is needed is to right the wrong." He naturally develops himself and helps his fellowmen also to develop.

Then there is the fourth man, who can never see what is called good without the possibility of its becoming bad, and who can never see what is called bad without the possibility of that bad turning into good. The best person in the world cannot hide his faults before him and the worst person in the world will show his merit to his eyes.

But when man has risen to the fifth grade of personality, then these opposite ideas of right or wrong, good or bad, seem to be like the two ends of one line. When that time has come he can say little about it, for people will not believe him; while he is the one who can judge rightly, yet he will be the last to judge.

There are three different ways that man may take in order to progress towards human perfection. But a person who is not evolved enough to adopt the third way or the second way, should not be forced to attempt them. If he were forced at this stage it would mean that he was only taught a manner. For these three ways are like three steps towards human perfection.

The first degree is the law of reciprocity. It is in this degree that one learns the meaning of justice. The law of reciprocity is to give and to take sympathy, and all that sympathy can give and take. It is according to this law that the religion and the laws of the state and of the community are made. The idea of this law is that you may not take from me more than you could give me: I will not give you more than I could take from you. It is fair business: you love me, I can love you; you hate me, I can hate you. And according to this law if a person has not learned the just measure of give and take, he has not practised justice. He may be innocent, he may be loving, but he has no common sense, he is not practical. The danger in this law is that a person may value most what he himself does and may diminish the value of what is done by another. But the one who gives more than he takes is progressing towards the next grade.

It is easy for us to say that this is a very hard and fast law. But at the same time it is the most difficult thing to live in this world and to avoid it. One must ask a practical man, a man with common sense, if it is possible to live in this world and not to observe this law of give and take. If the people of the world did no better than keep this law properly there would be much less trouble in this world. It is no use thinking that people will become saints or sages or great beings; if they became just it would already be something.

And now we come to the next step. This is the law of beneficence. And this law means being unconcerned with how another person responds to us in answer to what we do to him in love and sympathy. What concerns one is what can one do for the other person. It does not matter if a favor is not appreciated. Even if the favor were absolutely ignored, still the satisfaction of the beneficent man comes from what he has done, not from what the one who has received it has expressed. When this sense is born in man, from that day he begins to live in the world. For his pleasure does not depend upon what he receives from others but depends upon what he does for others. His happiness is not dependent on anything; his happiness is independent; he becomes the creator of his happiness; his happiness is in giving, not in taking.

But what do I mean by giving? We give and take every moment of the day. Every word we speak, every action we do, every thought and feeling we have for one another, is all giving and all taking. But it is the man who gives who will forget his sorrow, it is he who will forget his miseries, it is he who will rise above the pains and miseries of this world.

Then comes the third law, and that is the law of renunciation. To the one who observes this law giving means nothing. For he is not even conscious of the fact that he gives; he gives automatically. He never thinks "I give"; he thinks that it is being given. This person may be pictured as someone walking on the water. For it is he who will rise absolutely above the disappointments, distresses, and pains of life which are so numberless. Besides renunciation means independence and indifference; indifference to all things, and yet not by the absence of sympathy. And independence in regard to all things, and yet not independence in the crude sense of the word.

Renunciation, therefore, may be called the final victory. Only one in a million can attain to this ideal. And the one who has attained this ideal is he who may be called elevated, liberated.

Responsibility

In the Qur'an it is said that God offered His trust to the heavens and the earth and the mountains, but they refused, being unable to bear it; and then God offered His trust to man who did accept it. Trust in this case is responsibility. The value of man is as great as his responsibility, for what mountains cannot bear, mankind has carried through life; and that is why a responsible man naturally shows a spiritual quality in all connections, in all relationships. Be he our friend or our master or servant or relative, if he is responsible for the trust we give him, it is that which gives him value. Be he a minister or a king or a president of the state, his greatness, his value, is according to his responsibility, and according to the power with which he carries it out through life.

But there is another point of view from which to look at it: that man may become great by his responsibility. And at the same time he may fall, for there is a stumbling block: the more conscious man becomes of his responsibility, the less he recognizes the power of wisdom which is working beside him. It is because of this that at this time of materialism there are great personalities who accomplish many things, and yet in the end they show their limitation. This limitation comes from being drowned in the responsibility they have taken upon themselves and from having forgotten God, the other power that is working beside them.

However great man may be in wisdom, in power, yet he is limited; and if his wisdom and power are compared with divine wisdom and power, they are not even as much as a drop compared with the sea. Sa'adi, the Persian poet, has made a remark in his *Rose Garden* in simple words. He says, "The Constructor of this whole universe is active in constructing even my affairs. But my anxiety about my affairs is my illness." By this he means, "It is something I cannot help, but at the same time I recognize that all that I wish to accomplish is already done by someone else, who is far greater, more powerful and wise than I."

Jelal-ud-Din Rumi points out in his *Masnavi* that the smallest insect receives its proper nourishment; either it is attracted to its nourishment or the nourishment is sent to it. Man, who is responsible for himself and who takes the responsibility upon himself for other living creatures, would never even think of the small insects living at the bottom of the wall of the house, under the earth, hidden under leaves, covered by grass. But they receive what is needed to keep them alive; and so birds and animals all receive their nourishment and everything they need to build their nests without the help of man. The unfortunate task falls upon man of toiling and of earning his living, but it is the price that he pays for self-reliance, for self-dependence, for the responsibility that he takes upon himself. In so far as he takes a responsibility upon himself he undoubtedly does a great work for humanity; but if he becomes so absorbed in that responsibility that he relies only upon his limited resources, forgetting that source from whence his help comes, and if he is unaware of that power and wisdom which is beside him, then no doubt with his very great responsibility he will fail in the end, notwithstanding all the power and might he may have.

When a man asks today if there is not an energy, a force, working which is devoid of wisdom, the answer is that there cannot exist a quality, an attribute, without the possessor of that quality, of that attribute. Energy cannot exist without the energetic, to whom energy belongs. Might cannot exist without the mighty one whose attribute it is. Intelligence cannot exist without the intelligent one to whom that intelligence belongs. And then a person may say, "Well, is it not energy, a force, a power from which all this comes?" But he does not call himself energy, or force, or power. He says, "I am I, an ego, a being." If this being is produced from an object he cannot be a being; he should not claim himself to be a being. This shows that a being comes from a being; that there is a being behind it all. And that Being is perfect in His power and wisdom. But then a person is inclined to wonder if that being is a larger being than himself, for his ego compares that being with himself; he wants to see that other being, how it stands in comparison with himself. And the answer to this is that it is a Being that includes everyone and all things; and therefore there is nothing else that one can compare this Being with, nor can it be explained, for neither is His wisdom like our wisdom nor His power like our limited power.

Those who have tried to learn the life of dependence upon that Being have been saints and sages. They have practiced the recognition of the divine power and of divine wisdom by becoming passive to it, by becoming responsive to it. And by this practice their load of responsibility was taken away from them and their lives were made easy for them, and they experienced a great ease and peace.

Very often a thoughtful man envies a little child, who is so happy, without care, without anxieties. He realizes that the child represents the divine kingdom. It is as if all that is there belongs to it, all that is good and beautiful. But now the question arises as to how far one should depend upon divine power and wisdom, and how far one should feel responsible for oneself and for those who depend upon one. What sometimes happens is that man takes a principle and practices it; but in order to practice that principle one must prepare oneself. If one is not prepared for that principle one should not practice it. If a man who toils every day for his livelihood sits down and says that God must provide for his livelihood, the supply will not come so soon and he will be disappointed. In order to practice it he must first of all prepare himself to acquire faith; it is confidence and faith which will bring the supply. But confidence and faith should first be cultivated gradually, and the principle should not be practiced at once. If one has a business affair somewhere, and one says, "Well, it will all be done by itself, I shall not go there," that will be wrong, because that man has started by being responsible for it; he cannot suddenly take himself away like this. At the same time he should practice every day that principle of recognizing the wisdom and power which is beside oneself.

I would never advise anyone to give away one's responsibility in recognition of the might and wisdom of God. But one should be full of courage and confidence in the face of difficulty and seeming trouble by recognizing that there is a mighty power, that there is a perfect wisdom behind one, and that all will be well. Through this a person will rise above his limited power and wisdom, and will be able to draw power and wisdom from that unlimited source which in the end will lead him to success. Then even in the case of failure this recognition of a perfect power and wisdom working beside oneself will give one the strength to bear it, and to be resigned to the will of God.

The Aim of Life

The main object of life can only be one object, though there may be as many external objects as there are things and beings. There is one object of life for the reason that there is only one life, and this in spite of the fact that it appears outwardly to be many lives. It is in this thought that we can unite and it is from this thought that true wisdom is learned. No doubt that main object of life cannot be understood at once, and therefore the best thing for every person is first to pursue his object in life; for in the accomplishment of his personal object he will arrive some day at the accomplishment of that inner object. When man does not understand this he goes on thinking there is something else to accomplish, and he thinks of all that is before him that is not yet accomplished; that is why he remains a failure.

The person who is not definite about his object has not yet begun his journey on the path of life. One should therefore first determine one's object for oneself, however small that object is; once it is determined one has begun life. We find with many people that somehow they never happen to find their life's vocation. And what happens then is that in the end they consider their life a failure. All through their life they go from one thing to another, yet as they do not know their life's object they can accomplish so little. When people ask why they do not succeed, the answer is: because they have not yet found their object. As soon as a person has found his life's object he begins to feel at home in this world, where before he had felt himself in a strange world. No sooner has a person found his way than he will prove to be fortunate, because all the things he wants to accomplish will come by themselves. Even if the whole world is against him, he will get such a power that he can hold on to his object against anything. He will get such a patience that when he is on the way to his object no misfortune will discourage him.

There is no doubt that as long as he has not found it he will go from one thing to another, and again to another; and he will think that life is against him. Then he will begin to find fault with individuals, conditions, plans, the climate, with everything. Thus what is called fortunate or successful is really having the right object. When a person is wearing clothes which were not made for him, he says they are too wide or too short; but when they are his clothes he feels comfortable in them. Everyone should therefore be given freedom to choose his object in life, and if he finds his object, one knows that he is on the right path.

Also when a person is on the path there are certain things to be considered. When a person has a knot to unravel, and he is given a knife to cut it, he has lost a great opportunity in his life. It is a small thing, but by not accomplishing it he has gone backward. This is a minor example, but in everything one does, if one has not that patience and confidence to go forward, then one loses a great deal. However small the job a person has undertaken, if he completes it he has accomplished something great. It is not the work that a person has accomplished, it is the very fact of accomplishing which gives him power.

As to what is the main object of every soul, that object may be called spiritual attainment. A person may go through his whole life without it, but there will come a time in his life when although he may not admit it he will begin to look for it. For spiritual attainment is not only acquired knowledge, it is the soul's appetite; and there will come a day in life when a person will feel the soul's appetite more than any other appetite. No doubt every soul has an unconscious yearning to satisfy this soul's appetite, but at the same time one's absorption in everyday life keeps one so occupied that one has no time to pay attention to it.

The definition of spiritual attainment can be found in the study of human nature. For the nature of man is one and the same, be he spiritual or material. There are five things that man yearns for: life, power, knowledge, happiness, and peace, and the continual appetite which is felt in the deepest self yearns for one or other of these five things.

In order to fulfill the desire to live man eats and drinks and protects himself from all dangers of life; and yet his appetite will never be fully satisfied, because though he may escape all dangers, yet the last danger, which man calls death, he cannot escape.

In order to obtain power, which is the next thing, a man does everything to gain physical strength, influence, or rank; he seeks every kind of power. And he always runs up against disappointments, because he will find that wherever there is a power of ten degrees, there will always be another power of twenty degrees to run up against. Just think of the great nations whose military power was once so immense that one could never have believed that they would suddenly collapse. One would have thought that it would take them thousands of years to fall, so great was their power. We need not look for it in history, we have just seen this happen in the last few years; we have only to look at the map.

Then there is the desire for knowledge. This desire promotes a tendency to study. A man might study and study all through his life, but even if he read all the books in all the great libraries there would still remain the question, "Why?" That "why" will not be answered by the books he studies, by exploring the facts which belong to outer life. In the first place nature is so profound that man's limited life is not long enough to probe its depths. Comparatively or relatively one may say that one person is more learned than another, but no one reaches true satisfaction by the outer study of life.

The fourth kind of appetite is happiness. Man tries to satisfy it by pleasures, not knowing that the pleasures of this world cannot make up for that happiness which his soul really seeks after. Man's attempts are in vain; he will find in the end that every effort he made for pleasure brought greater loss than gain. Besides, that which is not enduring, which is not real in its nature, is never satisfactory.

Lastly there is the appetite for peace. In order to find peace one leaves one's environment which troubles one, one wants to get away from people, one wants to sit quietly and rest. But he who is not ready for that peace would not find it even it he went to the caves of the Himalayas, away from the whole world.

When considering these five appetites, which are the deepest man has, one finds that all the efforts man makes to satisfy them seem to be in vain. They can only be satisfied by spiritual attainment; that is the only answer to them. Thus the desire to live can only be satisfied when the soul realizes its eternal life. For mortality exists in conception rather than in reality. From a spiritual point of view mortality is the lack of the soul's understanding of its own self. It is like a person who had lived all his life in the conception that his coat was himself, and when that coat was torn from him he believed that he would die. One experiences the same in life. The soul gets from this physical body a kind of illusion and identifies itself with this mortal being; wise people of all times have practiced meditations to give the soul a chance to realize its independence of the physical body. Once the soul has begun to feel itself, its own life, independently of its outer garb, it begins to have confidence in life and is no longer afraid of what is called death. As soon as this phenomenon takes place a person no longer calls death 'death'; he calls death a change.

If one makes a study of the desire to live, one finds that one cannot have a desire if it is not in one's nature. If there is a desire there is an answer for it. Desire to live continually is a desire of the spiritual person as well as of the material person. A spiritual person will perhaps hope for the next life, and the pessimism of a material person works against his own desire; but the desire is there all the same. How does one attain to this continuity of life? It does not depend only upon a belief, although belief may help some to realize that experience, and those who have no belief will not be able to find the way. Nevertheless, the continuity of life is possible logically since every man desires to live. For it is natural that no one will desire what is not possible, and where there is a natural desire the possibility of its fulfillment is already there. If there were no possibility there would be no desire.

Naturally this does not apply to an unbalanced person; such a person can desire anything. But a person with reason will only desire what is possible to accomplish.

The secret of this question can be found by analyzing oneself. By studying the self one will find that the body is only a cover over one's real self. But by a still more profound study one will find that even one's mind is a cover over one's real self. As soon as one finds this out, one will become independent of the body as a means to live. Also, one will become independent of the mind to live. "But," one might ask, "if there is no body, then what is life?"

One asks this because man has limited himself by experiencing life through his body, and has not tried to experience life without its help. When man is not conscious of his body, then he is conscious of his mind. When the eyes are open he is looking at things before him. When his eyes are closed then he is pondering upon what his mind has gained. In both cases he is dependent either upon his body or upon his mind to live, and this dependence makes the soul limited. It not only limits it, but it makes the soul mortal. In reality the soul is not mortal, but if the soul believes in mortality it is just like being mortal.

The teaching of Jesus Christ, from beginning to end, is to rise above mortality, to find out about life, to learn the art, the science, of living. All the scriptures, every philosopher and mystic, teach this. And why do they teach this? Because if there is one thing undesirable it is mortality, death. No sane person would ask for death. Desire for death is not a natural desire, and even when the mind is craving for death the soul is longing for life.

The soul is living; it is life itself. Death is something foreign to it; it does not know death. That is why even the smallest insect protects itself in every way; it does not wish to die.

What we call death is our impression of a change. Life is subject to change, and death is only a change of life. But making people believe in immortality and making them rise above the fear of death should be done gradually and not suddenly, for otherwise this knowledge would frighten a person more than death itself. It is for that reason that the knowledge of this truth was made a mystical, secret science. Otherwise there would have been no reason for withholding something as precious as that knowledge from one's fellowmen. When a person is awakened suddenly he suffers a great shock, physically and mentally, and it takes him a long time to recover. It is the same with all spiritual truths; this is why there are initiations and a vow of secrecy. One cannot place a dinner before a newborn infant; he must first be fed with milk.

Then there is the desire for power. Man desires power, because it is natural for him to gain. Somewhere a power is hidden in him, he cannot help it; but man is powerless in spite of the power which is hidden in him. The powerlessness, the experience of being powerless, is his ignorance of the power within him. In order to open the doors, in order to see the power he has in store, it is necessary to seek the kingdom of God, as it is said in the Bible, for then he will find his divine heritage which is all power.

True power is not in trying to gain power; true power is in becoming power. But how to become power? It requires an attempt to make a definite change in oneself, and that change is a kind of struggle with one's false self. When the false self is crucified, then the true self is resurrected. Before the world this crucifixion appears to be lack of power, but in truth all power is attained by this resurrection.

As to knowledge, it has two aspects. One knowledge is what one gathers by learning the names and forms of this life. That cannot satisfy this appetite; it is only a stepping-stone to it. This outer learning only helps one to come to the inner learning, but the inner learning is quite different from the outer learning. How is it learned? It is learned by studying the self. One finds that all the knowledge one strives after and all that exists to study is all in oneself. Therefore one finds a kind of universe in oneself, and by the study of the self one comes to that spiritual knowledge for which the soul hungers.

In order to get that knowledge one must try to meditate and to dive into the sea of knowledge which cannot be taught by study. In this way one distinguishes two aspects of knowledge: one aspect of knowledge is intellect, the other aspect is wisdom. Therefore a wise man is not necessarily a clever man, nor a clever man a wise man.

Then there is the question of happiness. A person thinks that when his friends are kind to him, when people respond to him, or when he gets money, then he will be happy. But that is not the way to become happy; sometimes it proves the opposite. For lack of happiness makes him blame others, believing they are standing in the way of his becoming happy; in reality that is not so. True happiness is not gained, it is discovered. Man's way itself is happiness, that is why he longs for happiness. What keeps happiness out of one's life is the closing of the doors of the heart, and when the heart is not living, then there is not happiness there. Sometimes the heart is not fully alive but only partly; at the same time it expects life from the other heart. But the real life of the heart is to live independently in its own happiness; and that is gained by spiritual attainment, by digging deep into one's own heart.

The one who has found his peace within himself may be in a cave of the mountain or among the crowd, yet in every place he will experience peace. What generally happens is that in order to get peace we blame the other person who jars upon our nerves. But in reality the true peace can come only by being so firm against all influences around us that nothing can disturb us.

Now the question is how these five things can be gained. As I have said, the first thing needed is to accomplish the object which is standing before one immediately; however small it is, it does not matter. It is by accomplishing it that one gains power. As one goes further in this way through one's life, always seeking for the real, one will at the end come to reality. Truth is attained by the love of truth. When a person runs away from truth, truth runs away from him. If he does not run away, then truth is nearer to him than that which is without truth. There is nothing more precious in life than truth itself; and in loving truth and in attaining to the truth one attains to that religion which is the religion of all Churches and of all people. It does not matter then to what Church a man belongs, what religion he professes, to what race or nation he belongs; when once he realizes the truth he is all, because he is with all. The obstacle is the disagreement and the misunderstanding before he has attained to the truth. When once he has attained to the truth, there is no more misunderstanding. It is among those who have learned only the outer knowledge that disputes arise, but those who have attained to the truth, whether they come from the North or the South, from whatever country, it does not matter; for when they have understood the truth they are in at-one-ment.

It is this thought that we should keep before us in order to unite the divided sections of humanity, for the real happiness of humanity is in that unity which can be gained by rising above the barriers which divide men.

Knowing Life's Purpose

Every living being has a purpose in life and it is the knowing of that purpose which enables every soul to fulfill it. As it is said in the Gayan, "Blessed is he who knoweth his life's purpose."

Be not surprised if you find many groping in darkness all through life, doing one thing or another, going from one thing to the other, always dissatisfied, always discontented; and everything they undertake remains without result. The reason is the absence of that knowledge, the knowledge of the purpose of life.

Individuals apart, every object has its purpose. The mission of science is to discover the purpose in objects, and it is for this that science has come into being. Be it medical science or philosophy, all the various aspects of science are the result of the desire to discover the purpose of things. But the aim of mysticism is to find the purpose in the lives of human beings, the purpose in one's own life and the purpose in the lives of others. So long as a man has not found this purpose, though he may have success or failure, though he may seem to be happy or unhappy, in reality he does not live; for life begins from the moment a person finds the purpose of his life.

One finds people of great wealth, people who have position and every comfort and convenience, and yet who are missing something, missing the main thing which alone can make them happy:

knowledge of the purpose of their life. This is the very thing they miss. And yet at the same time mankind is ignorant of this. A man will be interested in a thousand things, he will be interested first in one thing and then pass on to another, and so on, but he seems never to come to that point where he finds the purpose of his life. Why? Because he does not look for it.

Coming to children's education, to the education of youth, very often the parents do not think about this problem. Whatever seems to them beneficial for the child to do, that it must do. They do not pay attention to the fact that it is in one's childhood that one has to find the purpose of one's life. How many lives have been ruined for this reason! A child may have been brought up with every facility and yet kept away from the purpose of his life.

However unhappy a man may be, the moment he knows the purpose of his life a switch is turned and the light is on. He may not be able to accomplish anything at once, but the very fact of knowing the purpose gives him all the hope and vigor and inspiration and strength to wait for that day. If he has to strive after that purpose all his life, he does not mind so long as he knows what the purpose is. Ten such persons have much greater power than a thousand people working from morning til evening not knowing the purpose of their life.

Besides, what we call wrong or right, good or bad, differs according to the purpose of life. The more one studies life, the more one realizes that it is not the action but the purpose that makes things right or wrong, good or bad. And as we progress we become more wide awake, and the greater becomes the purpose before us.

Beyond this is the purpose of all, the ultimate purpose. We begin our lives with an individual purpose, but we come to a stage where the purpose of every soul is one and the same. And that can be studied by studying the inclinations of men. Every man has five inclinations hidden in the depths of his heart. Being absorbed in the life of the world he may forget that ultimate purpose, but at the same time there is a continual inclination towards it. That shows that the ultimate purpose of the life of all is one and the same.

The first of these five inclinations is the love of knowledge. It is not only intellectual and intelligent beings who seek after knowledge. Even an infant wishes to know what every little noise is. Every child seeing a beautiful color or line in a picture inquires about it. And therefore in greater or less degree every individual is striving after knowledge. No doubt in life as it is today many are placed in a situation where they never have a moment in which to gain that knowledge which they seek after. From morning till evening they have their duty to perform; they are so absorbed in it that after some time that hunger for knowledge is lost and their mind becomes blunted. There are many thousands of people whom life has placed in a situation where they cannot help but concentrate on some particular work and never have time to think about things that they would like to think about, that they would like to know. We have made this life. We call it progress, freedom, but it is not freedom of mind. The mind is imprisoned in a limited horizon and we call it a sphere.

If all thought, all life, consists in studying something only in order to earn one's bread and butter, then when can one give one's thought and mind to what one's soul is seeking after? Among those who have a little freedom in life, who have time to think about gaining some knowledge, there are many who seek only after novelty. They think that to learn means only to get to know something they did not know before. There are very few seekers who discover that from every idea, however simple, a revelation comes when they give their mind to it, and that it then begins to teach them more and more things which they had never known.

I have experienced this myself. There was a couplet of a Persian verse I had known for twelve years. I liked it, it was a simple everyday conception, but after twelve years one day a glimpse of inspiration came and that very couplet became a revelation. It seemed as if there had been a seed and then a seedling sprang from it and turned into a plant which produced fruit and flowers.

The difficulty that so-called truth-seeking people experience is that when they have a little time to look for truth they are restless. One thing does not satisfy them and so they go from one thing to another. Thus instead of coming to the real notion of truth, they only get into confusion.

Someone asked an artist if he could make a really new picture. "Yes," he said, "I can." He put two horns and two wings on the body of a fish, and people said, "How wonderful, this is something no one has ever seen!" Everyone has seen wings on birds and horns on beasts; but there are many souls who need a novelty of that kind. Many admire it, and few think, like Solomon, that there is nothing new under the sun, especially when we come to the domain of wisdom, of knowledge. For one does not arrive at concentration, contemplation, or meditation by studying many things, nor by going from one idea to another.

The next inclination is the love of life, and not only in human beings, for even little insects escape if one tries to touch them; their life is dear to them. What does this show? It shows that every being wishes to live, however unhappy he may be, however difficult life may seem. Perhaps in the sadness of the moment a person might wish to commit suicide, but if he were in his normal condition he would never think of leaving this world. Not because the world is so dear to him, but because the soul's inclination is to live.

It is said in the Gayan, "Life lives, death dies." Since life lives, life longs to live, and nobody wishes for one moment that death should ever take him. The great prophets, masters, saints, sages, philosophers, mystics, what was their striving? Their striving was to find some remedy to cure man of mortality. But is his mortality his conception of his condition? It is a condition when seen outwardly; in reality it is a conception. The soul keeps the physical body as its garb only until its purpose is fulfilled and it wishes to leave this garb. For no one wishes always to carry his heavy coat. Even the king feels more comfortable when the crown is put in the cupboard.

The soul's happiness comes when it is freed from its physical burden; it can only be happy when it can be itself. As long as man thinks he is his body, so long is he mortal, being only conscious of his mortal existence. But this, intellectually understood, will not help. The soul must see itself, the soul must realize itself. How does the soul do this? In the scriptures it is said, "Die before death." What is this dying? This dying is playing at death. The mystics have all through their life on earth practiced playing at death; by playing at it they were able to see what death is. Then it was not only intellectual knowledge; they actually saw that the soul stands independently of this physical garb. Buddha has called it *Jnana*, which means realization. The absence of it is called *Ajnana*, the lack of realization.

Every thoughtful person, when he thinks of the day when he will have to depart from this earth where he has his friends whom he loves and his treasure, feels very sad. Not only that, but it makes him sadder still to feel that once he is gone he will be gone forever, for life does not wish to become death; life wants to live. But this shows ignorance and a false conception of life, a conception gained by the senses, by experience through the senses. The one who has realized life and things through the senses does not know life. Life can be very different from this.

The third inclination man shows is to gain power in any way whatever. Every person strives throughout life to gain power. The reason is that the soul strives to exist against the invasion of life, because life's conditions seem to sweep away everything that has no strength. When the leaf has lost its strength it falls from the tree; when the flower has lost its strength it is thrown away. Naturally the soul wishes to keep its strength; therefore, every individual seeks for power. But the mistake lies in the fact that however much power a man may have, it is limited. With the increase of power there comes a time when the man sees that another power can be greater than the one he possesses. This limitation makes man suffer; he becomes disappointed. Besides, when one looks at the power that man possesses, the power of the world, what is it? Powerful nations which were built thousands of years ago can be crushed in a very short time; then what is their power? If there is any power it is the hidden power, the almighty power. And by getting in touch with that power one begins to draw from it all the power that is needed.

The secret of all the miracles and phenomena of the sages and masters is to be seen in the power that they are able to draw from within. There are faqirs and dervishes who practice jumping into the fire or cutting their body and healing it instantly. But there exists a power even greater than that. Those who can really do such things do not do them openly; but at the same time there is this power which gives proof that spirit has power over matter, though spirit may be buried under matter for some time, which makes one powerless.

The fourth inclination man shows is to be happy. Man seeks happiness in pleasure, in joy, but these are only shadows of happiness. The real happiness is in the heart of man. But man does not look for it. In order to find happiness, he seeks pleasure. Anything that is passing and anything that results in unhappiness is not happiness. Happiness is the very being of man. Vedantists have called the human soul *Ananda,* happiness, because the soul itself is happiness; that is why it seeks happiness. And because the soul cannot find itself it is always looking for something that will make it happy; but what it finds can never make it really happy, perfectly happy.

Sin and virtue, good and bad, right and wrong, can be distinguished and determined on this principle. Virtue is what brings real happiness. What is called right is that which leads to happiness. What is good is good because it gives happiness; and if it does not do so it cannot be good, it cannot be virtue, it cannot be right. Whenever man has found virtue in unhappiness he has been mistaken; whenever he was wrong he has been unhappy. Happiness is the being of man; that is why he craves for it.

The fifth inclination man shows is for peace. It is not rest or comfort or solitude which can give peace. It is an art which must be learned, the art of the mystics, by which one comes to experience peace. One may ask why, if it is natural for the soul to experience peace, one must strive for peace by practice, by meditation, by contemplation. The answer is that it is natural to experience peace, but life in the world is not natural. Animals and birds all experience peace, but not mankind, for man is the robber of his own peace. He has made his life so artificial that he can never imagine how far he is removed from what may be called a normal, natural life for him to live. It is for this reason that we need the art of discovering peace within us. We shall not experience peace by improving outside conditions. Man has always longed for peace and he has always brought about wars; at the same time every individual says he is seeking for peace. Then where does war come from? It comes because the meaning of peace has not been fully understood. Man lives in a continual turmoil, in a restless condition, and in order to seek for peace he seeks war; if this goes on we shall not have peace till every individual begins to seek peace within himself first.

What is peace? Peace is the natural condition of the soul. The soul which has lost its natural condition becomes restless. The normal condition of mind is tranquility, yet at the same time the mind is anything but tranquil; the soul experiences anything but peace.

The question which arises in the mind of every thoughtful person is, what was the reason, what was the purpose of the creation of this world? The answer is, to break the monotony. Call it God, call it the only Being, call it the source and goal of all; being alone, He wished that there should be something for Him to know. The Hindus say that the creation is the dream of Brahma. One may call it a dream, but it is the main purpose. The Sufis explain it thus: that God, the Lover, wanted to know His own nature; and that therefore through manifestion the Beloved was created, in order that love might manifest. And when we look at it in this light, then all that we see is the Beloved. As Rumi, the greatest writer of Persia says, "The Beloved is all in all, the lover only veils Him; the Beloved is all that lives, the lover a dead thing."

Sufis have therefore called God the Beloved. And they have seen the Beloved in all beings. They did not think that God was in heaven, apart, away from all beings. In everything, in all forms, they have seen the beauty of God. And in this realization the main purpose and the ultimate purpose of life is fulfilled. As it is said in the ancient scriptures, when God asked Adam, "Who is thy Lord?" he said, "Thou art my Lord." This means that the purpose of creation was that every soul might recognize his source and goal, and surrender to it and attribute to it all beauty and wisdom and power, so that by doing so he might perfect himself. As the Bible says, "Be ye perfect even as your Father which is in Heaven is perfect.

Life's Demands

Every intelligent person comes to a stage in his life, sooner or later, when he begins to question himself as to what purpose there is in life, in being on earth. "Why am I here? What am I to accomplish in life?" he asks. No doubt the moment this question has arisen in a person he has taken his first step in the path of wisdom; before, whatever he did, not being conscious of his life's purpose, he remained discontented. Whatever be his occupation, his condition in life, whether he is wise or foolish, learned or illiterate, there is always discontent. He may have success or failure, but the desire that his life's purpose should be accomplished remains, and unless it is accomplished a person cannot be satisfied. That is why many people who are successful in business, doing very well in their profession, comfortable in their domestic life, and popular in society, yet remain dissatisfied because they do not know the purpose of their life.

After knowing the purpose of life we may be handicapped by many things, we may lack means, but the conditions will be favorable to go forward, in spite of all. When someone has found his life's purpose, no matter how difficult life is for him nor how many hindrances he has to contend with, from that moment there is nothing he will not withstand, no sacrifice he will not make, nothing he will not endure. He will wait with patience all his life, and if he does not succeed in this life he will wait even till the hereafter, happy because he is accomplishing his life's purpose. When a person knows, "I am here for this particular purpose," that knowledge in itself gives a great strength of conviction.

There is a story told of the Prophet Muhammad. At the time when the Prophet, who was born for that particular purpose in life, felt a kind of restlessness, a dissatisfaction with everything in life, he thought he had better go into the forest, into the wilderness, into the mountains and sit there alone to get in touch with himself, to find out why there was that yearning after something he did not know. He asked his wife if she would allow him that solitude which his soul longed for, and she agreed. Then he went into the wilderness and sat there for days together. And when the vibrations of the physical body and mind, which are always upset and in turmoil in the midst of the world, calmed down, and when his mind became quiet and his spirit was tranquil, when the heart of the Prophet became restful, he began to feel in touch with all nature there, the space, the sky, the earth; and then it seemed as if everything was talking to him, as if the water and the clouds were talking. He was in communication with the whole world, with the whole of life.

Then the word came to the Prophet: "Cry out in the Name of thy Lord." This is the lesson of idealism: not only being in touch with nature, but idealizing the Lord. In these days there is the great drawback that when people become very intelligent they lose idealism. If they want to find God they want to find Him in figures. There are many who would rather meditate than worship, than pray. In this way there has always been conflict between the intellectual person and the idealistic person. The Prophet was taught as the first thing to idealize the Lord; and when the ideal he thus made became his conception of God, then in that conception God awakened. And he began to hear the voice saying, "Now you must serve your people, you must awaken in your people the sense of religion, the ideal of God, the desire for spiritual attainment, and the wish to live a better life." Then he knew that it was now his turn to accomplish all those things that the prophets who had come before had been meant to accomplish.

We are all born in this world to accomplish a certain purpose, and as long as a man does not know this purpose he remains ignorant of life; he cannot call himself a living being. A machine has no choice, it cannot find its life's purpose, but an individual is responsible to a great extent. Very often out of weakness a man gives in to something which otherwise he would have refused to accept. This weakness comes through lack of patience and endurance, lack of self-confidence, and lack of trust. A person who does not trust in Providence, who cannot have patience, who cannot endure, will take what comes at the moment; he will not wait till tomorrow. Perhaps the purpose of his life would have opened up before him if he had had more power of endurance, more self-confidence, more trust in Providence. But when he possesses none of these things he is just like a machine. He is not pleased with what comes in life, he is grudging every day, he is confused; and yet he goes on like a horse which is not willing to go on, but is yoked to the cart and has to go on. The first knowledge we must gain is the knowledge of the purpose of our life.

It is a great pity that education as it is today pays very little attention to this question. Children, youths, and grown-ups all go through life toiling from morning till evening, studying or working, and at the same time not knowing what purpose they have to accomplish. Among a thousand persons there may be one exception, but nine hundred and ninety-nine are placed in a situation, whether they desire it or not, where they are working just like a mechanism, a machine put in a certain place which is made for it and where it must work. Out of a hundred perhaps ninety-nine are discontented with the work they are doing. Either it is their environment that has placed them there, or it is because they must work for their living, or because they have the idea that they should first gather what they need. By the time they have gathered the means to be able to do something in life, the desire of accomplishing something is gone.

It is a great drawback that in spite of progress individuals often have no opportunity to accomplish something they desire. Many youths never realize this; they think, "We must do that work and that is all"; and they have no time to think about the purpose of their particular life. Thus hundreds and thousands of lives are wasted. In spite of all the money they make their hearts are not satisfied, for it is not the wealth one gains that can give that satisfaction.

On hearing from the Prophet that all things and beings were created for a certain purpose, someone said, "O Prophet, I cannot understand why mosquitoes were created!" And the Prophet answered, "They were created so that you may get up quickly at night and engage yourself in prayer!" Everything is created with a purpose, in order that we may use it for its purpose. And so it is with people. Sa'adi says, "Every being is created for a purpose, and the light of that purpose is already kindled in his soul." As we need blacksmiths and goldsmiths and farmers and others, so we need philosophers and mystics and prophets. That creates the harmony, just as we need sharp and flat music. If it were not so there would be no beauty, for beauty is created through variety.

When we look at life with a philosopher's view we see that every person is like one note in this symphony of life; that we all make this symphony of life, each contributing the music which is needed in that symphony. But if we do not know our own part in the symphony of life, naturally it is as if one of the four strings on the violin is not tuned, and if it is not tuned it cannot give the music which it should produce. So we must each produce that part for which we are born. If we do not contribute what we are meant to and what we should contribute, we are not in tune with our destiny. It is only by playing that particular part which belongs to us that we shall get satisfaction.

Maybe many people will not think as I do; for instance, those who believe strongly in pacifism, in the peace ideal. They will say, "Is it not madness that anybody should make a war!" But everything one does, though it may look better or worse, yet belongs somewhere in the scheme of life, and we have no right to condemn it. The principal thing for every individual is to become conscious of the duty for which he is born.

There are in reality two purposes of life. One is the minor, the other is the major purpose of life. One is the preliminary, and the other is the final purpose. The preliminary purpose of life is just like a stepping-stone to the final one. Therefore, one should first consider the preliminary purpose of life.

In the East there are various stories told about sages and saints who have awakened someone to the purpose of his particular life; and the moment that person was awakened, his whole life changed. There is an account, in the history of India, of the life of Shivaji. There was a young robber who used to attack travellers passing along the way where he lived and he robbed from them whatever he could. And one day before going to his work he came to a sage and greeted him and said, "Sage, I want your blessing, your help in my occupation." The sage asked what his occupation was. He said, "I am an unimportant robber." The sage said, "Yes, you have my blessing." The robber was very pleased, and went away and had greater success than before. Happy with his success he returned to the sage and greeted him by touching his feet and said, "What a wonderful blessing it is to be so successful." But the sage said, "I am not yet satisfied with your success, I want you to be more successful. Find three or four more robbers and join together and then go on with your work." He joined with four or five other robbers who went with him and again had great success. Once more he came to the sage and said, "I want your blessing." The sage said, "You have it. But still I am not satisfied. Four robbers are very few. You ought to form a gang of twenty." So he found twenty robbers. And eventually there were hundreds of them.

Then the sage said, "I am not satisfied with the little work you do. You are a small army of young men, you ought to do something great. Why not attack the Moghul strongholds and push them out, so that in this country we may reign ourselves?" And so he did, and a kingdom was established. The next move of the robber would have been to form an empire of the whole country. But he died. Had he lived Shivaji would have formed an empire. The sage could have said, "What a bad thing, what a wicked thing you are doing. Go in the factory and work!" But the sage saw what Shivaji was capable of. Robbery was his first lesson, his a,b,c. He had only a few steps to advance to be the defender of his country, and the sage realized that he was going to be a king, to release his people from the Moghuls. The robbers did not see it, the young man did not think about it. He was pushed into it by the sage. The sage was not pushing him into robbery; he was preparing him for a great work.

Why in the East is the greatest importance given to a teacher in the spiritual path? For this reason: as Hafiz has said, "If your teacher says, 'Sprinkle your prayer rug with wine,' do it." A prayer rug is a holy object; wine is considered unwholesome; but Hafiz continues, "For the knower knows best which way to go." For instance if a person wishes to collect wealth, his whole mind is absorbed in it. He may be told, "No, that is not a good thing. What is wealth after all? It is unreal, useless. You ought to be devotional, spiritual!" But his mind will not be there. He cannot be spiritual. He is concentrated on that particular thing, and because he cannot collect the money he wants he is unhappy. If one forces upon him spirituality, religion, devotion, prayer, they will not help him. Very often people in place of food give water, and in place of water give food. That is not good. Spirituality comes in its time. But the preliminary purpose is what a man will contribute to the world as the first step before awakening to spiritual perfection.

All the great teachers of humanity have taught that preliminary purpose of life in their religions. Whatever teachings they have given to their followers, their motive has been to help them to accomplish that first purpose in life. For instance when Christ called the fishermen he said, "Follow me, and I will make you fishers of men." He did not say he would make them more spiritual. That was the first step. He wanted them to accomplish the first purpose of life; the next purpose was to become more spiritual. To the teachers of spiritual knowledge who look at it in this way, their first duty is to show someone how to accomplish the first purpose of life. When they have done this, then they show the second purpose.

There are four different ways people take in their lives. One way is the way of material benefit. By profession, by occupation, business, or industry, a person wants to make money. Something is to be said both for and against this ideal. Against it may be said that while working for money one very often loses the right track, thought, and consideration. One easily overlooks the rights of others when one is working for money. And what is to be said for it is this: that it is after all those who possess wealth who can use wealth for the best purpose. All charitable institutions, hospitals, schools, colleges, are raised by charitable people who have given generously to such organizations. There is therefore nothing wrong in earning money and in devoting one's time to it, as long as the motive is right and good.

Another aspect is duty. One considers that one has a duty to one's community, town, or country; one does social work, one tries to do good to others and considers it one's duty. It may be that one has a duty towards one's parents; one may be looking after one's mother and sacrifice one's life for her, or for one's wife and children. There is great merit in this also. No doubt what speaks against it is that very often such lives are spoiled, and they have no chance to do anything worthwhile in the world; but if it were not for the dutiful the world would be devoid of love and affection. If the wife had no sense of duty towards her husband, nor the neighbor towards his friend, then they would be living like creatures of the lower creation. It is the sense of duty that makes man greater than other beings; that is why we admire it. Heroes who give their lives for their country are not doing a small thing. It is something great when a person gives his life for the sake of duty. Besides duty is a great virtue.

At the time of the last war there was a young woman who was always displeased and in disagreement with her husband and she was always wanting a separation. When the call to arms came, her husband went to the battlefield, and he hoped that in his absence she would find someone else. As the war went on she thought that while her husband was fighting she would enroll as a nurse. And it happened that near the place where she was working, the husband was wounded; he lost his eyes, and she became his nurse. When she saw him in that condition she was astonished that it had come about that she was to be his nurse. She had just received a letter containing a proposal of marriage, but she tore it up and changed her mind in an instant; she said,

"Now that he has lost his eyes and that he is helpless, I shall remain his wife, I shall take care of him all his life."

Duty, the sense of duty, is a great virtue; and when it is perfected and deepened in the heart of a man it wakens him to a greater and higher consciousness. In that way people have accomplished noble things. The great heroes have lived a life of duty.

The sense of duty comes from idealism. The greater his ideal of duty, the greater the man. According to the Hindus the observers of duty are considered religious, because *Dharma*, the Sanskrit word which means religion, also means duty.

The third purpose one chooses in life is to make the best of the present. It is the point of view of Omar Khayyam who told one to "Drink the cup of life just now." There is a quatrain in the *Rubaiyat* where he says:

O my Beloved, fill the cup that clears
Today of past regrets and future fears.
Tomorrow! why, tomorrow I may be
Myself with yesterday's sev'nty thousand years!

It is the point of view of the person who says, "If I was great in the past, what does it matter? The past is forgotten. And the future, who knows what will come out of it? No one knows his future. Let us make the best of this moment, let us make life as happy as we can." It is not a bad point of view. It is a philosophical point of view. Those who adhere to it are happy and give happiness to others.

No doubt all these different points of view have a wrong side also. But when we look at their right side there is something in it to appreciate.

People nowadays use a phrase: "He is a jolly good fellow." In songs and on different occasions this phrase is used to show appreciation for that tendency of mind which tries to make this moment happy. It is difficult, very difficult, and not everyone can manage to do it; for life has so many conflicts, so many troubles. One has to face so many difficulties in life that to be able to keep on smiling is not everyone's achievement. In order to keep smiling a person must either be very foolish and not feel or thing about anything, but just close his eyes and his heart to the world; or a person must be as high as the souls meant by the story of the miracle of Christ walking upon the water.

There are some who sink and some who swim, and others who walk over the water. Those who are drowned in life's misery are those who cannot get out of it; they are tied down in the depths of life; they cannot get out and they are miserable there; they are the ones who sink. Then there are others who are swimming; they are those who strive through the conflicting conditions of life in order some day to reach the shore. There are, however, others who walk upon life. Theirs is the life which is symbolically expressed in the miracle of Christ walking upon the water. It is like living in the world and not being of the world, touching the world and not being touched by it. It needs a clear perception of life, keen intelligence and thorough understanding, together with great courage, strength, and bravery.

By this I do not mean to say that the man who makes the best of each present moment is the same as the man whom we call happy-go-lucky, the simple man. That man is the one who lives in another world; he is not aware of life's conditions, he is not awake to the conflicting influences of life; if he is happy it is not surprising, for he is happiness himself. I mean those who are awakened to life's conditions, those who are tender and sensitive to the thoughts and feelings of others. For them it is very difficult to go on living and at the same time to keep smiling. If a man can do it, it is certainly a great thing.

The fourth aspect is that of those who think, "What is life on earth after all! Is it not only a few days to pass somehow?" The day ends, the months and the years pass, and so time slips by. One comes to the end of life before one has expected it, and the whole past becomes like a dream in the night. Ask a man who has lived a hundred years, "What do you think about life on earth?" He will say, "One night's dream, my child, it is no longer than that."

If that is all there is to life, then those who consider it thus will realize they should think about the hereafter. Just as some think, "While we are able to work we must strive in order to make provision for our old age that we may be more comfortable," so those who think of the hereafter say, "Life is short, it is nothing but an opportunity. We must prepare something so that later we shall have the benefit of it." Maybe there will be some who have the right understanding, while others make too much of it and have a wrong conception of the hereafter; yet the wise ones who believe that they must use the time and opportunity which is given to them in this life to prepare for the next one, have accomplished a great deal. It is something to admire.

It is said that the earth and the sky and space do not accommodate a person who does not answer life's demands, although for exceptional souls there are exceptional laws, for the lives of exceptional beings cannot be explained in ordinary terms. One may ask what will be the future of those who have not fulfilled the demand of life; will they have to come back to learn their lesson once more? We must all learn our lesson right now. Life is lived right now, its demand is right now, and we must answer it right now. At every moment we are asked to perform a certain duty, to fulfill a certain obligation; and to become conscious of this and to do it in the most fitting and right manner, that is the true religion.

We understand life's demands by understanding life better. There are some who do not answer life's demands because they do not know what life asks of them; and there are others who do not answer life's demands although they do know. When the demands of the outer life are different from what the inner life asks of us, we should fulfill the demands of the outer life without neglecting those of the inner life, as it is said in the Bible, "Render unto Caesar the things that are Caesar's, and unto God the things that are God's."

We have to become like the ebb and flow. This is a symbolical expression. A certain thing is accomplished at one time by sympathy, and at another time by indifference; one situation we must meet by taking interest in it, in another situation we must become indifferent, not concerned with it. If in a sea there were always ebb and no flow, or always flow and no ebb, then this would be a dead sea. The living sea is both inhaling and exhaling; thus in everything we do in life, we should be able to meet every situation and event with the manner that the situation demands.

These are the four different ways people take in order to accomplish the purpose of their lives: making wealth, being conscientious in their duty, making the best of every moment of life, and preparing for the future. All these four have their good points. And once one realizes this there is no need to blame anyone for having taken another path than our own for the accomplishment of life's purpose. By understanding this one becomes tolerant.

And now we come to the ultimate purpose of life which is always one and the same: for every man has in the end to accomplish the same purpose, in whatever way he will. He will come to it either consciously or unconsciously, easily or with difficulty; but he has to accomplish it. That is spiritual attainment. One might wonder if a person who is so material that he never thinks about it and who refuses to consider this question will ever attain to spiritual realization, but the answer is yes; everyone, consciously or unconsciously, is striving after spiritual attainment. Sometimes he does not take the same way as we do, sometimes his point of view and his method differ, and sometimes one person attains to spiritual realization much sooner than another. It may be reached in a day, and another person may have striven for it all his life and yet not have attained to it. What determines it? It is the evolution of a particular soul.

There are stories told in India of how a person was awakened to spiritual consciousness after hearing one word from his Guru. That one word inspired him instantly to touch the higher consciousness. And then again we hear the stories in the East of people who went to the forest or to the mountains, who fasted for days and months, who were hanging by their feet, their head downwards, or who stood erect for years and years. This shows how difficult it is for one person and how easy for another. We make a great mistake today when we consider every man's evolution as the same. There are great differences between people. One is creeping, one is walking, one is running, and another is flying. And yet they all live under the same sun.

It is the custom in the East for those who begin to seek for a spiritual purpose to look for a spiritual teacher. They do not set forth of the spiritual journey by themselves, for thousands of years of experience have taught that to tread the spiritual path it is necessary to have some leader to whom one can give one's confidence and trust in order to follow him to the end. No doubt in the West there is a general awakening. Everyone wishes to know something about the spiritual path; but the difficulty is that everyone does not stick to one and the same thing. There are many who will go first to one esoteric school and then to another, and so on. In the end they have learned so much that they do not know what is true and what is false, which is right and which is wrong. It is just like visiting a restaurant and eating so much that one is not able to digest it. Besides when a person takes in all that is false and true, there remains no discrimination between false and true.

To realize the preliminary purpose of our life we must find our natural rhythm. Today people adopt wrong methods. They go to a clairvoyant and ask him about the purpose of their life. They do not know it themselves. Anybody else must tell them except their own spirit, their own soul; they ask others because they do not tune themselves to that pitch where they can feel intuitively what they live for. If another person says, "You are here to become a carpenter or a lawyer or a barrister," that does not satisfy our need. It is our own spirit that must speak to us. We must be able to still ourselves, to tune our spirit to the universal consciousness in order to know the purpose of our life. And once we know this purpose the best thing is to pursue it in spite of all difficulties. Nothing should discourage us, nothing should keep us back once we know that this is the purpose of our life. Then we must go after it even at the sacrifice of everything, for when the sacrifice is great the gain in the end gives a greater power, a greater inspiration. Rise or fall, success or failure does not matter as long as you know the purpose of your life. If ninety-nine times you fail, the hundreth time you will succeed.

Thus the ultimate purpose for which the soul is seeking every moment of our life is our spiritual purpose. And you may ask how to attain to that purpose. The answer is that what you are seeking for is within yourself. Instead of looking outside, you must look within. The way to proceed to accomplish this is for some moments to suspend all your senses such as sight, hearing, smell, touch, in order to put a screen before the outside life; and by concentration and by developing that meditative quality you will sooner or later get in touch with the inner self which is more communicative, which speaks more loudly than all the noises of this world; and this gives joy, creates peace, and produces in you a self-sufficient spirit, a spirit of independence, of true liberty. The moment you get in touch with your self you are in communion with God. It is in this way, if God-communication is sought rightly, that spirituality is attained.

The Secret of Life

Man's attitude is the secret of life, for it is upon man's attitude that success and failure depend. Both man's rise and fall depend upon his attitude. By attitude I mean that impulse which is like a battery behind the mechanism of thought. It is not man's thought which is man's attitude; it is something behind man's thought pushing it to the fore; and according to the strength of that impulse the thought becomes realized. Behind every word one speaks, the attitude is the most important factor in bringing what one says to its successful accomplishment.

There are three different aspects of this subject which one should observe. One aspect is one's attitude towards oneself: whether one treats oneself as a friend or as an enemy, whether one is in harmony with oneself or in disharmony. Not everyone is in harmony with himself, and not everyone treats himself as a friend, although he may think so. For man is generally his own enemy; he does not know it, but he proves it in his doings. One reads in the Qur'an, "Verily, man is foolish and cruel." Foolish because he does not even know his own interest, and cruel because he very often proves to be his own enemy. Apart from cruelty to others, man begins by being cruel to himself, and that cruelty is the cause of foolishness. Man may consider himself very practical and clever, yet he often proves to be his own enemy.

As Sa'adi says, "My cleverness, very often thou provest to be my worst enemy." Worldly cleverness without faith and strength and trust is usually nothing but a delusion. It is the development of trust in the heart, the development of faith, that first gives a man a friendly attitude to himself; and he becomes his own friend by bringing his external being into harmony with his inner being. For it is when the inner being seeks one thing, and the external being does something else, that there is disharmony in the self. When the higher self desires to go one way, and the lower self another way, then there is disharmony, the result of which is like a volcanic eruption. The two parts of his own being which should unite together in love, clash together and the result is fire. What causes people to commit suicide? What brings illness and depression and despair? Very often the conflict which exists within oneself, and therefore the attitude towards oneself must first be friendly, kindly, and harmonious. Even in spiritual matters one should not go against oneself. I remember that when beginning to get interested in spiritual matters I once asked my teacher, "Murshid, do you approve of my staying up most of the night for my vigils?" "Whom do you torture?" said my murshid, "Yourself? Is God pleased with it?" I had not another word to say.

When one thinks about one's dealings with friends, with relatives, with those with whom one comes in contact in everyday life, one will see that one attracts them or repulses them according to one's attitude. Whether a person is in business, in commerce, or in any other walk of life, he either repulses or attracts them, and on that depends his success or failure in life. The secret of magnetism depends on whether one considers oneself to be a friend or an enemy, a stranger; to him who considers everyone else to be a stranger, even a friend is a stranger, while to him who considers everyone else to be a friend, even a stranger is a friend. If one is afraid of someone who may harm one, then one inspires that person to do harm. If one distrusts someone, and thinks that one day that person will deceive one, he will certainly be inspired to do so; but if one has trust, the power of that trust may some day turn even an enemy into a friend.

Honesty and dishonesty are reflected in the same way in everything one does. If the attitude is not right then this wrong attitude is reflected upon whatever work one does or whomever one sees, and that person will respond in the same way. Therefore right and wrong doing is not only a religious teaching, something forced upon people; it is a scientific and logical truth. For with a wrong attitude nothing right can be accomplished, and with the right attitude nothing can go wrong, even if there are difficulties.

There is hidden in our heart a wonderful power. It is a divine power, a sacred power, and it can be developed and cherished by keeping our attitude right. No doubt it is not always easy to keep our attitude right. The influence of this life on earth, so full of changes, of temptations and of falsehood, continually upsets the steadiness of our attitude. Nevertheless the strength still lies in the steadiness of the attitude, and any lack of steadiness is the cause of every failure and disappointment. There is a Hindustani saying, "A steady attitude secures success," and when we enter the spiritual realm the same rule applies. It is not the prayer that a man says, it is not the house where he prays, it is not the faith that he claims, it is the attitude that counts in religion. It is just like the ticket one is asked to show at the railway barrier. They do not ask what position one has, what property or what ancestors. No, they say, "Ticket please!" and if one has it one is admitted. That ticket is man's attitude. In order to enter into the spiritual spheres that right attitude is needed, and it shortens the path.

Now the question is how to know the right attitude from the wrong. To know the right attitude from the wrong is as easy as seeing things when the eyes are open. When one does not realize the attitude is wrong it means that at that time one closes one's eyes. The eyes do not fail one; one closes them. Man does not like to admit his wrong attitude to himself; he is afraid of his own faults. But the man who looks his own error in the eye, the man who criticizes himself, has no time to criticize others. It is that man who will prove to be wise. But human nature is generally such that one does something quite different. Everyone seems to be most interested in criticizing another. If one would criticize oneself, there are endless faults, however saintly or wise one may be; there are no end of faults in a human being; and the consciousness of correcting one's faults, of making oneself better, of taking hold of the right attitude, is the only secret of success, and by it one attains to that goal which is the object of every soul.

According to the Sufi point of view there is only one teacher, and that teacher is God Himself. No man can teach another man. All one can do for another is to give him one's own experience in order to help him to be successful. For instance if a person happens to know a road, he can tell another man that it is the road which leads to the place he wishes to find. The work of the spiritual teacher is like the work of Cupid. The work of Cupid is to bring two souls together; and so is the work of the spiritual teacher: to bring together the soul and God. But what is taught to the one who seeks after truth? Nothing is taught. He is only shown how he should learn from God. For no man can ever teach spirituality; it is God alone who teaches it. And how is it learned? When these ears which are open outwardly are closed to the outside world and focused upon the heart within, then instead of hearing all that comes from the outer life one begins to hear the words within. Thus if one were to define what meditation is, that also is an attitude; the right attitude towards God.

The attitude should first be to seek God within; and after seeking God within, then to see God outside. In the story of Aladdin in the *Thousand and One Nights* we read that Aladdin went to look for a lantern; that lantern is the divine light within, and it is very difficult to find. Once a person has found that lantern the next thing is to throw that light on the outer life, in order to find God both within and without. Prayer, night vigil, any form of worship, all these things are helpful; but if a man is not inclined to make peace with his brother, to harmonize with his fellow men, to seek to please those around him, then he has not performed his religious duties. For what can a man give to God who is perfect? His goodness? His goodness is very little. His prayers? How many times will he pray? The whole day he spends for himself. If he prays two or three times, it is not much. If a man can do anything to please God, it is only to please His creatures, to seek their pleasure. There cannot be a better prayer and a greater religion than being conscientious in regard to the feelings of other men, being ready to serve them, to please them in every way, to forgive them, to tolerate them. And if when doing wrong he would realize that he was doing wrong to God, and in doing right that he was doing right to God, then his attitude would be right.

The end and the sum total of all mysticism, philosophy, and meditation, of everything one learns and develops, is to be a better servant to humanity. Everything from the beginning to the end in the spiritual path is a training to be able to serve mankind better, and if one does not do it with that intention, one will find in the end that one has accomplished nothing. There are many who seek wonderworking or great power to accomplish things. They may perhaps try and gain some power or other; but their soul will never be satisfied. The true satisfaction of the soul is in honest, humble service to another. If there were two people before me, one with great power of wonderworking who could perform miracles, and another humble and kind and gentle and willing to do anything he could for his fellow men, I would prefer this latter man. I would say: the first is wonderful; but the other is a sage.

The soul of man is goodness itself, if only he begins to love goodness. This is not something which is acquired; it springs up of itself. Right attitude towards God is a direct response to God. For His voice is continually coming as an answer to every call. The ears of the heart should be open and focused on that source whence the voice is coming. When that is done then the teacher within is found; then there is continual guidance, and one is guided to the extent that one keeps close to it. Then one needs no other guidance; but first the guidance of a spiritual teacher is necessary in order to come nearer to it.

Attitude forms a channel for an effort, and a right attitude makes a channel for a right effort. The world is the place of tests and trials. If one did not live in the world one would have no chance of doing good or bad; and even if one lived a very spiritual life in the wilderness it would do no good to anybody, not even to oneself; for one would not have gone through the tests and trials of the world. One can neither praise the life of a hermit, nor can one condemn it. If he is happy it is good. Everyone knows his own life, and if he is happy he will give happiness to others also.

Sometimes a man is born to live a hermit's life. In living that life he will not find any torture or trouble; let him live it; in that way he will prove to be his own friend. At the second step he takes he will be the friend of another. If someone asked me if the hermit's life is ideal, I would say it may be ideal for him, but you need not follow it. Is a hermit's life selfish then? If we observe life it is very difficult to say who is selfish and who is not. The life of a hermit is not a life for which one should sacrifice everything in order to follow it. I would be the last to recommend it to anyone. But if one followed it for one's own pleasure and found happiness in it, I would not prevent it, for a Sufi maintains from first to last the freedom of the soul.

What is Wanted in Life

If this question were asked of several people, each would perhaps make out a list of not less than a thousand things that he wanted in life. And yet even after writing them all down one rarely knows what one really wants. What one apparently wants in life is not what one really wants, for the nature of the outer life is illusion. As soon as one feels that one wants this or that, then the world of illusion will answer, "Yes, you want me, this is the particular thing you want in life"; but when a person thinks he lacks something in life, he only sees the outer lack; he does not find the lack which is within himself.

There is no doubt that what we lack most in life is to be tuned with the infinite and to be in rhythm with the finite; in other words to be in rhythm with the conditions of life and to be in tune with the source of our existence. Our perpetual complaints against all things in life come from our not being in rhythm with the diverse conditions of life that we have to face. And then we think that if these conditions would only change into something that we wish, it would make our life easier; but that is an inexperienced expectation. If we were placed in the very conditions that we had just desired, believing them to be the best, we would not even then say that we were quite satisfied; we would surely find something lacking in that condition also. For with all the errors and mistakes and shortcomings we find in our external life, we see a perfect hand working behind it all. And if we looked at life a little more closely than we generally do we would certainly find that all the lacks and errors and mistakes and faults add up to something, making life as complete as the wise hand which is working behind it wishes it to be.

There is a Persian saying, "The Gardener of this garden of the world knows best which plant to rear and which to remove." One might say that this comes close to fatalism, but I do not wish to take you further in that direction; we come now into the sphere of action. No doubt man has it in his power to improve his life's conditions greatly if only he does not lose patience before a desirable condition is brought about, if his courage has not been exhausted, and if his hope has endured.

And now the question is how can one become at one with the rhythm of life, in other words with the conditions of life? One's condition of life and one's own desire are generally two conflicting things. If desire gives in to the condition, then the condition gets the upper hand; and if the condition is mastered, then no doubt desire has the upper hand. But the condition is not always master when there is a conflict, a struggle; only one needs caution in fighting a condition in life. If harmony can be established peacefully it is better to avoid battling, though it is a fact that those who complain most about life and those who are most disappointed and troubled with life are the ones who struggle most with life's conditions. Therefore in achieving at-one-ment with the conditions of life one need not always use a weapon; one should first try to harmonize with a particular condition of life. The great heroes who have really fought through life and gained life's victory in the real sense of the word, have not been those who have fought against conditions; they made peace with the conditions of life. The secret of the lives of the great Sufis, in whatever part of the world they have been, was that they met conditions, whether favorable or unfavorable, with the aim of becoming at one with the rhythm of life.

A desire is sometimes our friend and sometimes our own enemy. Sometimes in unfavorable conditions desire becomes agitated and loses its patience, and wishes to break the condition; and instead of breaking the conditions it breaks itself. The great souls have extended their hand first to their worst enemy, because the one who makes his enemy his friend will make a friend of his own self. A condition as bitter as poison will be turned into nectar if we can get into the rhythm with that condition, if we can understand it, if we will endure that condition with patience, with courage, with hope. When there is a favorable condition we are very often afraid that it may pass, but when there is an adverse condition we do not generally think that it will pass; we think that it will last forever. This comes from fear, from agitation, from the desire to get out of this condition, and thus we lose even hope, the only source that keeps us alive. When we see the nature of life, and how from morning till evening everything changes, why should we not keep the hope that an unfavorable condition will change and turn into a favorable condition? A person gets into the habit of expecting the worst. He who has had some bad experiences in his life always thinks that whatever comes to him will not be good, that nothing good will come to him because he has once gone through bad times. He thinks anybody else can have a better time than he because he is born under an unfavorable star.

In the same way there are many imaginative and intelligent people who day after day read the newspapers and always come to the conclusion that there will be a war. Every insignificant struggle they read about gives them the idea that the world must go to pieces. There are other people interested in astrology who have gone further and are expecting the end of the world year after year, month after month. It gives people a topic to speak about at the dinner table, and at the same time it gives a shock to those who wish to live a little longer than the world's end. Many such threats of the world's destruction have passed, but the prophecy and expectation still remain and will continue. Therefore the best thing is to go through every condition that life presents with patience, with understanding, with open eyes, and so try to rise above it with every little effort we can make.

Tuning ourselves to the infinite is achieved by the way of silence, by the way of meditation, by the way of thinking of something which is beyond and above all things of this mortal world; by giving some moments of our life to the thought of getting in tune with that which is the source and goal of all of us, realizing that in that source alone is the secret of our happiness and peace. The nature of being in tune with the infinite is this: comparing our soul to a string of an instrument, it is tied at both ends; one is the infinite, and the other is the finite. When a person is conscious all the time of the finite then he is tuned to the finite, while the one who is conscious of the infinite is tuned to the infinite. Being in tune with the former makes us limited, weak, hopeless, and powerless; but by being in tune with the latter we obtain the power and strength that will pull us through life in whatever adverse conditions arise.

The work that a Sufi considers to be his sacred task has nothing to do with any particular creed, nor has it to do with any particular religion. It is only this simple thing: to be in rhythm with life's conditions and to be in tune with the infinite. And when one asks how one can arrive at being in accord with life instead of being frightened by life's conditions, the answer is: by meeting it and observing it keenly, and then by trying to harmonize oneself for the time being with that condition, while the next effort is to rise above it if it is an adverse one.

Once a young Arab was sleeping in a field and a serpent happened to crawl over his palm, and in his sleep he held the serpent with all his might. The serpent was helpless and could not bite, but as soon as the young man awoke from his sleep he was frightened at the sight of a snake in his hand and at once let it go. And when the serpent was out of his hand the first thing it did was to bite. One can manage a condition better when it is in one's hand than when it has been lost; then the situation is out of one's hand. For instance, if a person is cross, if he has lost his temper, the natural tendency is to pay him back in the same coin that he deals out. The outcome is a struggle, which will culminate in disappointment. But when a person is cross and has lost his temper, then he is the weak one, and that is the time that you can manage him. That is the time that the situation is in your hand, when he is weak and you are strong.

In our life in this world we are dependent on one another, and wealth, however powerful it seems to be, is in the end not so powerful as it appears. Its power is limited and it does not always take away the dependence of one person upon another. The point is to meet one's condition with understanding and with complete resignation. Thus the first thing is to meet the condition as it is and the second is to better the condition. The more one can avoid conflict the better; at the same time, we cannot always avoid a conflict, and we must not turn our back on it if it comes to us. After all, life is a struggle and we must be ready to struggle. Only, struggle must not make us drunk so that we lose the way of peace, which is the first thing to consider. We must not be like a boxer who is always looking for another person to box with.

The Battle of Life

Because life means a continual battle, one's success, failure, happiness, or unhappiness mostly depends upon one's knowledge of this battle. Whatever one's occupation in life, whatever one's knowledge, if one lacks the knowledge of the battle of life, one lacks the most important knowledge of all.

The question arises, of what does this knowledge of life's battle consist? It comprises the knowledge of warfare, how to fight and how to make peace. Human nature very often makes the mistake of taking sides, either the side of war or the side of peace. But if one studies the history of nations and races one will find that it was this mistake which often caused their failure. There have been times when nations and races have developed in their character the knowledge of peace, for instance people such as the Hindus with their most ancient civilization; but it could not bring them complete satisfaction as one side of human nature was neglected and misunderstood.

War comes from God in the same way that peace comes from God. A fruit has to go through many processes in order to become ripe and sweet. Sunshine and rain are both needed to make the fruit ripe; and that shows that war and peace both have their place. But with our limited understanding we do not always comprehend the justice of what is done to us. For instance, if a man had lived through all civilizations, he would think very differently from the ordinary man of today; and so it is with God in regard to His knowledge of the entire world. We are too limited to understand.

In this present age it seems that the knowledge of warfare has developed; but on the other hand the knowledge of peace is absent, for the full knowledge of warfare is both the knowledge of battle and the knowledge of peace. This can be learned according to the mystics by battling with oneself, and by bringing about peace with one's own soul. The life of an individual being is not very different from the life of the world. An individual person's home is not different from the world. An individual's body and mind and spirit form the whole universe. An individual life can fill the gap between the dawn of creation and the last day. Man does not realize how important is his own life, his self; and the study of his own life and his own self is a study of the greatest importance.

A healthy person has waiting at his door several illnesses, several diseases, waiting for the opportunity when they can attack him. A person with wealth has many who wait at his door for the chance to take away from him what he possesses. A person about whom good is said has many awaiting a moment when something bad may be said about him. A person who has power or position, how many are not waiting for the opportunity to pull him down and see him slide down from the place where he stands! And what does this show? Why is it so? One may give a thousand reasons, and yet no proper reason. The best explanation one can give is that life is a continual battle.

The process of creation began like this. According to science, light comes from friction. It is one power against the other power, fighting; and from these two different forces striking upon each other comes an effect, and that effect in reality may be called life.

In this lies the secret of both love and hate. One sees in the animal kingdom that the first tendency of the animals is instinctively to fight one another. This tendency becomes modified, and it is its modification and its reduced force that produce in them what we call virtues. As it is said in the Qur'an that the world was created out of darkness, so wisdom comes out of ignorance. And the best knowledge is not only the knowledge of all that is good and beautiful, all that is harmonious and peaceful, but also the knowledge of the causes that are behind all the conflicts and all the battles that one has to face in life. The reason why man generally lacks this knowledge is because when he is faced with a battle he wants to fight, instead of first wanting to learn how to fight. And the one who goes into life's battle without first acquiring the knowledge of warfare loses in the end. But one who learns about this warfare of life first, learns its reason and its causes, becomes more capable of fighting the battle of his life.

Christ pointed to this secret when he said, "Resist not evil." This means that if one resists or wants to fight a battle every time something in another person appears wrong or unjust, one will lose one's power. For the competent general is not the one who always attacks. The competent general is the one who stands firm in defence. His success is more secure than the one's who is continually attacking. Very often in everyday life one sees that by losing one's temper with someone who has already lost his, one does not gain anything but only sets out upon the path of stupidity. He who has enough self-control to stand firm at the moment when the other person is in a temper, wins in the end. It is not he who has spoken a hundred words aloud who has won; it is he who has perhaps spoken only one word.

For this battle in life the first thing that is necessary is to keep the army in order. And what is this army? It is one's nervous power. Whatever be one's occupation, profession, walk in life, if one has no control over one's own nerves one will be unable to control that walk in life. Today people study political economy or various other kinds of economy, but the most essential economy is economizing the forces which make one healthy and strong through life. This army must be drilled and made to work at command. And one will find the proof of this when one can sleep at will, when one can rest and eat and work at will; then that army is really at one's command.

The officers of this army are the faculties of the mind. These faculties are five: the faculty of retaining thought, the faculty of thinking, the faculty of feeling, the faculty of reasoning and judging, and that faculty in man which is the principal one, the faculty of 'I,' or ego. Even in a body with strong nerves, when these five faculties which work as the generals of the army are not in working order, not clear, one cannot expect success in life's warfare. One should further study, or practice the art of training these generals of the army in one's own body.

Even with an army and with competent generals one must, however, have the knowledge of what one is battling against. For very often man is battling with his own real interest. During the battle it is an intoxication; he is battling but he does not know where he is going, and at the end of the battle, even if he is victorious, he will find that his victory is a loss.

Today there seems to be a great seeking and enthusiasm everywhere; a new kind of urge seems to be aroused in humanity to understand life and truth. A very large number of people are looking for the best way of gaining the power needed to battle through life; and a small number again are looking for some way of bringing peace to themselves and to others. But both of these in their pursuit lack that balance which can only be brought about by understanding, by studying, and by practicing the knowledge of war and peace together. Without knowing about war one cannot thoroughly know about peace; without understanding peace one cannot thoroughly know about war. What is necessary at the present time is the study of life in general, and that means the knowledge of such questions as what is the purpose of life, what is really beneficial, what is nature, and where is the goal. It is no use practicing something before studying it. What does worldly wise mean? It means expert in this warfare of life; to know how to battle, how to make peace, why to battle, and what aim is accomplished by peace.

But it should be clearly understood that the battle with oneself means peace, and the battle with another war. If a person has not practiced this on himself he cannot be competent to battle with others. When one discovers what is the secret behind this creation, one finds that out of one life, the origin and the goal of all, this life of variety has come. That is why the nature of the life from which this world of variety has come is peace, and the nature of this life of variety is war. One can neither be without war nor without peace. One might say that all war in life should end, but this has no meaning; one might just as well say that the world of variety should not exist. Where there is plurality there must be conflict; and although conflict seems a tragedy, the true tragedy is ignorance. Instead of wanting to end the battle of life, or instead of opposing peace, one should gather knowledge of life and thereby attain to the wisdom which is life's purpose.

The Knowledge of Warfare

In this continual battle of life the one who stands firm through it all comes out of it victorious in the end. Even with all power and understanding, if one gives up through lack of hope and courage, one has failed. What brings bad luck in this life, in this battle, is a pessimistic attitude; and what helps man to conquer in the battle of life, however difficult, is an optimistic attitude. There are some in this world who look at life with a pessimistic view, thinking that it is clever to see the dark side of things. To some extent it is beneficial to see the difficult side also, but the psychological law is such that once the spirit is impressed with the difficulty of the situation it loses its hope and courage. Once a person asked me if I looked at life with a pessimistic attitude or if I was an optimist. I said, "An optimist with open eyes." Optimism is good as long as the eyes are open, but once the eyes are closed, then optimism can be dangerous.

In this battle drill is necessary. And that drill is the control over one's physical organs and over the faculties of mind. For if one is not prepared for this battle, however courageous and optimistic one may be, one cannot succeed. Another thing is to know something about this warfare, to know when to retreat and when to advance. If one does not know how to retreat and wishes always to advance, one will continually be in danger and become a victim of life's battle. There are many people who in the intoxication of life's battle go on battling, go on fighting; in the end they will meet with failure. Young people, strong and hopeful, who have had fewer difficulties, may think of nothing else but battling against all that stands in their way. They do not know that it is not always wise to advance. What is necessary is first to fortify the position and then to advance. One can see the same thing in friendship, in business, or in one's profession. A person who does not understand the secret of the law of warfare cannot succeed.

Besides one must protect one's own on all sides. Very often what one does in the intoxication of the battle is to go on and on without protecting what belongs to one. How many people in the courts and in law cases, for perhaps a very little thing, go on spending and spending money! In the end the loss is greater than the success. Again, how many in this world will perhaps lose more than they gain only because of their fancy or pride! There are times when one must give in; there are times when one must relax things somewhat; and there are times when one must hold fast the reins of life. There are moments when one must be persistent, and there are moments when one must be easy.

Life is such an intoxication that although everybody thinks that he is working in his own interest, hardly one among thousands is really doing so. And the reason is that people become so absorbed in what they are trying to get that they become intoxicated by it, and they lose the track that leads to real success. Very often people, in order to get one particular benefit, sacrifice many other benefits because they do not think of them. The thing to do is to look all around, not only in one direction. It is easy to be powerful, it is easy to be good, but it is difficult to be wise—and it is the wise who are truly victorious in life. The success of those who possess power or of those who perhaps have goodness, has its limitations. One would be surprised if one knew how many people bring about their failures themselves. There is hardly one person in a hundred who really works for his true advantage, although everyone thinks that he does.

The nature of life is illusive. Under a gain a loss is hidden; under a loss a gain is hidden; and living in this life of illusion it is very difficult for man to realize what is really good for him. Even a wise person, much of his wisdom is demanded by life and by its battle. One cannot be gentle enough, one cannot be sufficiently kind; the more one gives to life, the more life asks of one. There again is a battle.

No doubt the wise gain most in the end, although they have many apparent losses. Where ordinary people will not give in, the wise will give in a hundred times. This shows that their success is very often hidden in apparent failure. But when one compares the success of the wise with that of the ordinary people, the success of the wise is much greater.

In this battle a battery is needed. And that battery is the power of will. In this battle of life arms are needed. And these arms are the thoughts and actions which work psychologically towards success. For instance, a person says to himself every morning, "Everybody is against me, nobody likes me, everything is wrong, everywhere is injustice, all is failure for me, there is no hope." When he goes out he takes that influence with him. Before he arrives anywhere, at his business, profession, or whatever he does, he has sent the influence before him, and he meets with all wrongs and failure; nothing seems worthwhile, there is coldness everywhere. And there is another person who knows what human nature is, who knows that one has to meet with selfishness and inconsideration everywhere. But what does he think of it all? He thinks it is like a lot of drunken people. He thinks they are all falling upon each other, fighting each other, offending each other; and naturally a sober person who is thoughtful will not trouble with those who are drunk. He will help them, but he will not take seriously what they say or do. In this world of drunkenness a person who is drunk naturally has to fight more than he who is sober, for the latter will always avoid it. He will tolerate, he will give in, he will understand; for he knows that the others are drunk, and he cannot expect better from them.

Besides this, the wise know a secret, and that secret is that human nature is imitative. For instance, a proud person will always revive the tendency of pride in his surroundings; before a humble person even a proud man will become humble, for the humble one revivifies the humbleness in him. From this one can see that in life's battle one can fight the proud with pride, but also with humility and sometimes gain by it.

From the point of view of the wise, human nature is childish. If one stands in the crowd and looks at it as a spectator, one will see a lot of children playing together. They are playing and they are fighting and they are snatching things out of each other's hands, and they are bothering about very unimportant things. One finds their thoughts small and unimportant, and so is their pursuit through life. And the reason for life's battle is often very small when it is looked at in the light of wisdom. This shows that the knowledge of life does not always come by battling. It comes by throwing light upon it. He is not a warrior who becomes impatient immediately, who loses his temper suddenly, who has no control over his impulses, who is ready to give up hope and courage. The true warrior is he who can endure, who has a great capacity for tolerance, who has depth enough in his heart to assimilate all things, whose mind reaches far enough to understand all things, whose very desire is to understand others and to help them understand.

One may ask, how can one distinguish between the wisdom of the warrior and his lack of courage in the battle of life? Everything is distinguished by its result. There is a well-known saying in English that all is well that ends well. If at the end of the battle the one who was apparently defeated has really conquered, doubtless it was through wisdom and not through lack of courage. Very often apparent courage leads to nothing but disappointment in the end. Bravery is one thing; the knowledge of warfare is another. The one who is brave is not always victorious. The one who is victorious knows and understands; he knows the law of life.

What is sensitiveness? Sensitiveness is life itself. And as life has both its good and evil sides, so has sensitiveness. If one expects to have all life's experiences, these will have to come through sensitiveness. However, sensitiveness must be kept in order if one wants to know, understand, and appreciate all that is beautiful, and not to attract all the depression, sorrows, sadness, and woes of the earth. Once a person has become so sensitive as to be offended with everybody, feeling that everybody is against him, trying to wrong him, he is abusing his sensitiveness. He must be wise as well as sensitive. He must realize before being sensitive that in this world he is among children, among drunken men. And he should take everything, wherever it comes from, as he would take the actions of children and drunken people; then sensitiveness can be beneficial.

If together with sensitiveness one has not developed one's will power, it is certainly dangerous. No one can be spiritually developed without being sensitive; there is no doubt that sensitiveness is a human development. But if it is not used rightly it has a great many disadvantages. A sensitive person can lose courage and hope much sooner than another. A sensitive person can make friends quickly, but he can abandon his friends quickly too. A sensitive person is ready to take offense, and ready to take everything to heart, and life can become unbearable for him. Yet if a person is not sensitive he is not fully alive; therefore one should be sensitive, but not exaggeratedly so. The abuse of sensitiveness means yielding to every impression and every impulse that attacks one.

There must be a balance between sensitiveness and will power. Will power should enable one to endure all influences, all conditions, all attacks that one meets from morning till night. And sensitiveness should enable one to feel life, to appreciate it, and to live in the beauty of life. It is true that by the cultivation of will power one sometimes persuades oneself wrongly; there is that danger, but there is danger in everything. There is even danger in being healthy; but that does not mean that one must be ill. One must acquire balance between power and wisdom.

If power is working without the light of wisdom behind it, it will always fail, because power will prove to be blind in the end. What is the use of the wise person who has no power of action, no power of thought? This shows that wisdom directs, but that one accomplishes by power; that is why both are necessary for the battle of life.

What is most advisable in life is to be sensitive enough to feel life and its beauty and to appreciate it, but at the same time to consider that one's soul is divine, and that all else is foreign to it; that all things that belong to the earth are foreign to one's soul. They should not touch one's soul. When objects come before the eyes, they come into the vision of the eyes; when they are gone the eyes are clear. Therefore one's mind should retain nothing but beauty, all that is beautiful. For one can search for God in His beauty; all else should be forgotten. And by practicing this every day, forgetting all that is disagreeable, that is ugly, and remembering only what is beautiful and gives happiness, one will attract to oneself all the happiness that is in store.

The Struggle of Life

No one can deny the fact that life in the world is one continual struggle. The one who does not know the struggle of life is either an immature soul, or a soul who has risen above the life of this world. The object of a human being in this world is to attain to the perfection of humanity, and therefore it is necessary that man should go through what we call the struggle of life.

As long as an infant is innocent he is happy; he knows nothing of the struggle of life. The late Nizam of Hyderabad, who was also a great mystic, wrote, "What were those days, when my eyes had not seen sorrow! My heart had no desire and life had no misery." This is the first stage. From thence we come to the maturity of the intelligence, and then we see that no one can be trusted, neither the friend nor the relation. None can stand the test when it comes; all are false and none is true. At first a person believes that this is directed specially against him. A dervish once wrote these lines on the wall of the mosque where he had spent the night, "The world believes in the ideal of God, yet knows not whether He is friend or foe."

The waves of the sea go up and down; the atom believes that they rise and fall for it; it thinks, "The wave raises me, so it is favorable to me," or, "it lowers me, so it is unfavorable." In the same way man thinks a friend is favorable or unfavorable to him;

but then he realizes that this is the nature of the world. In all of us there is the *nafs*, the ego, and every ego fights against the others. There is a sword in every hand, both in that of the friend and in that of the enemy. The friend kisses before he strikes; there is no other difference. And then he realizes that nothing else can be expected of the world.

The great Indian poet Tulsidas has said, "Everyone does and says as much as he has understood." Why should a man blame another for what he cannot understand? If he has no more understanding, from whence can the poor man borrow it? Then a person begins to realize that whatever comes he should take it calmly. If an insult comes he takes it calmly; if a good word comes he accepts it with thanks; if a bad word comes he takes that quietly. If it is a bad word he is only thankful that it is not a blow; if it is a blow he is thankful that it is not worse. He is ready to give his time and services to all, to the deserving and the undeserving alike, for he sees in all the manifestations of God. He sees God in every form, in the highest, in the lowest, in the most beautiful, in the most worthless.

The Sufi says that if God is separate from the universe, he would rather worship a God who can be seen, who can be heard, who can be tasted, who can be felt by the heart and perceived by the soul. He worships God who is before him. He sees the God who is in everything.

Christ said, "I and the Father are one." That does not mean that Christ laid claim to Godhood for his own person. It is what the dervishes call *Naminaust*, which means all is He and He is all. There is not an atom in the universe that He is not. We must recognize Him, we must respect Him in every face, even in the face of our enemy, of the most worthless. Knowing that all is God by reading a few books on philosophy is not enough; our piety and our spirituality are valueless if we do only this. To read a religious book and feel pious is not enough. To go to some religious place and be pleased that we are religious is not enough. To give to charity and be conceited, believing that we have done something great, is not enough. We must give our services and our time to the deserving and undeserving alike, and we must be thankful to God that He has enabled us to give.

For this is the only opportunity we have of giving. This life is short, and we shall never have the same opportunity to give, to serve, to do something for others. In the Sermon on the Mount it is said, "Whosoever shall smite thee on thy right cheek, turn to him the other also." Someone may say or think that he should hit back; but a Sufi would not hit back. Why? Because he does not want twenty blows instead of one.

It is said that if a man asks you for your coat, you should give him your cloak also. Why? Because neither the cloak nor the coat are yours. If someone thinks, "This is mine, I should keep it, I should guard it," he will always be watching his goods. If they are yours, whose were they before? Whose will they be after you? Someone will take them after you, and all that you value so much will be in the hands of others.

Then it is said that if someone asks you to go with him one mile, you should go with him two miles. That means, if someone makes use of our services, let us not think, "Why should I, such an important person, serve another, give my time to another?" Let us give our services more liberally than we are asked to do. Let us give service, give our time; but when the time for receiving comes, do not let us expect to receive anything. Let us not expect our friend to be as we are to him; that will never be possible. We must then practice renunciation.

We must practice virtue because we like it; do good because we like to do it and not for any return; expect no kindness or appreciation; if we do, it will become a trade. This is the right way for the world in general, and the only way of becoming happy. Its moral is called the moral of renunciation.

There are two different attitudes that people adopt while going through this struggle of life. One struggles along bravely through life; the other becomes disappointed, heartbroken, before arriving at his destination. As soon as a man loses the courage to go through the struggle of life, the burden of the whole world falls upon his head. But he who goes on struggling through life, he alone makes his way. The one whose patience is exhausted, the one who has fallen in this struggle, is trodden upon by those who walk through life. Even bravery and courage are not sufficient to go through the struggle of life; there is something else which must be studied and understood.

One must study the nature of life, one must understand the psychology of this struggle. In order to understand this struggle one must see that there are three sides to it: struggle with oneself, struggle with others, and struggle with circumstances. One person may be capable of struggling with himself, but that is not sufficient. Another is able to struggle with others, but even that is not sufficient. A third person may answer the demands of circumstance, but this is not enough either; what is needed is that all three should be studied and learned, and one must be able to manage the struggle in all three directions.

And now the question is: where should one begin and where should one end? Generally one starts by struggling with others, and then one struggles all through life, and never finishes. The one who is somewhat wiser struggles with conditions, and perhaps he accomplishes things a little better. But the one who struggles with himself first is the wisest, for once he has struggled with himself, which is the most difficult struggle, the other struggles will become easy for him. Struggling with oneself is like singing without an accompaniment. Struggling with others is the definition of war; struggling with oneself is the definition of peace. In the beginning, outwardly, it might seem that it is cruel to have to struggle with oneself, especially when one is in the right. But the one who has penetrated deeper into life will find that the struggle with oneself is the most profitable in the end.

What is the nature of the struggle with oneself? It has three aspects. The first is to make one's thought, speech, and action answer the demands of one's own ideal, while at the same time giving expression to all the impulses and desires which belong to one's natural being. The next aspect of the struggle with oneself is to fit in with others, with their various ideas and demands. For this a man has to make himself as narrow or as wide as the place that one asks him to fill, which is a delicate matter, difficult for all to comprehend and to practice. And the third aspect of the struggle with oneself is to give accommodation to others in one's own life, in one's own heart, large or small as the demand may be.

When we consider the question of the struggle with others there are also three things to think about, of which the first is to control and govern people and activities which happen to be our duty, our responsibility. Another aspect is how to allow ourselves to be used by others in various situations in life; to know to what extent one should allow others to make use of our time, our energy, our work, or our patience, and where to draw the line. And the third aspect is to fit in with the standards and conceptions of different personalities who are at various stages of evolution.

Regarding the third aspect of this struggle, there are conditions which can be avoided, and there are conditions which cannot be helped, before which one is helpless. And again there are conditions that could be avoided, and yet one does not find in oneself the capability, the power, or the means to change the condition. If one studies these questions of life, and meditates in order that inspiration and light may fall on them, so that one may understand how to struggle through life, one certainly will find help and arrive at a stage where one finds life easier.

The Sufi looks upon the struggle as unavoidable, as a struggle through which he has to go. He sees from his mystical point of view that the more he takes notice of the struggle the more the struggle will expand, and the less he makes of it the better he will be able to pass through it. When he looks at the world, what does he see? He sees everybody with his hands before his eyes, looking only at his own struggles, which are as big as his own palm. He thinks, "Shall I also sit down like this, and look at my struggles? That will not answer the question." His work therefore is to engage in the struggle of others, to console them, to strengthen them, to give them a hand; and through that his own struggle dissolves and this makes him free to go forward.

How does the Sufi struggle? He struggles with power, with understanding, with open eyes, and with patience. He does not look at the loss; what is lost is lost. He does not think of the pain of yesterday; yesterday is gone for him. Only if a memory is pleasant does he keep it before him, for it is helpful on his way. He takes both the admiration and the hatred coming from around him with smiles; he believes that both these things form a rhythm within the rhythm of a certain music; there is one and two, the strong accent and the weak accent. Praise cannot be without blame, nor can blame be without praise. He keeps the torch of wisdom before him, because he believes that the present is the echo of the past, and that the future will be the reflection of the present. It is not sufficient to think only of the present moment; one should also think where it comes from and where it goes. Every thought that comes to his mind, every impulse, every word he speaks, is to him like a seed, a seed which falls in the soil of life, and takes root. And in this way he finds that nothing is lost. Every good deed, every little act of kindness, of love, done to anybody, will some day rise as a plant and bear fruit.

The Sufi does not consider life as different from business, but he sees how real business can be achieved in the best manner. The symbol of the mystics of China was a branch laden with fruit in their hand. What does is mean? It means that the purpose of life is to arrive at that stage where every moment becomes fruitful. And what does fruitful mean? Does it mean fruits for oneself? No, trees do not bear fruit for themselves, but for others. True profit is not that profit which one makes for oneself. True profit is that which one makes for others. After attaining all that one wants to attain, be it earthly or heavenly, one can place before others. *Propkar*, which, in the language of the Vedanta, means working for the benefit of others, is the only fruit of life.

The Inward Struggle

The only difference between spiritual attainment and the continual struggle of life is that in worldly life one struggles in another direction. In worldly life, be it in business or politics or industry or whatever be life's path, if a person proves to be lacking in that power which enables him to struggle along, he meets nothing but failure. He may be a good person, a saintly person, a spiritual person, but that does not count. It is for this reason that many in the world lose faith in goodness and in spirituality, when they see that this goodness does not seem to count in life. It is absurd for a spiritual person to say that by spirituality, goodness, and piety one's worldly struggle will be helped. One should have the inspiration and power to answer life's demands in life's struggle.

The seeker on the spiritual path should not forget that floating in the air is no good; standing on the earth is the first thing necessary. There are many who dream, who live in the air, but that does not answer our purpose. When they complain that they are doing spiritual work, yet are in bad circumstances, they forget that the language of these paths is different, the law of these paths is different. That is why I distinguish between these two paths, in order to make it clear that the one has little to do with the other. This does not mean that the wicked person will succeed or that success is gained by evil; if it were so, it would only be a mortal success. Nevertheless one should not blame the spirit for failure in worldly things, for worldly things belong to another inspiration; if it were not so all great sages would be millionaires.

The worldly struggle is outward struggle. The struggle on the spiritual path is inward struggle. No sooner does one take the spiritual direction than the first enemy one meets is one's own self. What does the self do? It is most mischievous. When one says one wants to fight it, it says, "I am yourself. Do you want to fight me?" And when it brings failure, it is clever enough to put the blame on someone else.

Do all those who have failed in life accuse themselves? No, they always accuse another person. When they have gained something they say, "I have done it." When they have lost something they say, "This person got in my way." With little and big things, it is all the same. The self does not admit faults; it always puts the blame on others. Its vanity, its pride, its smallness, and its egotistical tendency which is continually active, keep one blind.

I remember a Persian verse made by my murshid which relates to the self: "When I feel that now I can make peace with my self, it finds time to prepare another attack." That is our condition. We think that our little faults, since they are small, are of no consequence; or we do not even think of them at all. But every little fault is a flag for the little self, for its own dominion. In this way, battling makes man the sovereign of the kingdom of God. Very few can realize the great power in battling with and conquering the self.

But what does man generally do? He says, "My poor self, it has to withstand the conflicts of this world; should I also battle with this self?" So he surrenders his kingdom to his little self, depriving himself of the divine power that is in the heart of man.

There is in man a false self and a real self. The real self contains the eternal; the false self contains the mortal. The real self has wisdom; the false self ignorance. The real self can rise to perfection; the false self is productive of all evil. One can see both in oneself: God and the other one. By conquering the other one, one realizes God. This other power has been called Satan; but is it a power? In reality it is nothing. We should realize that this false self has no existence of its own. As soon as the soul has risen above the false self, it begins to realize its nobility.

But then there is the practical aspect. How does it show? What form has it? It rises up in support of its own interest. It defends itself from the attacks of others. It feels exclusive towards everyone. It knows itself as an entity separate from friend and foe. It concerns itself with all that is transitory; it is blind to the future and ignorant of the past. It manifests in the form of self-pity. It expresses itself in the form of vengeance. It lives by feeding upon bitterness and its life is always spent in obscurity. Its condition is restlessness and discontent. It has a continual appetite for all that is there; it is never satisfied. It has no trust in anyone, no thought for anyone, no consideration for anyone. It lacks conscientiousness and therefore manners. The little self thinks only of its own advantage and its own comfort. Giving to others, giving to those around it is dreadful to the self, for it knows no sacrifice. Renunciation for it is worse than death. That is the little self.

When we blame another person, when we dislike somebody, we overlook the same element in ourselves. There is no soul in the world who can say, ''I have not this in me.'' If only he were just! For mostly it is the unjust person who blames another. The more just we become, the more silent will we be in all circomstances. If outwardly we see faults in others, inwardly there is the sum total within ourselves. For instance, the little child cannot help loving. If a thief comes, or a robber, the child wants to love him and smiles at him. Why is it? Because a thief is not awakened in the child. The child is from heaven, the thief from the earth. There is no place for him there; that is why he is no thief to the child. We accept something because we already have it in us. If we consider our knowledge, a thousand things we seem to have experienced, we find that other people have told us most of them and we believed them at once. As soon as a person tells us about someone wicked, we think, "Now we know, we can be quite sure about it." But when a person comes along and says, "I have seen a most wonderful thing; this man is so good," everyone thinks, "Is it really true? Is it possible to be as good as that? Is there not anything bad in him?" Good is unnatural to many people.

One might ask whether the spiritual path is a tyranny over oneself. No, for it is by treading it that one molds one's character, that one makes one's personality. In this is all religion. When a person begins to think, "I must not bring harm to or hurt anyone I meet, worthy or unworthy, friend or foe," only then does he begin his work in the spiritual direction. Spirituality is not wonder-working. Spirituality is attained by right attitude.

Where is the shrine of God? It is in the heart of man. As soon as one begins to consider the feelings of another, one begins to worship God. One might say that it is difficult to please everyone. No doubt it is. It is more difficult still if one has in oneself the inclination to please everyone. There is a story of a murshid who was going with his mureeds to visit some village. And he was keeping a fast. The mureeds also had taken a vow of fasting. They arrived at the peasants' home where there was great enthusiasm and happiness and where a dinner was arranged for them. When they were invited to the table, the murshid went and sat down; but the mureeds did not dare because they had taken a vow of fasting. Yet they would never mention it to the murshid. They thought, "Murshid is forgetful; Murshid has forgotten the vow." After dinner was over and they went out the pupils asked, "Did you not forget the vow of fasting?" "No," was the murshid's answer, "I had not forgotten. But I preferred breaking the fast rather than the heart of that man who with all his enthusiasm had prepared the food."

The thirst for life makes us overlook little opportunities of doing good. Every moment of life brings an opportunity for being conscious of human feeling, in prosperity, in adversity, in all conditions. It costs very little; only a little thought is necessary. A person may be good but at the same time not be conscientious about little things. There is no greater religion than love. God is love; and the best form of love is to be conscientious regarding the feelings of those with whom we come in contact in everyday life.

The further one goes, the more difficulties there are; one finds greater faults in oneself as one advances along the spiritual path. It is not because the number of faults has increased, but the sense has become so keen that one regards differently faults which formerly one would not have noticed. It is like a musician: the more he advances and the better he plays, the more faults he notices. He who does not notice his faults is in reality becoming worse. There is no end to one's faults. To think of them makes one humble.

To say, "God is in me" before one has realized this other, metaphysical aspect of truth, is not humble but profane. God is in the depth of the heart, but to know this is of no use when the doors of the heart are not open. It is the realization of the innumerable faults which makes one humble and effaces the little self from one's consciousness. And it is in the effacement of the self that real spiritual attainment lies.

Life, an Opportunity

When we look at the world today and at the condition it is in, we begin to wonder if we understand any better than those who lived before us the idea that life is an opportunity. In spite of our present stage of evolution and the scientific advancement of the world, the war which humanity went through not long ago shows that never in the history of the world was such a great catastrophe caused by mankind. It seems as though the whole evolution of humanity had been intended to prepare and to create such means of destruction that the greater part of humanity has been ruined by it. And when we think of the distrust that exists today among nations and how one nation has allowed another nation to be ruined, we begin to feel that we understand the idea that life is an opportunity much less than those who lived before us.

Regarding education, year by year the study in the schools and colleges is becoming more difficult; to pass their examinations the students have to work so hard that it seems that by the time they have got a degree their nerves and finer forces are shattered, and that they are then unable to make full use of their qualifications.

When we look at the political world we see the same: each political party is striving for its own welfare just as each individual is trying to get the better of another; and nations follow the same principle.

Domestic life seems to be declining every day. Life is becoming more and more a hotel life. Very few in the world today experience and enjoy home life, or are even capable of appreciating it, for they do not know it. Those who lived before us were much happier, for they knew the simplicity and affection of home life and the joy and the pleasure of a home. The pleasures today are not like the enjoyments of the more intelligent and wise in ancient times. They used to enjoy poetry and higher music; today jazz has become more popular. It is the same with all the other entertainments. When we go to the theater we find the plays more and more limited in scope; there is no depth, no height, no ideal. They show life as it really is, but that does not inspire or uplift mankind. What is needed is to show life better than it is so that man may follow that example. Besides the tendency of the writer, of the poet, of the artist, of the musician, is now to appeal to the most ordinary person, to the man of the lowest evolution, "the man in the street." If everything that should educate man, theater, books, poetry, and art, pull him down to his lowest stage of evolution, it means going downward instead of upward. When a person writes good music or poetry with more lofty themes, there is no market for it. Whenever a person brings something higher he is told that it is not wanted. It seems that education, higher ideals, everything, is becoming commercialized; and by being commercialized it is lowered. And at the same time, if we stand in the midst of the crowd and look at the people hurrying by, we would think that never before have people tried so hard to make the best of life's opportunity.

But the opportunity of life should be considered from a different point of view. The wiser we become the more our outlook changes. There are four different stages in life: childhood, youth, middle age, and advanced age; and each of these four stages shows a great opportunity. For instance in childhood the consciousness is in paradise. The child living in the same world of woe, treachery, and wickedness as the grown-up is happy because it is not yet awakened to the other aspect of life. It only knows the better side of it, the beauty of life. And therefore that same world is the Garden of Eden for the child till it grows and is exiled from the Garden. Before that it enjoys paradise on earth; it is unaware of the wickedness and the ugliness of human nature. It still maintains in itself the heavenly air and angelic innocence and the tendency to appreciate all beauty and to love every being.

As it grows it begins to lose that tendency; nevertheless the child shows by its words and actions and by every tendency the angelic essence in its soul. This is the opportunity for every child to experience kingliness in life; and this opportunity is taken away by parents who send the child to school too early and burden it with study. We need not be anxious to prepare the child for its studies so that it will be able to answer in school. That kingliness that God has given to it, that joy and beauty for which it is born and which it longs to have, are thus taken away from it. This period of its life should be made free of anxiety and worry. The parents burden the child with studies, but after all what do these studies lead to? The child's strength and intelligence are only lessened when it is burdened with unnecessary studies before the mind is developed, and this tendency is increasing more and more.

People also want to teach a child concentration, but they have forgotten that a child is born with concentration. It is the grown-up whose concentration is weak. Every soul is born with concentration; it loses this faculty as it grows up.

Once I was travelling in England and someone invited me to see a school where concentration was taught. They brought before me ten or fifteen children, and each child was asked to look at a blank curtain, and say what was there. One child looked and looked and said, "A lily." Another child said, "A rose." The teacher asked a third child to tell her what was there. The child answered, "I don't see anything!" I thought, "That is much better; at any rate he says what he sees!" And so the teacher asked ten or twelve children questions about what they saw. It was a lesson in hypocrisy, in exciting the imagination. It could never help a child, for the child's concentration is already there; if the child is kept a child that is enough. We want to make the child into a grown-up person, but it is only happy when left to run about or to be cheerful. The child should not have this burden. We have made it for ourselves; it is not born with us.

If life were not so complex there would have been no need of war and of such difficulties as we have today. Because we have spoiled ourselves we want more and more; and yet we make it so difficult to get what we want that in the end we cannot get it at all. And at the same time, by wanting more than is necessary we make life miserable, and the life of others also.

The amount of study with which a youth is loaded is the greatest wrong done to him today. But the culture of the youth seems to have disappeared and inspiration is lacking. We have not realized what is necessary for young people; they are not given the inspiration of lofty ideals, nor those impressions which make them do great things. Today there seems to be a kind of uniformity in all youths. Youth has no admiration for a hero; no stimulus is given to youth to become a wonderful or an inspired person, a great poet or musician. Because of this uniform education the child does not get the nourishment for its soul which it needs to become that for which it was born.

Besides, youth is an opportunity during which time a beautiful manner, a high aspiration, and lofty ideals can be taught. And it is youth which has the enthusiasm to take everything that comes, assimilate it and express it in return. But when the time of a youth is spent only in working hard all day long and trying to pass examinations, and little time is left for recreation or for other things, that does not suffice for his life's purpose.

Those who understand these ideas realize that youth is the greatest opportunity that comes in life; it never comes again. Life's spring time never returns; it comes only once, and when that opportunity is taken away and the youth has not been inspired as he should be, it is just like keeping a plant without watering it. For that is the very time it should be watered, that is the time for it to be reared; and that time should not be neglected. There are thousands and millions of young people in the colleges who have had no good manners taught to them, and no inspiration given to them. When they are grown-up they can show that they have passed examinations, that they have gained a lot of knowledge; yet the knowledge which enables the soul to develop has been neglected during their youth, during the time when the mind is receptive, and when the child with all its enthusiasm and capacity for concentration can grasp everything that is good and beautiful.

The inspiration of the musicians and poets who have done great work in the world was created during their youth. Either they saw an example, a living example which impressed them, or they were told or they studied something that was just like sowing the seed in their heart. For youth is the only time which destines the child to become great in life; and if this time is past it will never come again. Whether a person wants to be a businessman, or a politician, a professional man, a scientist or a musician, it is in youth that he should start and that he should be inspired with that ideal. At that time the ground is fertile. But when that time is gone, the chance does not easily come again.

Besides the training for various professions and occupations, there remains another capacity which is neglected in youth: the cultivation of the heart quality. Today there is hardly one person in a hundred whose heart quality has been cultivated. Although instinctively the heart quality is always there, every effort is made to blunt it. What is meant by the heart quality? There is intuition, there is inspiration, and there is revelation. All these come from the culture of the heart, from the heart quality. A person may be most cultivated, may have studied much, and yet may not be intuitive. A person may learn all the techniques of music and poetry without having the heart quality. Heart quality is something which must be developed within oneself; and when no attention is given at the time of youth to developing that particular quality, what happens when a person is grown-up? He will be selfish, proud, mannerless, and not ready to sacrifice. He believes that these characteristics guard his interest best, and one calls such a person a man of common sense or a practical man. But if everybody were like that, what could one expect of life except constant conflict as there is today? Religion or the devotional side of man's nature is also dying out for the reason that the heart quality is lacking. Even if people go to church or to another place of worship, their piety is intellectual. People can only enjoy something intellectual. When there is a mathematical explanation of something it is wonderful; but when it comes to feeling blessed and uplifted, to feeling the raising of the consciousness towards the higher spheres, that they cannot experience for they live in their intellect.

There are two principal experiences of life: one experience is called sensation and the other exaltation. What is generally known and experienced by the average man today is what is called sensation: all the beauty that one sees, of line or color, all that one sees with the eyes or that one tastes and touches. It is living in sensation that makes man material, and after some time he becomes ignorant of the spirit.

Exaltation, which is a greater bliss, a higher pleasure, and which makes man independent of the outer life for his happiness, does not seem to be known by the majority. What is exaltation? The soul can go through four different experiences which are all in reality the longing of the soul. Mistakenly man does not seek those four experiences but instead he experiences something else. For instance, it is a constant yearning of the soul to experience happiness, and instead of that it becomes connected with what one calls pleasure; but pleasure belongs to sensation and happiness to exaltation. Pleasure is only the suggestion; happiness is reality.

After that comes knowledge. Every soul yearns for knowledge, that knowledge which will give exaltation. But the soul cannot be satisfied by the knowledge one gathers from books, by learning, or by the study of outside things. For instance the knowledge of science, the knowledge of art, are outside knowledge. They give one a kind of strength, a kind of satisfaction, but this does not last. It is another knowledge that the soul is really seeking. The soul cannot be satisfied unless it finds that knowledge, but that knowledge does not come by learning names and forms. On the contrary it comes from unlearning. Do not be surprised therefore if you read in some books of the East that Mahatmas went into the mountains and sat there for many years. I do not say that we should follow their example, but we can appreciate what they have brought from there. They went there to explore life, that aspect of life which is unseen and remains unexplored. They sat there for years in meditation. They lived on leaves and fruits, on what they could find in the forest. They contemplated. What they have thus gathered is not a knowledge learned from this world, but a greater knowledge which can be learned from within.

One can see pictures of Buddha, with closed eyes, sitting cross-legged. What does that symbol convey to us? That there is a knowledge that can be learned by closing not only the eyes but also the mind from the outside world. Closing the eyes does not make the concentration any greater. Most people go as far as closing the eyes, and no further; but if the eyes are closed and the mind is pondering over things, that is not concentration. Those who can concentrate can do it without having to close the eyes. I once saw, when travelling in the East, a person working in a telegraph office; and however busy he was, his concentration continued. I said, "It is very wonderful, that with all this work you can go on concentrating." He smiled and said, "That is the way of concentration."

The third thing one experiences in life and for which the soul yearns is happiness. That can be gained also by getting in touch within oneself. And the fourth thing is peace. It cannot be gained by outer means, by outer comfort and rest alone. It can only be gained when the mind is at rest.

After youth comes the stage of middle age. Middle age is the time when one has gathered knowledge, when one has experienced life, when one has gone through joy and sorrow, when one has learned lessons from one's profession, from one's occupation, from one's home, from every side of life. It is the opportunity to make the best use of what one has gathered by experience. But what generally happens is what Sa'adi, the Persian poet says, "O my self, you have come to middle age, and yet you are no better than a child!" If a person has not learned by that time all he ought to learn, he has indeed lost life's opportunity. Because it is that age during which he earns not only money, but experience and knowledge; and the more he has learned, the richer he is at that time, and the better he knows how to make use of what powers he has, the more successful and fruitful he becomes.

Besides, that is the age when one begins to know life's obligations, and if one does not know them even then, one has not learned anything. To know one's obligation towards those who look up to one, who surround one, who expect some help, some advice, some service from one, that is the time when one must be conscious of these things. It is the beautiful age when the tree comes to full maturity, when it begins to give fruit to the world. Not only is this the time for the singer when his voice is in full blossom, not only is this the time for the artist or the thinker when he can express himself fully, but for every person that age is the promise of the ripened mind expressing itself to the best advantage; and if that opportunity is not taken then man has missed a great deal in life.

Advanced age too has its own blessings. People do not appreciate the blessings of every period of life; therefore, they appreciate one and dislike another. In the East, especially in India, great respect is given to age; and it would be good if that ideal were more widespread. Old age is the time when man is the record of his whole life: whether he has been sympathetic, kind, wise, foolish, or whatever he has been, whatever he has done, advanced age brings the record of it. One can read it in his face, in his features, in his atmosphere. He has a greater opportunity to inspire, to bless, and to serve those who want his service or who want to be directed. He can show them a better way of looking at life. But when man does not realize his opportunities, he will act like a child in middle age, while in childhood he was given the work of an old person, and in youth he was burdened like someone of middle age.

If we only understood that every moment in life, every day, every month, and every year, has its particular blessing; if we only knew life's opportunity! But the greatest opportunity that one can realize in life is to accomplish that purpose for which man was sent on earth. And if he has lost that opportunity, then whatever he may have accomplished in the world, whether he has gathered wealth, possesses much property, or has made a great name for himself, he will not be satisfied. Once man's eyes are opened and he begins to look at the world, he will find there is greater opportunity than he had ever thought before.

Man is as poor as he is, as limited as he is, as troubled as he is; yet there is nothng in this world which could not be accomplished by man if he only knew what thought can do. It is ignorance which keeps him from what he ought to accomplish. Man should know how to operate his thought, how to accomplish certain things, how to focus his mind on the object that should be accomplished. If he does not know, then he has not made use of his mind, but has lived like a machine. If man knew the power of feeling, and realized that the power of feeling can reach anywhere and penetrate anything, he could achieve whatever he might wish.

There is a Persian story of Shirin and Farhad. Once Shirin, the girl whom Farhad admired, in order to test his love said, "Farhad, do you love me? If you love me, you will have to make a way through the mountains." Farhad said, "Yes, I was waiting for that test." He went to the mountains full of the feeling of love he had for her. Every time he broke the rock with his hammer, he said the name of Shirin, and the strength of his hammer became a thousand times greater because it was joined by the feeling of his heart.

Today man has forgotten the great power there is in feeling. It can break rocks. There is nothing that cannot be accomplished by the power of feeling. But generally there is no feeling; feeling has become drowned, it no longer exists. To realize the power of feeling and to express it is a great opportunity which life offers; but a still greater opportunity of life is to free oneself from the captivity of limitations. Every man is a captive in some form or other; his life is limited in some form or other; but one could get above this limitation by realizing the latent power and inspiration of the soul.

Kabir, the great poet of India says, "Life is a field and you are born to cultivate it. And if you know how to cultivate this field you can produce anything you like. All the need of your life can be produced in this field. All that your soul yearns after and all you need is to be got from the field, if you know how to cultivate it and how to reap the fruit." But if this opportunity is only studied in order to make the best of life by taking all that one can take and by being more comfortable, that is not satisfying. We must enrich ourselves with thought, with that happiness which is spiritual happiness, with that peace which belongs to our soul, with that liberty, that freedom, for which our soul longs; and attain to that higher knowledge which breaks all the fetters of life and raises our consciousness to look at life from a different point of view. Once a person has realized this opportunity he has fulfilled the purpose of life.

Desire, Wish, and Will

Will is the development of the wish. When we say that something happened according to the divine will, it means that it was a command, a wish which developed into action. When the wish develops into action it becomes will, it becomes command. One might think it is only one's wish, and indeed it is a wish as long as it is still; although it is there it has not sprung up, it is inactive just like the seed in the ground. But the moment the seed comes out of the ground as a seedling and is in the process of becoming a plant, then it is a will. Therefore, wish and will are two different names for the same thing, in its undeveloped state and in the process of its development.

Desire is a weaker or a more primitive stage of the wish. When an idea or a thought that one would like a certain thing is not yet made clear in one's own mind, when one's own mind has not taken a decision, then it is a desire, a fancy. When it is a little more developed then it is a wish; then it stays there and is not dispersed like the clouds. It is tangible, it is there, and yet it is not fulfilled, because for fulfillment it must develop.

There are some people in this world who say that all their lives they have had bad luck; never have their wishes been fulfilled. Also, they very easily imagine that an antagonistic spirit is hindering them, or that God is against them, or the stars, or something else which has prevented their wish from being fulfilled. But generally this is not so. In the first place, God wishes the same that we wish; if God wished differently from our wish, we could not worship that God who was always against us. Besides there is no benefit in opposing the wish of man, and there is no advantage in opposing the wish of God. It is true that there may be planetary or cosmic conditions which oppose the wish; as it is said: man proposes, God disposes. God is then put in the place of the cosmic forces, but in reality God, with His mercy and compassion, never desires to oppose anyone's wish. And apart from God, even a kindhearted man would never want to oppose anybody's wish; he would do everything possible to help a person's wish to come true.

What usually happens is that man proves to be the worst enemy of his own desire, for many reasons; and one reason is that he is never sure of what he desires. Among a hundred persons we will find perhaps one who really knows what he desires, while ninety-nine are not sure. One day they think they desire something and the next day they do not, and thus the desire disintegrates in the confusion of the mind.

There is another kind of person: those who have adopted a passive attitude. Such people say it is a sin to desire; and yet they cannot be without some desire. In this passive attitude they decide not to desire; they thwart any desire that was there. And there is a fourth kind: those who desire something but by lack of concentration cannot turn their desire into a wish, and therefore their desires always remain in their primitive stage. Finally there is the fifth kind of person who develops desire into a wish; he goes so far and no further. Thus the desire is not carried through, so to speak, and it never comes to its culmination, which only happens when the wish is developed into a will.

This question is of the greatest importance in the life of everyone. No person can exist in the world without wishing for something. And if there is anyone who has no wish, he should not stay in the world, he should avoid the crowd as he cannot exist there; he should go into the mountains, somewhere away from the world, and even there he should turn into a tree or into a rock in order to exist, because to be a living being without a wish is not possible.

There is a saying in the Gayan, which not everybody is able to understand, "To repress desire is to suppress a divine impulse." Those who distinguish between *divine* and *not divine* certainly make the greatest error, as either all is divine or nothing is. The only difference is the same as that between the machine and the engineer. The mind of God is working and at the same time the instrument, the machine of God is working; therefore that which arises as a desire has God as its source and is thus a divine implulse. The pious man in his ignorance has a false conception of this idea and makes of God a captive in heaven.

Another saying in the Gayan is, "All that produces longing in the heart deprives it of its freedom." The truth is that when there is a longing one is tied by a chain, a chain which is stronger than iron. To desire is to be bound; this is not a moral but a philosophical statement. On the other hand, one cannot live without desire; one might just as well be a rock. No doubt if one were free from desire one could have the same freedom as the rock; but even the rock is waiting for the day when it will feel desire. The desire of fulfillment will come with the development of the human form.

The difference between people is according to the wishes they have. One wishes for the earth, the other wishes for heaven. The desire of the one takes him to the height of spiritual progress, and the desire of the other takes him to the depths of the earth. Man is great or small, wise or foolish, on the right road or on the wrong road, according to the desire he has.

According to the Sufis there is Kaza, universal will, universal power; and Kadr, the individual power. Certainly the individual power compared with the universal power is like a drop compared with the sea. It cannot stand against the sweeping waves of the sea that come and destroy it. Nevertheless the drop, being from the same source as the sea, has also a certain amount of strength, and it has the individual will to hold out against opposing forces.

If we want to make this question of the individual will and the universal will more clear, it is in small things that we can do so. A person who is walking in the street and says, "I feel hungry, I should like to go to a restaurant and have a meal," shows individual will. Another person who goes into the street and sees a poor man says, "This man seems poor, can I not do something for him? I want to see him looking happier," and as soon as he thinks of the good of another person his will at once becomes the universal will. The reason is that the boundary that limits the will of an individual is the thought of the self; as soon as one has forgotten the thought of self, as soon as one thinks of another, that boundary breaks down and the will becomes stronger. Where did the masters of humanity, those who have been able to do great things in the world, get their will from? It was their own will which was extended by the breaking down of the boundaries of the thought of self. This does not mean that one should entirely give up the thought of self, that one must never think of oneself, never think of one's lunch and dinner. The self is there, one has to think about it. But at the same time in order to expand, in order to let the will grow, the more one forgets oneself the more one is helped.

There are some who take the path of resignation, doing good neither to themselves nor to others. They take the attitude that it will come from somewhere or that somebody will do it, that if they are hungry or in need somebody will come and feed or help them. Their wish is inactive, they do not let their wish become a will, they remain where they are, they are passive. There is no doubt that an intelligent passiveness and resignation can also bring about a wonderful result. But many of these people practice it intellectually. The quality of the saints is to be resigned to all that comes, but then they do not even form a wish. They take all that comes, flowers or thorns; everything that comes they accept. They see thorns, and look upon them as flowers. They are contented with both praise and blame, with both rise and fall; they take life as it is. That is the intelligent way of doing it; the unintelligent way is to say that everything is difficult, and that somebody else will come and do it. This is nothing but a kind of laziness, not passiveness.

In India there is a story of a man who was lying under a cherry tree, and some ripe cherries were falling near him. But he did not move. When he saw a man coming from a distance, he called out, "Please come here, will you put this cherry in my mouth?" There are many to be found like this, who give in, who have no enthusiasm, no courage. In this way their will power is broken down, and in the end they are helpless. There is no comparison between the saintly spirit and the spirit of the helpless, although both become resigned. But the latter is not resigned; he would like the cherry in his mouth, but only if the other gives it to him. The saint does not care if he eats it or not; it is just the same to him.

Then there are others who are overanxious for their wish to come true. This destroys their wish because they put too great a pressure upon their wish. It is just like guarding a plant against the sun and the rain. If one guards it against the very thing which should help it to grow, then the plant cannot prosper, and it is the same with the wish. If one is too eager about one's wish, and at the same time always afraid that perhaps it will not come true, then one is thinking with doubt and fear and suspicion, and in that way one will destroy one's own wish.

And, again, there is the person who is willing to sacrifice anything or to persevere as much as necessary for even a small wish, which in reality he does not value very much. Yet he gives every thought to it, and he does everything in his power to make that wish come true. That person is taking the same path as the path of the Master. He will meet with success, and it is success which brings further success. If once a person is successful, this success attracts more success; but if once a person fails then this failure attracts further failure. It is the same when one is on the path of accomplishment: each accomplishment gives one a greater power to go forward, and when one is on the downward path then every step leads one downward.

The question arises as to which desire and wish one should give up, and which one should nourish. One must have discrimination; if there is no discrimination, then one will take a wrong path. It may lead to success but it will be a wrong kind of success. If one fostered every desire and wish, and believed they should all be accomplished, then it might sometimes be right and sometimes not. The sense of discrimination should first be developed in order to understand what leads one to a lasting happiness, a greater peace, a higher attainment. But once a person has discrimination and has chosen a wish, then he should not analyze it too much. Many have formed a habit of analyzing everything all day long. If a person holds a wish for ten years and analyzes it every day in his mind, he acts against it; he looks at it every time from a new point of view and tries to find what is wrong with his own wish, and thus in the end he crushes it in every possible way. In ten years time his wish, which should have come true, will be broken to pieces. There are many intellectual people, people who doubt, people with analytical minds, who are the greatest enemies of their own wishes.

Some think that it is wrong for a person to express his wish in prayer since God knows everything. Why should one tell God that something should happen? God knows the secret of every heart. Besides is it not selfish to bring our wish before God? If it is a good wish it must come true of itself! The answer is that prayer is a reminder to God, prayer is a song before God, who enjoys it, who hears it, who is reminded about something. But how can our prayer, our insignificant voice, reach God? It reaches God through our ears. God is within us. If our soul can hear our voice, God can hear it too. Prayer is the best way, because then the wish is put in a beautiful form which harmonizes with God, and which brings about a closer relationship between God and man.

Furthermore, one can never think too often or too much of the wish one has. One should dream about it, imagine it, think about it, keep it continually in mind, and do everything possible towards its fulfillment; but one should do this with poise, with tranquillity, with patience, with confidence, with ease, and not by thinking hard about it. The one who thinks hard about his wish destroys it; it is just like overheating something or giving too much water to a plant. It is destroyed by the very thing which should help it. If a person worries about his wish he certainly either has no patience, or he has some fear or some doubt; all these things destroy the wish. A wish must be cherished easily, with comfort, with hope, with confidence, and with patience. Doubt is like rust to the wish: it eats into it; and fear is still worse: it destroys it. And when a person has no discrimination, and is not sure whether it is a right wish or a wrong wish, whether it should come true or not, one day he will say, "I should so much like it to come true," another day he says, "I do not care if it comes true or not," after a week he says, "I wish it would happen now," and after a month, "I do not care any more." It is just like making a fire and then putting it out; every time one extinguishes the fire it is gone, and one will have to make it anew.

The question whether a wish is desirable or not depends upon our stage of evolution. A person whose evolution is such that he has no wish other than for the needs of his daily life, must not think that he should wish for something higher. If his heart is inclined to that kind of wish he should not worry about it. But if he feels in his heart, "No, I really cannot wish for this, I can think of something much higher," then he must accept the consequences. And the consequences will be that he will have to go through tests and trials; and if he does not mind this, so much the better.

There are many things in this world which we want and which we need, and yet we do not necessarily think about them. If they come it is all right, and if they do not come we may feel uncomfortable for a time, but that feeling passes. We cannot give our mind and thought to them if we are evolved and are thinking of something higher and greater than what we need in everyday life, and that slips from our grasp. This is why great poets, thinkers, and saints very often lacked the things of everyday life. With the power they had, they could command everything, even gold to come to their house, or the army to come or to go: they had only to command. Yet they could not give their mind to it, they could only wish for something which was in accordance with their particular evolution.

So each person can only wish for something equal to his evolution; he could not properly wish for something which is beneath his evolution, even if he were told to do so. Very often to help a person in a certain situation I have said to him, "Now concentrate on this particular object." But being more evolved, he thought with his brain; his heart was somewhere else and so it never came true. One can give one's heart and mind and whole being to something which is on a par with one's evolution, but if it is not on a par one cannot give one's whole being to it, maybe only one's thought. What is thought? Thought without feeling has no power; if the soul and the spirit are not at the back of it, there is no power.

It must be understood that our higher wish should be apart from what we need in everyday life. We should never mix it, but always think of what we need in everyday life as being something practical, though if it really is our wish, then it is all right. But we should cherish and maintain our higher wish as something sacred, something given to us by God to cherish, to bring to fulfillment. For it is in the fulfillment of one's highest and best and deepest wish that the purpose of life lies.

Divine Impulse

The first question that arises when one reflects upon the subject of divine impulse is where does every impulse come from? Every movement, every vibration, every motion has one source. The Bible hints at this when it says, "The Word was God." The Word means vibration, and vibration means movement.

Vibration was the first or original aspect of Brahma, the Creator. Every impulse, every action on any plane of existence has its origin in the one source. In the Qur'an it is said, "God is all power; there is no power but God's." All that is done is done by His power.

If all the scriptures state this, then where does Satan come in? What is the meaning behind the power of Satan? Another power is suggested besides the power of God, and sometimes the power attributed to Satan seems mightier than the power attributed to God; this is a puzzle to many. The explanation is to be found in the understanding of metaphysics and of the laws of nature. There is one law which is the natural law; all that happens and is directed by nature's law is harmonious. The gardens made by man may seem superficially to be an improvement upon the wild country-side, but eventually, on closer examination, the garden with its artificial layout appears limited in beauty and harmony. The inspiration one can get in the woods, in the countryside, is much greater than in the manmade garden, for there man has limited possibilities of inspiration, as the life he radiates is limited. Man makes a law and finds he cannot keep it, so he makes another law, and is never satisified; for he does not take into account nature's laws of peace and harmony.

It is said that nature is cruel; yes, but man is far more cruel than the animals. Animals have never destroyed lives on the scale that man has. All the apparent cruelty of nature cannot compare with the cruelty, ignorance, and injustice of man. Jesus Christ said, "Thy will be done." There is much for us to learn from this. Man makes the world in which he lives different from the plan of God and the laws of nature, and so the will of God is not done; this prayer teaches man that he must find out what is the will of God. It is not necessary for animals and birds to find out the will of God, for they are directed by nature's impulse; they are closer to nature than man, but man's life is so far removed from the life of nature that every movement is difficult. At the present time we do not realize this; with all our knowledge we make life more and more complicated, and so the strife becomes greater and greater. For every person, old or young, rich or poor, life is a difficult struggle, for we go further and further from the impulse which comes direct from the source from whence every impulse comes.

From the metaphysical point of view, there are different rhythms describing the condition of man, and these are called in the Vedanta Satva, Rajas, and Tammas. Tammas is a rhythm which is chaotic, destructive, and every impulse that comes to man while he is in this chaotic rhythm is followed by destructive results. Any impulse coming from a person who is in the rhythm of Rajas will be accomplished, but the impulse that comes when he is in the rhythm of Satva is inspired and is in harmony with the rhythm of the universe.

All religions have taught that there will be either punishment or reward for our deeds. But if we examine more closely we shall see that the punishment or reward is the outcome of our deeds; it is our tendency towards idealization that causes us to name as punishment and reward what is simply the outcome of our actions. Good cannot be the outcome of evil, neither can evil be the outcome of good. If a thoughtless child is sent to buy eggs, and on the way home becomes so interested in its surroundings that it does not notice where it is going and falls and breaks all the eggs, we are apt to say, "You have broken all the eggs, and this is a punishment for your carelessness"; but in reality there was no one who dealt out this punishment; it followed as the natural result of carelessness.

If we look down deeper within ourselves, we shall find that our deeds have a great effect on our inner being, and react and manifest on the surface as good or bad results. This explains right and wrong, good and evil. In other words, our body, mind, and heart, the factor of feelings, react on each other. If the body controls the mind, or the mind the feelings, the result is bad, for it is the lower plane having a control over the higher plane of existence. On the other hand, when the heart controls the mind, and the mind the body, the result can only be good, as the higher self then has control over the lower self. The body having control over the mind is as if the horse were to ride on the man, and not the man on the horse. If the horse were to ride on the man, he would lead him astray, but if the man rides on the horse he will guide it rightly.

For instance, if the soldier were to control the sergeant, and the sergeant the captain, matters would naturally go wrong. The captain must have control over the sergeant, and the sergeant over the soldier. To take another example: a kindhearted person when controlled by his thoughts, may lose his kindness, and may keep another from some good thing by thinking that he should have it for himself; but when his kind feelings have risen above his thoughts, he may repent and say to himself, how could I have thought such a thing?

The extreme intensity of Tammas is bad in all its aspects, for the vibrations increase so in speed that they clash together and cause destruction. When there is an intense love on the part of one for another, something usually happens to destroy it. This is also the case with intensity of desire or action, which ends in destruction.

Rajas, the balanced activity, is always desirable. The result of our action may be good or bad, but it can never be very bad, as there is a balance.

Satva, the activity that always results in good, is the controlled activity, when we have a rein over it. This is the most difficult to attain, and needs the work and effort of a whole lifetime. All the saints and sages have had to journey through these grades and learn from experience, and they understand how difficult it is to attain control over our activity in life.

There are two ways in which we may attain control over our activity. The first is confidence in the power of our own will; to know that if we have failed today, tomorrow we will not do so. The second is to have our eyes wide open, and to watch keenly our activity in all aspects of life. It is in the dark that we fall, but in the light we can see where we are going.

So it is in life: we should have our eyes wide open to see where we walk. We should study life, and seek to know why we say a thing, and why we act as we do. We have failed perhaps hitherto because we have not been wide awake. We have fallen, and felt sorry, and have forgotten all about it, and perhaps may have fallen again; this is because we have not studied life. A study of life is the greatest of all religions, and there is no greater and more interesting study. Those who have mastered all grades of activity, they above all experience life in all its aspects; they are like swimmers in the sea who float on the water of life and do not sink. It is they on whom the deed has no effect; they are both the doers of the deed, and the creators of its effect.

The active life of man gives little time for concentration, and for getting the mind and body into the state in which he can experience the rhythm which gives inspiration and meets with the will of God. This experience comes in answer to the prayer of Christ already mentioned, "Thy will be done on earth as it is in heaven." By producing that condition of mind and body, one tunes oneself to a certain pitch which is harmonious and heavenly, and in which the divine will is as easily done as it is in heaven. It is in this rhythm alone that the will of God can be done.

It was not because of any prejudice against the world that the great ones left the world and went into the forests and caves; they went in order to tune themselves to that rhythm in which they could experience heaven. Heaven is not a country or a continent, it is a state, a condition within oneself, only experienced when the rhythm is in perfect working order. If one knows this one realizes that happiness is man's own property. Man is his own enemy; he seeks for happiness in the wrong direction and never finds it. It is a continual illusion. Man thinks, "If only I had this or that, I should be happy forever," and he never arrives at it because he pursues an illusion instead of the truth. Happiness is only to be found within, and when man tunes himself he finds everything which his soul yearns for within himself.

The nature of every impulse is that it goes through three stages, and having done so it is realized as a result, whether right or wrong, beneficent or harmful, as soon as the impulse springs from within. There is no impulse which in its beginning is wrong or purposeless or out of harmony, for in the sum total of all things every impulse has its purpose. It is our limited outlook that judges. The justice which is behind everything is so perfect that in the ultimate result everything fits into its proper place. It is during the process through which the impulse passes that it becomes right or wrong, but not at the beginning or the end; for the beginning has a purpose, and the end has answered the demand. This is a question of metaphyics, and one must study it from different points of view or one will be very much confused. Man with so little knowledge is ready to condemn or to admire, and thousands of times he fails to judge rightly. All great souls who have attained illumination have realized this. Christ says, "Judge not." Then tolerance comes, and when one realizes what is behind the impulse one says very little.

An impulse first rises in the region of feeling, and in this region it is either strengthened or destroyed. The feeling may be love or hatred, kindness or bitterness; but whatever the feeling may be, the impulse which has risen either gains strength to go forward or is destroyed. For instance a person may have a great feeling of kindness; then the impulse of revenge rises, but it is destroyed before it can materialize. Another person has a great feeling of bitterness, but while the impulse is to forgive, it will be destroyed before it ever touches the reason; he will not have to call on his thought to judge, for his feeling will destroy it. Or a person has a great feeling of bitterness and the impulse rises to do a kind service, but it is destroyed before it reaches the realm of thought, which is the second region through which the impulse rises. Or if the impulse rises till it reaches that realm of thought one may reason, "Why should I help? Why should I serve? Does he deserve it? Will he benefit by it? Is it right?" All these problems are settled in this region. Then third comes the realm of action. If the mind consumes it, it goes no further; but if the mind allows it, it comes into the region of action and is realized as a result.

One may ask how sages and thinkers have distinguished the divine impulse among the different impulses that arise in the heart of man. First we must understand what the word 'divine' means. Divine means a state of perfection. This state is experienced by God through man; in other words, when a man has risen to the stage of development where he can be the perfect instrument of God, when nothing of his own being stands in the way of the direct impulse that comes from within, that spirit may be called perfect. That which is most precious, that which is the purpose of man's life, is to arrive at that state of perfection where he can be the perfect instrument of God.

When a man has reached this stage, he at first begins to realize God only at certain moments; then as he develops he does it for a longer time; and those who develop still further pass most of their time in that realization. Then their feeling and thought no longer hinder the divine impulse, for it rises freely and reveals the divine purpose. The message of the prophets and teachers of all times has been to teach man how to make peace with God. The fulfillment of life's purpose is in harmonizing with God, and this is done by distinguishing the divine impulse.

One can distinguish a divine impulse from others just as in music one can distinguish the true note from the false, the harmony from the discord. It is only a matter of training the ear. When the ear is trained one can distinguish the slightest discord; the greater the musician, the more capable he is of distinguishing harmony and discord, the true and the false note. Many think that what we call right or wrong, good or bad, is something we learn or acquire. That is true when it is manmade right or wrong, but every child has a sense of what is naturally right and wrong. The child feels the wrong vibration at once. The infant feels whether its surroundings are harmonious or not, but man confuses himself so that he can no longer distinguish clearly. For man to learn to know for himself is a great advance along the spiritual path. When a man is clear as to the feeling he gets from every impulse, he has advanced far. There are some who say after a bad result, "I am sorry," but then it is too late, it was not true "ear training."

The divine impulse is an impulse full of love; it gives happiness, it creates peace. The difficulty is that not every man observes the beginning of the impulse; most men only observe the result. They are like an intoxicated person, and so in time, as with a drunken man, they become confused and depressed, and there is struggle and strife. But man was not born for this; he was born for happiness. Peace, love, kindness, and harmony are parts of his own being, and when a person is unhappy it means that he has lost himself, that he does not know where he is.

Man is seeking for phenomena; he wants miracles, communication with ghosts or spirits, he is looking for something complex; and yet the simplest thing and the most valuable thing in life is to find one's true self.

Self-discipline

What counts most in the path of truth is self-discipline, for without this our studies and practices cannot produce great results. This self-discipline has many different aspects. By studying the lives of the acsetics who lived in the mountains and forests and in the wilderness, we learn that those who have really sought after truth have done their utmost to practice self-discipline; without it no soul in the world has ever arrived at a higher realization. No doubt it frightens people living in the world, accustomed to a life of comfort, even to think of self-discipline; and when they do think of it they imagine it only in its extreme forms. But it is not necessary for us to go to the mountain caves or to the forest or to the wilderness in order to practice self-discipline; we can do so in our everyday life.

There are four principal ways in which self-discipline can be practiced. One way is the physical way, the practice of remaining in the same position, of sitting in the same posture for a certain time. And when one begins to do it one will find that it is not as easy as it seems. One may sit without realizing it in the same posture or stand in one position for a certain time, but as soon as one begins consciously to practice it one finds it very difficult. There are various positions in which to hold one's hands or legs or eyes or head; and these practices help one to develop the power of self-discipline.

The fantasy of the whole of creation is apparent in the direction of every movement; it is in accordance with that direction that a thing takes form. Where do all the opposites such as sun and moon, man and woman, pain and joy, negative and positive, come from? Since the source and goal are one, why such differences? They belong to their direction; the secret of every difference is direction. It is an activity, an energy working in a certain direction which makes a certain form. That is why the way one sits makes a difference; it makes a difference whether one sleeps on the right side or on the left, whether one stands on one's feet or on one's head. Mystics have practiced various postures for many, many years; and they have discovered different ways of sitting while doing certain breathing exercises. They have made a science out of this; there is a warrior's posture, a thinker's posture, an aristocratic posture, a lover's posture, a healer's posture, different postures for the attainment of different objects. These postures make it easier for man to learn the science of direction; posture does not denote anything but direction.

Then there is another aspect of self-discipline which is connected with eating or drinking: one avoids certain things in one's everyday food or drink, and makes a practice of being able to live without them, especially things that one feels one cannot live without. This is one of the reasons, apart from the psychological and physical ones, that some adepts live on a diet of fruit and vegetables; that for days or weeks or months they go without certain things that they are accustomed to eat or drink.

Fasting is also one of the ways by which the denseness of the body can be diminished. And when one knows the right way of fasting, when one is under the direction of someone who really knows when and why and how a person should fast so that he is benefited by it, a great deal can be achieved by fasting. Surgeons keep their patients without food for several hours or days knowing that it will help them to heal more quickly. In the same way spiritual teachers may prescribe a fast for their pupils: sometimes going without meat and sometimes without bread; sometimes living on milk or fruits and sometimes for a limited time without anything at all, according to the capacity and endurance of the pupil. But in point of fact, I am myself the last person to prescribe fasting. I hardly ever do so; I only give some advice to my pupils if they themselves wish to fast. I once knew a disciple who went to a murshid, and the murshid told him that in order to begin his practices he should start with a three days' fast; but after the first day he felt so hungry that he left the city, so that he might never see that teacher again!

There is always a meaning to it if the teacher prescribes a fast. In Baghdad there lived a Sufi who was known for his wonderful attainments. Once he told a young pupil of his to live on a vegetarian diet. The mother of this young man, having heard that since going to that teacher the boy only ate vegetables, went to the teacher's house to tell him what she thought about this. She arrived just when he was at table, and there was chicken in front of him. So the mother said, "You are teaching your pupils to live on a vegetarian diet and you yourself are enjoying chicken!" Upon this the teacher uncovered the dish, and the chicken flew away; and he said, "The day when your son too can do this, he may eat chicken!"

There is yet another aspect of self-discipline and that is the habit of thinking and of forgetting. This means on the one hand to be able to think of whatever one wishes to think of, and to continue to do so and to be able to hold that thought; and on the other hand to practice the forgetting of things, so that certain thoughts may not get a hold over one's mind; and in the same way to check thoughts of agitation, anger, depression, prejudice, hatred. This gives moral discipline and by doing so one becomes the master of one's mind.

After one has practiced these three aspects of discipline, one is able to arrive at the fourth aspect which is greater still; it is greater because by it one arrives at spiritual experiences. This discipline is practiced to free one's consciousness from one's environment. It is the experience of the adepts and they have spent much of their lives arriving at this. In the old school of the Sufis, and even today, there is a custom that when they enter or leave the room of meditation, one among them says, "Solitude in the crowd." The suggestion is that even when one is in the midst of the crowd one can still keep one's tranquillity, one's peace, so that one is not disturbed by the surroundings. It is this which enables one to live in the midst of the world and yet progress spiritually, and it is no longer necessary to go into the wilderness, as many souls did in ancient times, in order to develop spiritually.

No doubt this is difficult, but at the same time it is simple; and in a small way everyone experiences it, although unconsciously. A person engaged in something that interests him very much, or that completely occupies his mind, is often not conscious of his environment. A poet, a writer, a composer, a thinker, when he is entirely absorbed in something that he does, is unconscious of his environment. And it very often happens that one is so absorbed in something one is doing or thinking about, that one is not conscious of one's body or one's self. Only what a person is thinking of exists for him, not even his self. This is the stage which is termed by Sufis *Fana*. The word Nirvana, about which so much has been said, is simple to understand in this way. It is only an experience of the unconscious; in other words it is the freedom of the soul, reaching a stage where one is not thinking about oneself, nor about one's environment.

One might ask if these practices are not dangerous in any way. Everything in this world is dangerous. If we think of the danger there could be in eating, drinking, going out or coming home, there could be danger every moment. It is dangerous to go into the water, but when one can swim that counteracts it. It is even dangerous to be in the street, but if one can walk and run then that counteracts the danger. It is in being able to meditate and to raise one's consciousness above one's environment that the secret of spiritual development lies.

Once a person is accustomed to the practice of self-discipline he will find that though in the beginning it may have seemed difficult, it gradually becomes easier. It does not take long to experience its wonderful results. Almost everyone complains that the person who is closest to him does not listen to him. He is continually saying that the other does not listen to him! But by self-discipline one rises above this complaint, because one begins to realize that it is one's own self which does not listen to one. Then one finds the mischief maker: it was not the other person, it was the self; and as one begins to get power over it, one begins to feel a great mastery. It is a mastery over one's kingdom; it is a feeling of kingship. And naturally as one begins to experience this phenomenon, everything becomes more and more easy.

Control

Life has two aspects, of which one is known and the other unknown except to a few. This unknown aspect of life may be called the immortal life, the eternal life; and the known aspect may be called mortal life, as it is the experience we have through our physical being which gives us the evidence of life. The immortal life exists but most of us do not know it. This is because of our lack of knowledge, and not because the immortal does not exist. Everything we have in this life, whether an object, a living being, a thought, a condition, a deed, or an experience, breaks up and dies away. Every one of these things has its birth and death; sooner or later what is composed must be decomposed, what is made must break, what is built must be destroyed, and what is visible must disappear.

This shows that there is a struggle between what we call life and the life which is behind it. In Sufi terms we call these two aspects of life *Kaza* and *Kadr*: Kaza, the unlimited aspect of life, and Kadr, the limited aspect in the background. Kadr draws upon the life of Kaza for its existence, and Kaza waits, its mouth open to swallow whatever comes into it. Therefore the adepts and the wise, those who are called mystics or Sufis, have discovered the science of how to withhold the experience of life from the mouth of Kaza, the ever-assimilating aspect of life. If we do not know how to withhold it, it will fall into the mouth of Kaza; for Kaza is always waiting with open mouth, just as an illness awaits the moment when a person is lacking energy. So in all different forms Kaza is waiting to assimilate everything that comes, which is then merged in it.

The question arises: how can we withhold, how can we keep something from falling into the mouth of Kaza? And the answer is: by controlling our body and our mind. In the East I have seen a man lifting a heavy stone on one finger. One might wonder how that can be possible, but it is the power of will alone which sustains the heavy stone; the finger is only an excuse. I have seen those who experiment in the field of spirit and matter, jumping into the raging fire and coming out safe, cutting the muscles of their body and healing them instantly. It is not a fable that the mystics know how to levitate; it has been seen by thousands of people in India. I do not mean that this power is something which is worth striving for; I only wish to point out what can be accomplished by the power of will.

If the divine will is working through all things and beings, and man is but the instrument through which the divine will works, he is helpless, and how can he be responsible for his deeds? Man is nevertheless held responsible, for the free will of the individual is the perfect will, working through the intelligence of the individual. This may be illustrated in the following way. A merchant who owns a factory employs many hands to work in it. It is his will and wish that all shall work harmoniously together, but the success of the factory is equally the responsibility of each individual worker, for the owner of the factory runs it by means of the workers. If anyone works contrary to his will, things go wrong, and the one working thus is responsible for it. In like manner the will of the whole Being works through all, yet it is the responsibility of the individual to carry out that will; if we consider this carefully we shall find that this will is also our will, and when we act contrary to it we get no satisfaction, for we have not carried out our own will. We are, as it were, a pole, at one end of which is the limited individual and at the other end the perfect Self.

In seeking to carry out the will of God our attitude should be that of a child who is kept from doing wrong by the thought that he might vex his parents. In the same way we should watch our every thought and action lest they should be displeasing to God, the perfect Self. The question may be asked, "Is it just that human beings with intelligence should have to give in to the perfect or divine will, which seems so contrary to the ideal of freedom?" This question may be answered in the following way. Let us suppose that one wishes to move forward, and the feet move in the opposite direction, or one wants to look straight up while the eyes, against one's will, look down; would life be happy although the feet and the eyes in acting so are only using their free will? The answer is no, for in so doing they are working against the will of the whole individual being. In like manner the inharmonious free will, which may be called sin, disturbs the whole Being, the harmony of which is maintained by each individual, from greatest to least, and from highest to lowest.

To establish the reign of will power over the physical body the first thing necessary is physical control. The scriptures say that the body is the temple of God, but this means that the body is made to be the temple of God; a temple cannot be called a temple of God if God is not brought and placed there. So naturally when a soul feels depressed there is something wrong with the vehicle. When the writer wishes to work and the pen is not in order, it annoys him; there is nothing the matter with the writer; it is the pen which is not right. No discomfort comes from the soul; the soul is happy by nature; the soul is happiness itself. It becomes unhappy when something is the matter with its vehicle, which is its instrument, its tool with which it experiences life. Care of the body, therefore, is the first and the most important principle of religion. Piety without this thought is of little significance. The soul comes into this world in order that it may experience the different phases of manifestation and yet not lose its way, but regain its original freedom with the added experience and knowledge it has gained in this world.

Among the various kinds of physical culture known to the modern world there is nothing that teaches the method or the secret of sustaining action. For instance to be able to sit in the same posture without moving, to be able to look at the same spot without moving the eyes, to be able to listen to something without being disturbed by something else, to be able to experience hardness, softness, heat, or cold, while keeping one's vibrations even, or to be able to retain the taste of salt, sweet, or sour. Ordinarily these experiences come and go, and man has no control over the extent of his pleasure or joy; he cannot enjoy an experience through any of his senses for as long as he would wish. He depends upon outer things and he does not know how to sustain any experience he may have; he does not realize that the only way of sustaining an experience is by control.

There is another side to this question. Being unconsciously aware that every experience which is pleasant and joyful will soon pass away, man is overanxious; and instead of trying to retain the experience he hurries it and thereby loses it. For instance the habit of eating hastily or of laughing before an amusing sentence is finished, is caused by the fact that a person fears that the pleasure or joy will pass away. In every experience man loses the power to sustain it because of his anxiety about losing the pleasure it gives. To give another example: the great joy of watching a tragedy in the theater lies in experiencing it fully, but people are sometimes so thrilled that already at the beginning of the tragedy they begin to shed tears, and then afterwards no tears are left. When once the zenith has been reached, there is no more experience to be had; and so instead of keeping every experience from being swallowed by the mouth of eternal life, man throws it into the life behind him without discovering its secret.

The mystic, therefore, by sitting or standing in different postures, have gained control over their muscles and nervous system, and this has an effect on the mind. A person who lacks control over his nervous and his muscular systems has no control over his mind; he eventually loses it. But by having control over one's muscular and nervous systems one gets control over the mind also.

The means by which life draws its power is the breath. With every breath one draws in, one draws the life and power and intelligence from the unseen and unknown life. And when one knows the secret of posture, and draws from the unseen world the energy and power and inspiration, one gets the power of sustaining one's thought, one's word, one's experience, one's pleasure, one's joy. When one asks what is the cause of every tragedy in life, the answer is: limitation. All miseries come from this one thing, limitation. Therefore the mystics have tried by exercises, by practices, and by studies to overcome limitation as much as possible. There is no worse enemy of man than helplessness. When a person feels that he is helpless, this is the end of his joy and happiness.

Furthermore, in order to gain physical control one needs thought power as well as both posture and breath. One cannot get above one's likes and dislikes, for they cause much weakness in life. When one says, "I cannot stand this," "I cannot eat this," "I cannot drink this," "I cannot bear this," "I cannot tolerate," "I cannot endure," all those things show man's weakness. The greater the will power the more man is able to stand everything that comes along. It does not mean that one has no choice; one can have one's choice, but when one gives in to one's ego then life becomes difficult. There is a false ego in man, which the Sufis call nafs, and this ego feeds on weakness. This ego feels vain when one says, "I cannot bear it, I do not like it," it feeds the ego, the vanity. It thinks, "I am better than others," and thereby this ego becomes strong. But the one who can discriminate, distinguish, choose, while at the same time having everything under control, and who although enjoying sweet things can yet drink a bowl of something bitter, that person has reached mastery.

Also, impulses weaken a person when he gives in helplessly to the impulse. For instance perhaps he has an impulse to go to the park, but instead of waiting till it is the right time to go to the park he quickly puts on his hat and goes along. By following his impulse immediately he loses power over himself. But the one who subordinates his impulse, controlling it, using it for the best purpose, attains mastery. Besides, indulgence in an impulse towards comfort, towards one's own convenience, always looking for the path of least resistance, brings weakness. However small the work may be, if a person takes it seriously and finishes it with patience, he gains much power over himself.

Patience is one of the principal things in life, although sometimes patience is as bitter, as hard, as unbearable as death. Sometimes one would prefer death to patience. But it is of the greatest importance for the human race to develop patience in all conditions of life, in all walks of life. Whether we are rich or poor, high or low, this is the one quality that must be developed. Besides it is patience that gives endurance, it is patience that is all-powerful, and by lack of patience one loses much. Very often the answer to one's prayer is within one's reach, the hand of Providence not very far off, and then one loses one's patience and thereby the opportunity. Therefore impatience, in whatever form, is to be avoided. It makes one lose one's equilibrium, and when that is lost nothing can be accomplished. There is no gain to be had from impatience; yet patience does not necessarily mean sloth, negligence, or laziness.

In conclusion, physical control makes a foundation for the character and the personality, a foundation upon which to build spiritual attainment.

Struggle and Resignation

There are two distinct paths by which one attains to the spiritual goal, and one is quite contrary to the other. One is the path of resignation; the other is the path of struggle. No doubt in the path of struggle there is also resignation, and in the path of resignation there is also struggle, but generally the one who is treading the path of resignation has only one thought, to be resigned; whereas to the one who strikes the path of struggle, struggle is the main object. Both paths are essential; it is not possible to ignore one of them or to accept only one of them. People often think Sufism means being passive, but it is not so; it is being both active and passive. It is the knowledge of the secret of man's life on earth, of what he needs for his character, for his condition.

When we reflect upon these principles, we find that there are things in life to which we can only be resigned. It is easy to be resigned to things one cannot help, but if one has the power to struggle it is difficult to be resigned. The one who is resigned in easy conditions may not find it difficult, but he does not know what resignation means. For instance a man may have poor relations who want a part of his capital because they are in great need, but in spite of this he cannot resign himself to let them have it; yet when during the night thieves come and break into his house and leave with his whole fortune, he may resign himself very quickly to his loss. This kind of resignation is no virtue. To resign oneself means to do so even when one has the power to resist. All the great ones have recognized the value of resignation and have taught it. Christ said that if someone wants us to walk a certain distance with him, we should walk with him further still. What does this teach? Resignation. One might think that resignation is impractical and that this selfish world will take advantage of one. This is true, but the loss is small compared with the gain, if only the heart can sustain the loss. Yet if one is not contented with what has been done, it is better not to be resigned.

If one can be resigned, so much the better; but one should not force one's nature. A man once asked another man to lend him his raincoat. It was immediately given, but at the same time the giver was very much annoyed that the other should have asked for it, and when he himself was obliged to go out in the rain he was vexed at having to get wet. It would have been much better for him to have said at once that he was sorry not to be able to lend the coat. Once having given it, however, he should not have grudged it, but should have been glad to get wet having helped the other man; if he gave it, he should have done so with his whole heart.

One who is really resigned does not show it. It is not easy. How many people is this world try to learn wonderful spiritual things! But this resignation which is such a simple thing is yet miraculous; this virtue is not only beautiful, it is a miracle. There is resignation in so many little things; we do not always recognize it, but it is there. Those around us may ask us to do something which we do not like. Perhaps they say something to us that we do not wish to take in silence; we want to answer back. Then there are the little pin pricks from all we meet in everyday life. If we were not resigned, we would feel irritated all the time. Therefore to be resigned is not weakness, it is a great strength. As one goes further, one finds that one can be resigned even to cold and heat,

to places which are congenial or uncongenial, and all this resignation has a meaning and we benefit by it. We should form a habit
of being resigned; not having resigned ourselves to an experience
means the loss of an opportunity.

There are also two forces working: the individual power and the
collective power. In Sufi terms the one is Kaza, the other Kadr.
Very often the individual power will not surrender and consequently it is crushed. For instance if a man is called upon to fight
for his country but says that he will not join the army, he is
helpless before the might of the whole nation however fine his
idealism may be. Here he must resign himself to the condition
in which there is a conflict between a lesser and a greater power;
here resignation is the only solution.

Of course everything must be understood rightly. Resignation
preached foolishly is not profitable. A mureed, who was learning
the lesson of resignation from a murshid, was once walking in the
middle of the road engrossed in the thought of resignation when a
mad elephant came from the other direction. A wise man told him
to get out of the way, but he would not because he was trying to
resign himself to the elephant, until he was roughly pushed aside
by it. They brought him to his murshid who asked him how he
came to be injured. He answered that he was practicing resignation. The murshid said, "But did nobody tell you to get out of the
way?" "Yes," he answered, "but I would not listen." "But," said
the murshid, "why did you not resign yourself to that person?"
Often fine principles can be practiced to great disadvantage.
Nevertheless, resignation has proved to be the path of the saints,
because it develops patience in man. And what is patience? It is all
the treasure there is. Nothing is more valuable, nothing a greater
bliss than patience.

A story is told about the Prophet when he was very ill; he had
been suffering for many years. Through his trial his insight

became clearer, but his suffering was so great that those around him could not stand it anymore, and so he had to seek refuge with God in the forest, to spare them from seeing his pain. As his sight was keen and the ears of his heart were open, he heard a voice coming from the trees, "I am the medicine for your disease." The Prophet asked, "Has the time of my cure come?" The voice answered, "No." He said, "Why should I take you then?" Later he had the same experience. Again he heard the voice. But when he asked if the time of his cure had come, this time the answer was yes. But the Prophet still said, "Why should I take you?" for he still could not resign himself.

When we think of an extreme ideal, we may wonder if it is not impractical, especially at this time where there are so many treatments and so many mechanical things. But the thoughtful person will consider how many people have ruined their lives by going from one treatment to another, lacking the patience and resignation in which resides their complete cure. The remedy is not always the answer to the difficulty; often patience is the answer. It seems that man becomes more and more impatient every day owing to this superficial life. There is hardly any resignation to little things, even though it is so much better to be resigned than to worry.

When we throw the mystic light upon this subject, we find that by being resigned we form a harmonious connection with the Infinite. And how should we learn this? Should we do it by being resigned to God? No, that is still a greater lesson to learn. The first lesson to learn is to resign oneself to the little difficulties in life, not to hit out at everything one comes up against. If one were able to manage this one would not need to cultivate great power; even one's presence would be healing. Such a person is more precious than the branch of the rose, for that has many thorns but only a few flowers.

Resignation is the outcome of the soul's evolution, for it is the result of either love or wisdom. The truth of this can be seen in the lives of a child and of a grown-up person. As soon as a child becomes attracted to an object, the only thing it knows is that it wants it; and if it is denied this object the child is dissatisfied. Yet as the child grows up and evolves in life it learns resignation. That is the difference between an unripe soul and a soul advanced on the path of wisdom; for the ripened soul shows in its nature the development of the power of resignation. Man certainly has a free will, but its power is very small in comparison with the all-powerful will of God, which manifests in the form of more powerful individuals, of conditions which cannot be changed, and in many other ways. Resignation does not mean giving up something; resignation means being contented to give it up. To be resigned means to find satisfaction in self-denial.

Self-denial cannot be a virtue when it is the result of helplessness and culminates in dissatisfaction. The nature of an unevolved ego is to resent everything that arises in life which hinders the accomplishment of a certain object; but when a person accepts being resigned in the face of a difficulty, and at the same time feels satisfaction, then even without having accomplished his object he has risen above it. In this way for the truly resigned soul even a defeat is really a success.

Resignation is a quality of the saintly souls. It is bitter in taste but sweet in result. Whatever a man's power and position in life may be, he has always to meet with a more powerful will, in whatever form it may manifest. In truth this is the divine will. By opposing the divine will one may break oneself; but by resigning oneself to the divine will one opens up a way. For resignation has the nature of water: if anything obstructs it it takes another course; and yet it flows on, making its way so as to meet the ocean in the end. This is what the saintly souls do who tread the path of resignation and yet keep their own will alive. That will has the power to make its way. A person who is resigned by nature becomes in the end a consolation to himself and happiness for others.

Resignation is not necessarily weakness or laziness or cowardice or lack of enthusiasm. Resignation is really the expression of mastery over one's self. The tendency to submit to the will of another or to certain conditions does not always work to the disadvantage of the resigned one. It may sometimes seem to be unprofitable, but in the end the benefit of such a virtue is realized. Lack of power of endurance is the cause of souls not being ready to resign themselves, for they cannot endure their pain or sustain their loss. Those who are resigned practice resignation even in the small things of everyday life. They avoid using their power of will needlessly in every little thing they do. Resignation is passivity, and sometimes it seems to be a disadvantage in the life of an active person who has an object to accomplish. But a continual activity kept up by power and energy very often results in disaster. Every activity should be balanced by passivity. One should be active when it is time to be active, and become passive when the conditions ask for passivity. It is in this manner that success in life is attained and that happiness, which is the quest of every soul, is gained.

The symbolical meaning of the story of Christ riding on a donkey on Palm Sunday is that the donkey, which has a cross on its back to indicate that it has to bear all burdens, shows its resignation by submitting to the will of its master. That is the privilege of the one who serves: however humble, he will have the privilege of serving God.

The Privilege of Being Human

Mankind is so absorbed in life's pleasures and pains that a man has hardly a moment to think what a privilege it is to be human. Life in the world no doubt contains more pain than pleasure, and that which one considers to be pleasure costs so much that when it is weighed against the pain it costs, it too becomes pain. Since man is so absorbed in his worldly life he finds nothing but pain and grievance in life. Thus, until he changes his outlook, he cannot understand the privilege of being human.

Yet however unhappy a person may be in life, if he were asked if he would prefer to be a rock rather than a human being, his answer would be that he would rather suffer and be a human being than be a rock. Whatever the condition of a man's life, should he be asked if he would rather be a tree than a man, he would choose to be a human being. And although the life of the birds and beasts is so free from care and troubles and so free in the forest, yet if a man were asked whether he would prefer to be one of them and be in the forest, he would surely prefer to be a man. This shows that when human life is compared with the various other aspects of life, it reveals its greatness and its privilege; but when it is not compared with those other forms of life, then man is discontented and his eyes are closed to the privilege of being human.

Another thing is that man is mostly selfish, and what interests him is that which concerns his own life; not knowing the troubles of the lives of others, he feels the burden of his own life even more than the burden of the whole world. If only man in his poverty could realize that there are others whose sufferings are perhaps greater than his; in his troubles that there are others whose difficulties are perhaps greater than his! Self-pity is the worst poverty. It overwhelms a man, and he sees nothing but his own troubles and pains; then it seems to him that he is the most unhappy person, more so than anyone in the world.

Sometimes we find satisfaction in self-pity. The reason is that it is our nature to find satisfaction in love; and when we are confined to ourselves we begin to love ourselves, and then self-pity arises because we feel our limitation. But the love of self always brings dissatisfaction, for the self is not made to be loved; the self is made to love. The first condition of love is to forget oneself. One cannot love another and oneself at the same time, and if one says, "If you give me something I will give you something in return," that is another kind of love; it is more like business.

Man's ego is the false ego; God's ego is the true ego. But what is the ego? Ego is part of a line: one end of the line is God's ego, the other end is man's ego. The latter is false because man has covered it by his illusion, calling it himself. Therefore, when that ego is broken by love or by wisdom or by meditation, then the clouds that cover it are dispersed and the true ego, the ego of God, manifests itself.

Sa'adi writes in the account of his life, "Once I had no shoes and I had to walk barefoot in the hot sand, and I thought how very miserable I was; and then I met a man who was lame, for whom walking was very difficult. I bowed down at once to heaven and offered thanks that I was much better off than he, who had not even feet to walk upon." This shows that it is not a man's situation in life, but his attitude towards life that makes him happy or unhappy; and this attitude can even make such a difference that one man would be unhappy in a palace while another would be very happy in a humble cottage.

The difference is only in the horizon that one sees. There is one person who looks only at the circumstances of his own life; there is another who looks at the lives of many people: it is a difference of horizon.

Besides, it is the impulse that comes from within which has an influence on one's affairs. If there is an influence always working from within, if there is discontent and dissatisfaction in life, one finds its effects in one's affairs. For instance, a person impressed by an illness can never be cured by a physician or medicines. A person impressed by poverty will never get on in life. A person who thinks that everybody is against him, everybody ill-treats him, and everybody has a poor opinion of him, will always find that it is so wherever he goes. There are many people in the world, in business, in professions, whose first thought before they go to their work is that perhaps they will not be successful. The masters of humanity, at whatever period they came to the world, always taught faith as man's first lesson: faith in success, faith in love, faith in kindness, and faith in God. This faith cannot be developed unless man is self-confident, and it is essential that man should learn to trust others. If he does not trust anyone, life will be hard for him. If he doubts, if he suspects everyone he meets, then he will not trust the people nearest to him, even his closest relations, and he will soon develop such a state of distrust that he will even distrust himself.

The trust of someone who trusts another but does not trust himself is profitless. But someone who trusts another because he trusts himself has the real trust, and by this trust in himself he can make his life happy whatever his conditions may be.

In the Hindu traditions there is a very well known concept, that of the tree of the fulfillment of desires. There is a story in India of a man who was told that there was a tree of the fulfillment of desires, and he went in search of it; after going through forests and across mountains he arrived at last at a place where he lay down and slept under a tree without knowing that it was the tree of the fulfillment of desires. Before he went to sleep he was so tired that he thought, "What a good thing it would be if I had a soft bed to rest upon and a beautiful house with a courtyard around it and a fountain, and people waiting upon me!" And with this thought he went to sleep. When he opened his eyes he saw that he was lying in a soft bed and there was a beautiful house and a courtyard and a fountain, and there were people waiting upon him; he was very much astonished, for he remembered that before going to sleep he had thought of all this. But as he went further on his journey and thought deeply about his experience, he realized that he had actually slept under the tree he was looking for, and that the miracle of that tree had been accomplished.

The interpretation of this legend is a philosophy in itself. It is man himself who is the tree of fulfillment of his desire, and the root of this tree is in the heart of man. The trees and plants with their fruits and flowers, the beasts with their strength and power, and the birds with their wings, are unable to arrive at the stage which man can reach; and it is for this reason that he is called "man," which in Sanskrit has the same root as the word "mind."

The trees in the forest await that blessing, that freedom, that liberation, in stillness and quiet; and the mountains and the whole of nature seem to await the unfoldment, the privilege of which is given to man. That is why the traditions tell us that man is made in the image of God. Thus one may say that the most fitting instrument for God to work with is the human being; but from the mystical point of view, one may also say that the Creator takes the heart of man through which to experience the whole of creation. This shows that no being on earth is more capable of happiness, of satisfaction, of joy, of peace, than man. It is a pity when man is not aware of this privilege of being human, for every moment in life that he passes in this error of unawareness is wasted and is his great loss.

Man's greatest privilege is to become a suitable instrument of God, and until he knows this he has not realized his true purpose. The whole tragedy in the life of man is his ignorance of this fact. From the moment that a man realizes this he lives the real life, the life of harmony between God and man. When Jesus Christ said, "Seek ye first the kingdom of God, and all these things shall be added unto you," this teaching was in answer to the cry of humanity; some were crying, "I have no wealth"; others, "I have no rest," or, "My situation in life is difficult," or, "My friends are troubling me," or, "I want a higher position." And the answer to them all is what Christ said.

One may ask how we can understand this from a practical, a scientific point of view. The answer is that external things are not in direct connection with us, and so they are often unattainable by us. We can sometimes attain our wish, although frequently we fail; but in seeking the kingdom of heaven we seek the center of all, both within and without, for all that is in heaven or on earth is directly connected with the center. In this way we are able to reach all that is on earth and in heaven from the center, but whatever we seek which is not at the center may be snatched away from us.

In the Qur'an it is written that God is the light of the heavens and of the earth. Besides the desire to obtain the things of the earth, there is that innermost desire, working unconsciously every moment of life, to come into touch with the infinite. When a painter is painting, or when a musician is singing or playing, if he thinks, "It is my painting, my playing, my music," he may have a certain satisfaction, but it is like a drop in the ocean. If, however, he connects his painting or his music with the consciousness of God, if he thinks, "It is Thy painting, Thy music, not mine," then he connects himself with the center, and his life becomes the life of God.

There is much in life that one can call good, there is much to be contented with, and there is much that one can admire, if one can only adopt this attitude; this is what can make a man contented and give him a happy life. God is the painter of all this beautiful creation, and if we do not connect ourselves with the painter we cannot admire his painting. When one goes to the house of a friend whom one likes and admires, every little thing is so pleasant; but when one goes to the house of an enemy, everything is disagreeable. Our devotion, our love, our friendship for God can make the whole of creation a source of happiness. In the house of a dear friend, a loaf of bread, a glass of milk, is most delicious; but in the house of someone we dislike, even the best dishes are tasteless. And as soon as one begins to realize that the mansions in the house of the Father are in this world with its many relgions, races, and nations, which yet are all in the house of God, then, however humble and difficult the situation in life, it must sooner or later become happier and better; for we feel that we are in the house of the one we love and admire, and all that we meet with we accept with love and gratitude because it comes from the one we love.

For all his claims to civilization and progress, man seems to have fallen into the greatest error. For centuries the world has not been in such a state as it is now, one nation hating the other, looking with contempt on another. What do we call it? Is it progress or is it a standstill? Or is it worse that that? Is this not the time when thoughtful souls should awake from sleep, and devote themselves to doing whatever good they can to humanity in order to better the conditions of the world, instead of each one thinking only of his own interests?

Destiny and Free Will

Very often those who believe in destiny do not believe in free will. There are some who have had some success in their work and have recognized it as the outcome of that work. Then they think that if anything exists it must be free will, that they have achieved results according to what they have done. And there are others who have tried and not succeeded. In that case they feel that there is something holding them back from getting results, and then they think that there must be such a thing as destiny, and it is that which is holding them back. Many people think that it is a form of laziness to be a fatalist and they call destiny a superstition; and there are others who admit that free will is a conception, an idea, but that in reality all is governed by destiny.

The idea of free will has its meaning, and belief in it has its peculiar benefit in life. At the same time the idea of destiny is very profound; whether a person believes in it or not, there is always an attraction about it. The one who reads the future will always attract both the one who believes in destiny and the one who does not. The believer bows to him with faith; the unbeliever goes his way with a smile. Both are attracted because it is the greatest mystery there is. One's own life in which one is most interested always remains a secret and a mystery, and this mystery is greater than any other in the world. No one can say, ''I have no interest in knowing about my life, in knowing why I have had that past, why I have this present, and what future I shall have.'' To know about it is one's greatest desire.

When one thinks about destiny, the question arises whether there is a plan drawn up, and whether every occurrence in life must happen according to that plan; and, if it is drawn up, on what ground, and by whom? If it is God who has drawn it up, how far can He be called just for making one happy and another miserable, one great and another small; letting one enjoy himself and at the same time making another suffer, though living under the same sun and walking on the same earth? And if it is not destiny but man's action, is it then the action of the past which brings about the action of the present, and if it is so, to what degree is man responsible for it? These questions take one to the depths of life's mystery, and once they are solved a great philosophical problem is solved.

The mystic finds the secret of life by knowing how to make a plan according to what he wishes. However, he arrives at this stage by first giving up his plan. For a person who has no power over his plan, it is better to give it up into the hands of God. The more one depends upon the Maker of the plan, the more one is able to make it oneself. It is just like the mother who, as long as her little child cannot walk by itself and depends on holding her hand, does not allow the child to go alone. And even when she allows it to walk alone she holds her hands around it so that it may not fall. When a man takes his own responsibility into his hands, calling it free will, he loses, so to speak, that dependence on God which holds him and which makes God responsible. Therefore it is a saintly person who arrives at resigning himself to the will of God; and afterwards this may develop into his free will, which will then be the will of God. This is what marks the difference between the saintly character and the character of the master: the character of the saint is to be resigned fully to the will of God, and the character of the master is to find the will of God in his own free will.

Very often we ask why, if there is a God and if God is love and is kind and merciful, there should be so much suffering as if people were being punished. But that is our small way of looking at it. In reality if our eyes were open and we could see deeper into life, we would realize that there is no such thing as punishment. In all things there is the mercy of God, but we only call that God's mercy which we can perceive and understand; that which we cannot see and understand we think of as a punishment from God. Whether the parents scold the child or caress it, in both there is their love and nothing else. As Tagore says, "When Thou tunest me to a higher pitch, then I feel pain. But I know, Lord, that pain is to attune me to the right pitch."

When we arrive at stilling our agitation and becoming peaceful, resigning our will to the will of God, then we begin to see the love of God in all things, and never again think that God can be anything other than love. That is why the Sufi does not always think of God as a Creator, as a King, or as a Judge; but as a Beloved, as a Lover, and as Love itself.

Most people have a preconceived idea and keep this idea like a wall before them; they do not try to think any further and are content with what they know about it. There is no doubt that a man is born with a plan which is to be accomplished in life; not only of what his instincts or merits or gifts will be, but also the whole plan of how his life will turn out. There is a saying in the East that you can read the life of an infant by looking at its feet. Even the little feet of the infant show the sign of the plan that it is to follow through life.

There is a story that throws some light upon the relation between destiny and free will. There was a seer working as a porter in a rich man's house. Now there is a belief in the East that no sooner is a child born than angels come and write on its forehead the whole plan of its destiny. This porter was a wonderful man. At the door, as soon as the angels came, he said, "Stop, where are you going? I am master here, you cannot go in unless you promise to tell me about the plan." So the angels told him. And again the next time that a child was born in that house, the porter took down notes of what was going to happen.

After some time the parents passed away. They had been rich, but they lost their money for some reason or other, and the children had to leave their home and were without a refuge. Then this old porter took upon his shoulders the burden of looking after them, but as soon as they were a few years older the children each went to different countries. One day the porter thought that it was his duty to go and see how they were getting on. Also, for a seer it is most interesting to observe the material phenomena of something he has seen inwardly as a vision; it is a satisfaction to him, a delight, when all that he has felt inwardly becomes materialized and he sees it happening on the outer plane. It gives him the greatest pleasure.

So the porter went and saw one of the children working as a horse groom, and he was very sorry about this. He went to the young man and said, "It could not be avoided, it was meant that you should be what you are. But I want to give you some advice, because it makes me sad to think that you, at whose house there were so many horses, have to work as a horse groom. Here is a little money, take it and go to another city and try to work there as a horse trainer. The horses of the rich men will be given to you to train, and I am sure you will be successful." The young man asked, "Can I do anything else?" He said, "No, that is the only way. You would have been a groom all your life if I had not told you this. There is nothing else you can do; this is the only door open for you. Do it, and then you will have success." The young man did as he was told and was very successful.

The porter went to the other son and asked, "What are your circumstances?" He said, "My circumstances? I wander about in the forest and catch birds and sell them in the city but I make hardly enough money to live." In those days there was a fashion among kings to keep a certain bird as a pet; that bird was called Shabaz, the king's bird. And the porter said, "You must not look for game birds, you must look only for this bird Shabaz." The boy said, "But if I cannot find it, then I shall starve and die!" The old man said, "Do you know what your father was, and what you are?" "Yes," he said, "I know, I have had bad luck." The man said, "You will have better luck if you will only listen to me. You need not change; your profession is still catching birds. But catch Shabaz. You can sell it for millions. That is the bird you ought to catch."

This story makes us realize what the seer does. A definite plan was made for those two young men; at the same time there was scope for free will to work, but within that plan. And if they had not realized that scope they would have had to continue leading a miserable life. It is a great lesson and those who can understand this lesson can benefit immensely by it.

Sa'adi, the great poet of Persia, has said, "Every soul is born for a certain purpose and the light of that purpose is kindled in that soul."

The Hindus believe a person is born with what they call Karma; some action of the past or an impression he has brought with him to the earth as a good influence or a bad influence or as something that he has to pay back. No doubt there is some truth in this idea, and we can see the proof of that truth very often; for instance, when a person is placed in a situation where he has to serve, as if he has to pay a debt to someone. He may not have the slightest desire to do so; but at the same time it falls on his shoulders, he cannot help it. It is as if the highest Power has determined that it should be so; whether he does it willingly or unwillingly he must give his time, his thought, his sympathy, and his service to someone else.

Then one sees a person receiving money, comfort, love, and sympathy from someone else, regardless of whether he deserves it all or not. This shows that although from one's birth there is a relation between give and take, yet a man is born with certain obligations. It also shows that however powerful and great a person may be, however good the circumstances might seem, when there is to be a difficulty, one cannot help it; the difficulty comes. And then at other times in life, in spite of all obstacles, a way opens; we do not have to do much and everything goes smoothly. This also shows that there is a plan, that it is not only qualifications and cleverness that make us successful. But there are times where we are meant to have an easy life, success, and all we wish; and there are other times when we have to do without it, we cannot help it.

Is it something a person is born with, or is it the effect of a person's action of the earth? Both. Suppose an artist first thought out a design for a certain picture, and while he was making that picture he became so inspired that it suggested to him that he should change the design. And as he went on he changed it to such an extent that it became quite different from the picture he had originally conceived. To the same extent life may be changed by action. A right action, a good action, is productive of power and is creative and it can help far more than man imagines.

The question is to what extent can man help himself. Man has two aspects in him. One aspect is his mechanical being, where he is but a machine controlled by conditions, by his impressions, by outer influences, by cosmic influences, and by his actions;

everything working mechanically turns his life accordingly. He has no power over conditions, he is just a tool of influences. The more pronounced this aspect is in man, the less evolved he is. It is the sign of a lesser evolution. But there is another aspect in man which is creative, in which he shows he is not only part of God but linked with God, because his innermost self is God. Be not surprised therefore if you hear stories of sages, masters, saints, and prophets whose command affected the cosmos and by whose will whole peoples moved as they wished them to move. It is nothing to be surprised at. Outwardly every man is about the same size; no man is as tall as a camel or as large as an elephant. Outwardly men vary only a little. But inwardly there is no comparison in the size of the spirit; no comparison between the understanding of one man and of another. One walks, one runs, one flies, and one creeps; yet all walk on the same earth, all live under the same sun, and they are all called men. Nevertheless there is no man who has not a spark of this power, who has not the possibility of changing conditions by his free will, if only he can realize what it is. It is the absence of this realization which makes a man a machine.

As to man's destiny, it is not only his own action but also the thought of another that can change a man's life. I have seen for instance many cases where a loving mother was not pleased with her growing child who did not satisfy her. This will always make it suffer in some way or another. The child may become a qualified man, a capable man, but if he has not satisfied his mother, that is quite enough for him to have bad luck. A keen study will make one understand how these things work; but from childhood we have been so absorbed in our own life and our own interests that we do not think very much about how we are affected by the thought and feeling of those around us.

A rich man, if he is displeased with his servant and speaks roughly to him or insults him, may not realize it at the time, but perhaps the feeling of this servant who is dependent on him and who is bound to that particular place is hurt. And when this rich man goes to his office, to his affairs he may get back that pinprick which he gave. He does not know it; he believes he has given a pinprick to a servant who could not return it; but someone else returns it without his realizing that this is the answer to what he has done. The more we think about this the more we shall understand how God works through all beings, even through animals and birds. And then when we are able to believe this, we cannot help believing what Buddha has said: that the essence of religion is harmlessness. Harmlessness does not only mean to refrain from killing. Many are killed without killing; in order to kill a person one does not need to murder him. A glance, a word, a thought can kill a person, and that is worse that death.

It is this experience that I had in mind when I said in the Gayan, "My bare feet! Step gently on life's path, lest the thorns lying on the way should murmur at being trampled upon by you."

There is no end to consideration, once a person begins to think about it. If there is any religion it is in consideration, considering that feeling which can be hurt by a moment's thoughtlessness. If there is any abode of God, it is in the heart of man. If the heart is touched wrongly it has an effect upon destiny. One does not realize to what extent destiny can be changed by the feeling of another person; it can change it more than our own feeling. One always wishes good for oneself; no one wishes to be unhappy.

There are also planetary influences. What are these planetary influences and what relation do they have to us? The answer is that man is a planet also; and as one planet is related to the other, so in the same way the planets are related to mankind. Naturally a change in the condition of a planet and the effect produced by that planet have an influence upon man's life. One might ask if man is really so small as to be under the influence of a planet. Yes, outwardly; outwardly man is as small as a drop in the ocean. If the planet is an ocean, then the individual is a drop. But inwardly the planet is a drop in the ocean of man; that is the heart of man. Asif, the great philosopher, says, "My ignorance, the day you depart my heart will be open, and this whole universe will become a bubble in the ocean of my heart."

Limitation, smallness, and imperfection are the outcome of ignorance. But when the heart is open the whole universe is in it, and the source of destiny, its secret and its mystery, are in the hand of man. What, then, is the way in which to believe in destiny and free will? The best way of believing in destiny is to think that all the disagreeable things we have gone through are part of destiny and belong to the past; to think that we are free from it. And the best way of looking at free will is to keep in mind that all that is to come, all that is before us, is the outcome of free will. To keep before us as a concentration that nothing wrong will touch us, that all that is good for us lies before us. It is wrong to think that worse things are in store for us because destiny has preserved our Karma and ordained that we must suffer, and that one has to pay according to one's Karma. For the one who is conscious of Karma will have to pay a high interest; the more conscious he is of it, the higher the interest he will have to pay.

In conclusion one comes to understand that there are two aspects of will working through all things in life. One is the individual will, the other is the divine will. When a person goes along ignoring the divine will, naturally the human will fails and he finds difficulty, for he is swimming against the tide. The moment a person works in consonance, in harmony, with the divine will, things become smooth.

One may object that life has not been smooth for great personalities such as Christ. From childhood there were difficulties; his parents had to flee to the desert, and when the young Jesus was brought among people there were still greater difficulties. And all the great saints and sages had great difficulties all through life; things were not all smooth for them. Did they work against destiny, against the will of God? This question makes us realize that the will of God meets with difficulty on the material plane. In the Bible we read, "Thy will be done on earth, as it is in heaven," but it is not easy for His will to be done on earth as it is in heaven.

This suggestion teaches us a great lesson, and that lesson is that there is a conscious will working and that there is an unconscious will working. But conscious working is divine working. It may be that the divine will has difficulty, but at the same time this difficulty has a meaning in it. In other words, success or failure of God and of God's power means nothing because ultimately both are success; but success and failure of man means nothing because in the end both are failure.

If a man succeeds in collecting much wealth or in attaining a high position, what is the end of it? It will belong to someone else who will snatch it from his hand. Therefore whether we have success or failure in life, if it is individual in the end it will be failure. But in the case of godly things, whether it is failure or success, it is always success in the end. It cannot be otherwise; it is the only gain there is. As Nanak says, "The grain that takes refuge near the center of the grinding mill is saved." So is the man who keeps close to God. He draws his power and inspiration from God, and when his life is directed by that power and inspiration, whether he has difficulties or not, the way is always smooth and the end is what it ought to be.

Man's Aim in Life

If we have studied the chapter on the Silent Life in *In an Eastern Rose Garden*, it may seem contradictory to speak of the other aspect of life. We might ask: Why did creation take place? Why is man on earth? Is it to seek the silent life, or what is the reason of all this happening? Are we to throw out everything that we call life, our position, our rank, our strength, and everything we have so far thought worthy of pursuit? Shall we continue to seek to attain these things, or should we discard them all in favor of the pursuit of the silent life?

The answer to these questions is found in the words of the Lord's Prayer: "Thy will be done on earth, as it is in heaven." We can extend this to: Thy perfect will be done on earth as well as in heaven, or: That which Thou desirest in heaven we must do on earth, or: I will do as Thou desirest me to do. Yet at the same time the mystic thinks, "My soul is not separate from Thy spirit; therefore my will is not separate from Thine; therefore my will be done on the earthly plane as Thine is done on the heavenly plane, namely on that of my mind. Thus that which I have been thinking to do will happen on the plane of the earth."

Omar Khayyam said, "Heaven is the vision of fulfilled desire; hell is the shadow of a soul on fire." The fulfillment of desire, however small or great it be, is the first step towards perfection. Unfulfillment of desire, however high or low, is a going back.

We may ask: But what if the desires we have are not worthwhile? Our desires may indeed be imperfect ones; they may not be right; but what of that? We cannot desire things which lead to our destruction. Is there no good desire in our heart? Is not the heart the vehicle of good through which one desires? So we see that our desire is God's desire, and that creation's whole purpose is the fulfillment of that desire. As the Vedanta say, this life is the dream of Brahma. The creative faculty or power desired what Brahma desired; it produced what He desired. This is why the Sufi regards as the first lesson to learn through concentration and meditation: that my desire shall be accomplished.

Religion teaches the same in the Lord's prayer: Give us our daily bread. In another place the Gospel says: "Knock and it shall be opened unto you," and again: "If his son ask bread, will he give him a stone?" If you tell yourself that you do not desire anything, you go back. Your progress lies in desiring whatever you wish. The fulfillment of your desire is the first proof that your concentration is successful. This is called *Vilayat.* A person may be able to see into things and yet not be a master; to be a master implies being master of all situations in life. Although a seer is one who can see, yet unless he has mastery also he can only see and nothing else. Mastery is greater than seership, because the master both sees and accomplishes.

This whole creation is the result of desire. The purpose of creation, therefore, must be the fulfillment of this desire. Thus your first step towards accomplishment or attainment, whether it be spiritual or worldly, will also be to proceed with purpose towards the goal of your desire.

You may think, "But if I keep on with the pursuit of my material desire, perhaps I may never reach the spiritual goal and will never get beyond my desires.'' The answer to this is that if you let the desire go unfulfilled and you lack the patience needed to accomplish the desire, your progress will be arrested. This failure will keep you back from spiritual progress. When once you have accomplished one desire, you will have that something which is needed for the accomplishment of something greater. Every desire you accomplish is one step further towards that final goal which every soul ultimately has to reach.

Thus the way to go is this, even for attaining spiritual perfection. Those who renounce their desires for God, for spiritual perfection, bury their own desires in their heart. It is more than renouncing; it is killing them and burying them; but they are there all the same. They are entombed in the heart, and there they will produce all sorts of germs and worms, and they will decay. There will only be pain and nothing else, and so spiritual accomplishment cannot be attained in this way.

The steps you take towards the goal by accomplishing your desires, your patience in doing this, your perseverance with it, these are what teach you. One may compare it with playing with dolls. The child who plays with a doll is learning to be a mother; learning how to be kind to children, putting them to bed, waking them up and dressing them. When once a little girl has learned this she will later be a good mother; this means she will accomplish her desire.

The man who has become rich or powerful, material though this may be, has attained something all the same; something has been accomplished; the mind gets strength and confidence. Then he can take the next step, which is the spiritual step.

A person has prepared himself for renunciation when he has risen above the object he demands. He is only entitled to say that he does not want the sweet when he has had so much of it that he cannot eat any more. If he is still longing, well, he may say, ''No,'' but it will be only a formality; perhaps it would not be good etiquette to say "Yes," but he longs for it just the same!

So it is that you have to rise above everything that you renounce. You have not really renounced until you have done that. You go on seeking as long as you have a desire for a thing.

Gain and Loss

To the view of a mystic a gain is not a gain nor is a loss a loss; for that which appears to be a loss at one time may appear at another to be a gain. The more deeply we think about it, the more we see that in every gain there is a loss, and in every loss there is a gain. That which seemed to be a gain yesterday may prove to be a loss tomorrow, and that which is a loss at one time proves to yield a gain at another. Consequently the mystic realizes the joy of the gain and the sorrow of the loss in their right aspect; he discerns what it is that turns a gain to a loss, or converts a loss to a gain. The more deeply we consider the subject, the more do we discern that there are certain gains which are only transient, because material, and that to attain them we may have sacrificed a greater gain. Of course if we do not see that greater gain, we do not mind the loss. We can only see what we have lost or what we have gained after we have discerned whether the gain we have sacrificed really was a greater one or not.

Every experience in life has three aspects: that in which it is in the state of a motive; that in which it is in the process of achievement; and that in which the experience is an accomplished fact. In the first aspect, where the experience is as yet only in the form of a motive, we can have no clear conception as to whether it is a gain or a loss. We start out, for instance, with the thought, "I wish to start a business; in this business I shall make a profit." That represents the initial motive. The next step will be the actual building up of the business. It is now that the gain or the loss becomes more clearly perceptible. But the gain or loss is most clear after the business is accomplished. The experience is now realized. Hitherto the person has not realized the benefit or otherwise, but in the final stage he is able to form a true estimate as to whether the idea of his life has led to gain or loss.

In life we discriminate between two things: the real and the false. We think more of the real and less of the false. We discriminate between imitation gold and real gold; we pay more for the real gold because it is more lasting. The two samples of gold may be equally bright; hence it is evident that the value we attach to things is in proportion to their lasting power. Similarly, if we could see what things in life are lasting or passing, we should discriminate between real loss and false loss, real gain and false gain. The gain or loss which is momentary is not real. So, too, joy or sorrow is a momentary state; the joy over a gain today may tomorrow prove to be a sorrow. If we knew the realities, we should never grieve over the loss of things which experience shows to be only of a transient character.

On the one hand we are working for our own individual benefit and interest; but on the other hand there is a universal power which is more mighty than ourselves, and more just in its working. When these two powers, the Kaza, or universal, the Kadr, or individual, are working harmoniously, things come right. But when they clash, that which is thought right by Kaza will happen without regard to what Kadr may think right or wrong. Those who know this, and harmonize their will with Kaza, the universal Will, begin to experience divine impulses, and they begin to feel every time what is and what is not harmonious in the Kadr also. To such as these there come fewer failures in life. Life is easier because they swim with and not against the tide.

Our sense of justice is partial, because it is obscured or shadowed by our likes and dislikes, by our personal interest and lack of interest in people and things.

In the Bible it is written, "Where your treasure is, there will your heart be also." If our gain is only in objects of a passing nature, our heart will find no gain in this life or in the hereafter. Those who trust in transitory gain must accept the inevitable disappointment, both here and in the hereafter. Everybody in this world is selfish; for is it not true that the sages who renounce that which is valued by worldly people, after all only take up that which they understand to be really the greater gain? The only difference between their action and that which seems entirely selfish in those who are not sages is that they sacrifice what they perceive to be a false gain. For anyone to do otherwise is to be like the dog which was running after its own shadow.

The privilege of having life on earth in this delicate human vehicle is too great to risk wasting it on something which will leave one the loser in the end, however rich and ample the false gain may appear. What gain is it to have the object we have gained snatched from our hands in the end? What gain is it to have an object which has to be constantly guarded and watched against the rapacity of others? Everyone is on the watch to take our gain away and make it his; and this he can do with any transient gain. We always desire dependable objects and friends. It is our nature to long for something we can depend on for life. Our own nature teaches us that if we realize our life's desire, that which we consider important, we realize only transient things. Has not war shown us how artists lose their art, poets their poetry, kings their thrones and many a man falls from his heaven to the earth, all in a moment's time? What, then, is there in this world that can be depended upon? Have we not seen how parents have even sacrificed their lives in order to give the desired happiness to sons and daughters? Have we not seen that friends whom one relies on, in their turn depend on someone else and are disappointed?

When we really think about these things we are bound to see that after all we are only like children in understanding. We think ourselves clever and wise, and yet we do not really think deeply about life. Some day we begin to think, and then we see ourselves as a parent sees his children's acts. The child thinks its sand and toys are such important things, things that we grown-ups attach no importance to. And we too begin to see how childish our own life is when we can assess at their true value these actions and desires which seemed so important to us yesterday. We think little things so important: dignity, ill-treatment, insults, reputation; and what do they matter in the end? Do we not see people praised and raised up high in vanity and greatness one day, and next day they are quite forgotten? Before the revolution every shop in Moscow had a picture of the Czar in one window, and of Jesus with the Virgin in the other. Within three years, what a change there was! Even a whole race will change its attitude in a moment's time.

Praise, honor, love, kindness, are they lasting, are they dependable? Are we not seeking after wealth, or fame, or love, or kindness, or some help from morning until evening? However evolved we may be with our education and experience, yet what are we really seeking? Things from which we cannot derive any lasting gain. From these false things we gain the experience that the things to which we have hitherto attached importance and which we have valued are things that do not last. We learn at length that it would be wise to remember that all these objects and ideals and aspirations which we have in life should be judged according to whether they are dependable or not, lasting or not. After we have perceived the truth that this or that is not to be depended upon, we find that it is not necessary to renounce them all, to give up everything in life. We can be in the crowd just as well as in seclusion in the wilderness. We can have all good things, wealth, friends, kindness, love to give and love to take, once we have learned not to be blinded by them, learned to escape from disappointment, learned to escape from repugnance at the idea that the things are not as we would want them to be. A man can still attend to business, he may attain wealth, he can carry out all those things, but now his eyes are wide open; before, they were blind. This is the teaching of life. Thus it is that when we study life in the East, we will find that a Sufi may be a king or he may be a faqir. A Sufi means a seer; and a Sufi may still be a king. It is not the actual literal renunciation which counts, it is the personal abandonment of belief in the importance of transient things.

A person who pretends to be unselfish is generally foolish-selfish. It is the wise-selfish who are right; they are selfish, it is true, but they are selfish with true wisdom. They think out what it is in life that will benefit them most. The foolish-selfish man never puts money by, and thus never has any to give away. The wise-selfish man will obtain money in order that he can express his generosity with what he has collected. He who remains a pauper all his life has never achieved anything for anyone. Therefore he is wise who not only understands what is real gain and what is false, but also understands the price there is to pay for the gain. What determines our success is weighing whether one's gain is of more value than the price one has to pay for it, or whether the price one has to pay is greater than the gain one can obtain. He who perceives this clearly has learned the true business of life very well.

For every gain, however, there is a need for sacrifice. To gain anything we have to sacrifice something; to pursue two gains is to lose both. Therefore it is necessary to decide once and for all what is false, and then to follow the real and leave the false.

If there is such a thing as saintly renunciation, it is renouncing small gains for better gains; not for no gains, but seeing with open eyes what is better and what is inferior. Even if the choice has to lie between two momentary gains, one of these would always be found to be more real and lasting; that is the one that should be followed for the time. When we take the torch of wisdom to show us our faith through life, we will end by realizing what is really profitable in life and what is not.

Will Power

When the mind inquires into the nature of will power, it becomes a question whether it is a power of the mind, a power of thought, or a power of the brain. Those who cannot see beyond the power of the brain, call it brain power; those who cannot see beyond the mind, call it a power of the mind. Those who cannot conceive of the existence in man of anything above the feelings, consider will power to be a power of feeling. A Sufi understands it to be the divine power.

It is the divine will that is manifested throughout the whole universe, which has created the whole universe; and it is part of the divine will that manifests itself through us. Everything we do in life is governed and directed by that power. Were it not that there is but one power to govern and direct, how would it have been if one foot determined to go to the North, and the other to the South? Our two eyes might have turned in opposite directions, one to the West, the other to the East, had there not been one will power behind them to direct their gaze towards one object. When lifting a certain thing, one hand might have gone up and the other down, had there not been one will power to govern both, and cause them to join in the one movement. This shows that each individual has one will power which governs several organs of our physical existence as well as our thoughts and imaginations; all are directed consciously or unconsciously by the one power. We could not have accomplished one single thing in life had will power not been at work.

But there are two ways in which the will power works: first, when it is lighted with the light of intelligence; second, when it is not so lighted, but works by itself. When it works by itself, we call it accidental. We do things accidentally which we have not intended to do. But when will power makes our mind and body work consciously, then the light of intelligence is followed and the will power is acting consciously. This is the difference between various happenings. In the one we are conscious of what we are thinking, we are conscious of what we are speaking and of what we are doing in proportion to our will power and to the light that is thrown upon it from the light of our intelligence. But we have acted without will power when we have to say, "I have done something I should not have done; I have said something I should not have said; I have thought something which I should not have thought." When a person says, "What I did is terrible; I said something I should not have said," it means that during the time he said or did it the will power was there, but the strength and light of intelligence had not fallen upon it to the extent to which they should.

There are two aspects of our being: the will power or governing power, and the vehicles, the mind and the body. Both are governed and controlled by that one governing power. In one aspect of our being we are king, in the other aspect we are minister, and in a third aspect we are servant. We are minister when our mind works, and we are servant when the body works. We are king when the will power works.

When this power loses its control over the mind, then our thoughts become disordered; they dwell in any regions and wander on any lines, even those which our moral standard has perhaps not drawn for them. And our body also works in a disorderly way when the power of the will is lost. Therefore all illnesses, all failures, all disappointments and faults in life are caused by just one thing: weakness of will power.

Man, not knowing this, sometimes considers the will power to be a power of thought and mind. He does not know that behind mind there is something else. When the will is behind it, the body is powerful too. There was a well known Indian faqir who was able to lift an elephant. How can a man lift an elephant? However strong he may be, what comparison can there be between the two? What power is at work? It was his will power that was greater than the elephant's.

The great and wonderful things that man has done in this world that we see around us, are all the outcome of man's will. Animals, with all their strength, have not that will. Therefore puny man stands before the elephant and says, "Sit down," and the elephant sits down; "Stand up," and the elephant stands up. With all the strength in its body, still the elephant listens to him. That is how the faqir lifted the elephant. Man makes tigers, lions, horses work; he even makes his thought and will act through inanimate things; even through objects his will power can be manifested. But when man does not realize its effect upon living creatures, how can he experience his power over objects?

Jelal-ud-Din Rumi, in his *Masnavi,* speaks of fire, air, water, earth, and ether as beings, while man calls them things. To man they are things; to God they are beings, obedient servants. Whatever He wishes, they do. As the servant acts according to his master's desires, so these elements act as God desires. Further, not only does the will of God work through elements, but the will of man also, in proportion to the power of his will. A loaf of bread given with will power can cure a man's disease more successfully than a medicine, if there is enough will power with it. The lesson of Christ, that if one has faith even as a grain of mustard one can remove mountains, can be understood after one has realized that it is the will power which does the work.

In the East there are superstitions which have a mystical meaning. When a person goes into a new business, or goes on a journey, his relatives give him flour or rice in his hand, or some betel nuts, with the wish that he may meet with success. The token itself is nothing; but behind it there is will power, and the person who received it has believed; therefore he has responded to the will power attached to the gift. There is a harmony. The one who wishes to have good luck receives it.

Nevertheless, it is not to be inferred from this that a man should be prepared to believe in superstitions or become superstitious. It is to show that he must know the value of will power, and use it in his profession, his business, his home, in all things. Is it not a desirable thing to have will power; is it not desirable to have physical strength? If we are satisfied with feebleness of body, it may be that we are also satisfied to be without will power.

All light is for us, inspiration is for us; why not use it as long as we know how to use it to make the best of life? If one wishes to abuse power, one may abuse bodily power, fighting everybody, boxing and wrestling. But that is another part of life. Power is necessary and should be developed; but when man is anxious to develop power, either of body or of mind, he ought to remember that the will power is behind it all; that if the will is developed, the physical and mental power can easily be obtained. The will power governs the body and the mind.

Now coming to the question of the will of man as opposed to the will of God: which is which? We understand the difference when we perceive that the nature of will power differs only according to whether it exists in its fullness, or whether it is limited. The will power in its fullness is divine power; the will power in its limited state is the individual will. And if there is anything that can be called the source of the whole creation, it is the divine will, the will of the absolute Being. If we do not desire to call it will, we may call it force, strength, or might. But force, strength, might, energy, are all dead words. Force can be without intelligence, energy without intelligence, mind without intelligence; but will means force, energy, might, with intelligence. Therefore it is called divine will instead of divine energy. A person with a materialistic mind would call it energy. But why energy? Is our intelligence energy? It is beyond energy. Is our will only energy? It is energy with intelligence. Therefore divine will is energy, but with divine intelligence. In all there is intelligence.

If we observe nature keenly, we see how divine wisdom is working. The animals and birds of tropical countries have fur and feathers which differ from those one finds in the Himalayas and other cold regions. They have suitable bodies, suitable skins; their life, their whole existence is adjusted to the place where they live.

Man's desire, the desire of his senses, is matched by the possession of every sense, every organ of sense, each suited to gratify the desire of his being. The eye meets the requirements of the sense of sight. With all our intelligence and great research no one can make a new eye so adaptable and fitted for the purpose. This wisdom makes us understand and believe that behind all this there is an intelligent God and Creator, not only a life or energy or force; it makes us ask why anyone should want to call Him force or energy, and not God.

The light which we see of the planets is not their own. It is the light of the sun which illuminates the planets and is reflected from them; it is the same light that they receive which they reflect. So it is with man: it is the will of God that is reflected in man. Although every star is not necessarily a sun, yet its light ultimately comes from a sun.

If man has divine light in him, why should he commit sin or do evil, and why should there be anything that we call wrong or a sin? If it is God's will, how can it be sin? We understand this when we consider the difference between wrong and right, sin and virtue, good and evil. These differ with different people. It depends upon the standards of each one's evolution; it depends on the goal or ideal which each one has placed before him. That is why the Prophet said, "The religion of each person is peculiar to himself." It is a great fault on our part when we accuse another person of an untrue or false belief, an untrue or false religion. We do not know that perhaps he has a religion which is suited to himself. His evolution or attainment in life, his temperament, his standard of morals are different; therefore we ought, if only we could, to keep to our own religion. The standard that we believe in for our own good is quite enough.

Our intelligence and experience of this life on earth create within us a world of experiences; and these experiences teach us, by comparing one with the other, that this one is for happiness, that one is not. That which is for our happiness we call virtue, and that which does not contribute to our happiness we call vice. In this way the world which we make into our own is a world of personal experiences, either in our own lives or seen through the lives of others. Therefore it is quite natural that a person in Tibet should have a different religion from a person in France; and a man in Persia a different one from a man in Colombo. Although mankind is the same everywhere, a man's religion is his experience in life, and therefore his own evolution, his own experience, added to the temperament of the people with whom he lives. He can see what is good for him, and what is not; what is right and what is not right; what gives him happiness, and what keeps him from it. The world itself becomes a scripture or book to the soul. If he does not consult it, he is thoughtless. But the one who consults with the world that he has created within himself is wise. Sometimes in his world he has decided a certain thing is a sin or evil, and yet when it comes to an action, or thought, or speech, he cannot follow the moral he has already made for himself, either because of the weakness of his mind or body, or because of the weakness of his will. He fails to fulfill the law of his own world, of his own scripture that he has written. Thus he falls, and that is considered by him to be sin. It is the same with virtue. We have our own sins, our own virtues, which we have made from our own experiences.

If a child throws a knife at somebody, it has not committed a crime, because it has not yet set that action down as a crime in its world of experiences; it has not gathered it into that world. It only becomes a crime when the child knows it to be criminal. After that it becomes responsible for its deed. "Judge not, that ye be not judged; for with what judgment ye judge, ye shall be judged." We judge others according to our world of good and bad; the same world, the same scripture that is our religion judges us also, when we do wrong. And no one would do wrong if his will power helped him to do right, for how could he do something which the scripture of his own heart tells him to be wrong, had not his will power failed him? Therefore those who repent after their crimes, faults, and failures show thereby that it is not that they wanted to do or have these things, but that their will power failed them. The will power was not strong enough to help them to carry out their own standard of good, as it should help all men through the journey of life.

How can will power be developed? Are there any exercises by which it can be developed? Are there any rules to follow? Is there any knowledge to acquire? All these three are required.

The first exercise to help the will power to develop would be to check every act, word, and thought which we do not wish to occur; to avoid unintentional actions, speech, and thoughts. The other exercise that is necessary for the development of the will power is that of seeing that neither our mind nor our body rules us, but that we rule our body and our mind. Desires such as appetite, thirst, sleep, even the desire of moving or standing or walking, all these desires should be under control. There should be a time in every day when every desire of the body is checked. See if you can do it; and then as long as you can let the body go without listening to it, do so. It takes a great deal of trouble to rule the body, for it is not willing to be ruled.

Yogis, faqirs, Sufis may be seen sitting, standing in one posture for hours together. All the postures adopted are to control and govern every atom of the body, so that it may be under the control of the will. I do not mean that one should devote all one's time to those things, or even that one should have certain exercises for this. When one understands the matter, and carries it out in one's everyday life, then one's life becomes a continual progress.

Next, there is the control of the mind. The mind sometimes does not listen. We want to think of our business, and perhaps the mind thinks of the state of our health, or about a neighbor. It insists on thinking of something else. It may be as unruly as a wild horse which cannot be controlled. So the next step to gain control of it is by concentration, by absorption, by meditation. Concentration should be practiced in everyday life. It is necessary that our bodies and minds should act according to our will in our profession, in our office, in our ordinary life.

There is a tradition of the Brahmins that Rama had two sons, Kusha and Lahu. They went with their mother to a city, where they dwelt with a great hermit of the time. Lahu, a young lad, went out to wander through the town and look at its beauty. To his great surprise he found a beautiful horse running without a rider. And when he inquired whose horse it was, people said,

"This horse is let loose with the intention that anyone who can catch it shall be crowned as king of this country."

The lad, with the enthusiasm of growing strength and hope in life, thought, "What a good thing it would be if I could catch this horse." So he ran after it and tried to catch it; but every time he approached the horse, it slipped away. Again he ran after it. And again when the horse was only a little distance away, he was just able to touch it but again it slipped away. This went on for a long, long time. He was away so long that his mother became uneasy about him, not knowing where he had gone. So she told Kusha that his younger brother had gone out and not returned. Kusha went out and discovered that Lahu was after this horse. He was very glad to note his brother's ambition. He knew, however, that he would never catch the horse unless he were instructed what to do. Finally, Lahu, knowing now how to catch the animal, succeeded and was able to bring it before the authorities, who declared him to be their king.

This story tells us about will power. The mind is just like a wild horse, and the will is the only thing which can catch it. The thoughts and imaginations are all so unruly that we cannot think or feel what we wish. If we were able to do so, then neither could sorrow touch us again, nor could unhappiness come near, because it is the thoughts and imaginations which bring sorrow. If we could think what we wished to think, if we could feel what we wished to feel, life would be a heaven for us. When we do not feel what we wish to feel, when we do not think what we wish to think, it is just because of lack of will power. That which is the governing power cannot hold it.

The elder brother of the story is the teacher who shows the path to his younger brothers who are groping in darkness. He is sent with a message from God, the Father and Mother of His children on earth, to guide his younger brethren. Those who are seeking after the power to control this vehicle, and have the ambition or desire to obtain the crown of life, to them will be granted the inheritance of the kingdom of their country.

The Will, Human and Divine

The will is the same, whether it be human or divine. The only difference is that in one aspect it is the whole, in the other aspect it is a part; in one aspect it is almighty, in the other it has only a certain might, or a certain power; in one aspect it is unlimited, in the other it is limited.

The difference between the divine and the human will is like the difference between the trunk of a tree and its branches; and as from the boughs other branches and twigs spring, so the will of one powerful individual has branches going through the will of other individuals. In a tree there is a trunk, and there are some prominent or large branches; from these there spring many smaller branches. So there are the powerful beings, the masters of humanity. Their will is God's, their word is God's word, and yet they are branches, because the trunk is the will of the Almighty. As the branches grow, so we too grow; as the branches develop, we develop; as the branches flourish, we flourish; as the branches bear fruit, we bear fruit; as the branches are capable of rising, we too rise. Whether the branch be large or small, every branch has the same origin and the same root as the stem. Therefore, whether a person be holy or wicked, wise or foolish, he has in his innermost spirit the same essence and the same power that the wise have.

There is no reason for anyone to feel discouraged by his weakness or deficiencies, or by his actions that have dissatisfied him, or by anything in life that has failed. He should forget the past that has failed him, and begin to construct and mold his future as he would wish it to be, considering that as a branch is not separate from the bough, and the bough is not separate from the stem, so with all our limitations we are not separate from the will of the Unlimited One.

In Sufi terms these two aspects of will are called *Kaza* and *Kadr*. Sometimes we think, "If I could see that friend it would be so pleasant," and at the same time there comes a desire, "If I could have some nice flowers," and then a friend comes bringing a bunch of our favorite ones. Or we may desire to have fish to eat, and the cook brings a savory dish of fish. Sometimes this is due to the strength of one's own will, and sometimes it is the soul working in harmony with the divine will. One only knows when it is in harmony with the divine will and when not by noting the results, and the one who knows beforehand is the seer.

Sometimes things are accomplished without the least effort. When it is the divine will it is like something floating on water; it advances without effort. Problems and actions may be achieved in a moment then, whilst at other times the smallest problem cannot be solved without great difficulty. One finds that some persons are very clever and experienced in industrial work or in politics; they have striven very hard to attain their goal, and yet have accomplished nothing; they are always a failure. And there are others who take up a thing, and without much effort, without much worry on their part, they complete it and attain their goal.

All this is accounted for by harmony with the divine will. Everyone experiences such a thing at some time or other. When things are in harmony with the divine will, everything is there; we just cast a glance towards a thing and it is found, as in the saying,

"Word spoken, action done." When we strive with all the material in our hands and yet cannot achieve our desire, that is when the matter is contrary to the divine will. Our success or failure all depends upon the harmony or disharmony of our individual will with the divine will.

But if our individual will is a branch of the divine will, if its source is the same, how can it ever be out of harmony? Sometimes the hand sympathizes with the foot, at other times it does not. We hurt ourselves many times just because of disharmony; we may cut ourselves, our fingers for instance. If then I, who am one person, can cause harm to myself, and suffer thereby, why should it not be possible that the human will should be out of harmony with the divine, so that the divine suffers thereby? It is possible to act in a way contrary to the divine will, even though one is only a branch of it. In a fountain there is a big stream which flows up and then breaks into many drops. The stream is like the divine will, and the different drops like the wills in us. One drop goes higher, another lower; one falls to the left, another to the right; one goes north, another south. But the source of all this activity is one; it is one thing that turns into so many, scattering in all directions. Thus from unity there has come variety.

The sages have therefore taught the part played by contentment. It is said, "Resist not evil," and yet how many give in to evil instead! The real meaning of the scripture is: suppose a person is angry with us, if we partake of his anger we resist him; the fire that he sets alight in our minds we allow to become alight in ourselves, and we have resisted. Do not resist evil in that way. Do not partake of the evil of another. If you are quiet and calm, your calmness and quietness will have a greater effect on the other than his anger, so that true resistance is practice of contentment. Patience is the best quality that man can cultivate. We are always apt to become excited or annoyed when another person does not understand us. Why get excited if he cannot understand us? If a person is foolish or cannot do things right, by becoming excited we make him still more foolish, still more stupid. We cannot help him in that way, and we partake of his quality by allowing ourselves to oppose him. If we kept our mind tranquil, if we had patience, we should keep in harmony. Harmony is the greatest thing to learn in life. All the disagreement between couples, friends, people in business and politics, comes from lack of patience. If we just had patience and contentment, we could teach ourselves much better.

Contentment teaches resignation. But this resignation is not exactly what people mean by fate. The true recognition of fate is like the drop realizing that it is foolish to fight against the ocean. The drop is part of the ocean. Why want to fight it? If the drop does not resign itself, of what profit will it be? Why believe that what we think is right, and no one can be right who thinks otherwise? We should remember that another person does not see as we see, because each one sees only a reflection of the highest Ego that works in man though he is unconscious of it. To him it is right, but to the other it need not appear right. It is only right for that one person, for that one moment; later it may not appear so. The limited being cannot claim the perception of the Unlimited; thus we cannot regard our own will as being the universal Will unless our will is in harmony with the will of God. We should therefore practice harmonizing our will with that of our fellow men, by tolerance, patience, endurance; because in this world every ego is working for itself, however near or dear another may be. Everyone thinks, "What can I make another person do for me?" He wants everybody to be in harmony with his way of life. That is why there is a world full of rebellion, like the thorns in the rose bush.

It may seem a great sacrifice and torment to practice patience, but it is the only way to get out of the whirlpool; it is the only way that one can conquer life's difficulties. If anybody has ever conquered, he has only done so by this means; never by the means of resistance, but always by the way of resignation. All teachers have taught this way, saying, "Prostrate thyself on the ground; prostrate thyself before God; kneel down." Some of us fail to appreciate this, but the messengers do not leave anything unspoken; it is we who do not understand what they say. People fight for their religions; if we were just to learn them instead! The question should always be: have we learned our own religion? To have learned it means to practice it and see its benefit. However fast we may try to run away from it, we will still find this lesson to learn. We have to make ourselves strong and prepared to withstand all that befalls us. Therefore we must develop our will power first by such morals, and be able to harmonize our will with others.

One thinks one can develop will power by fighting, but that is not so, because by fighting we make very little progress; by fighting with ourselves we progress a hundred times more. Our greatest enemy is ourself. All weakness, all ignorance keeps us from the truth of our being, from all the virtues hidden in us and all perfection hidden in our souls. The first self we realize is the false self. Unless the soul is born again it will not see the kingdom of heaven. The soul is first born into the false self; it is blind. In the true self the soul opens its eyes. Unless the false self is fought with, the true self cannot be realized. Therefore endurance is necessary, patience is necessary.

If only we could fight with ourselves so that we became able to give pleasure to others! Sages are as harmonious with a pious person as with a wicked one, as harmonious with a wise man as with a foolish, with a rich as with a poor man. We feel friendly towards some, not towards others; we get on well with some, but with others there is always disharmony, while with others again everyone feels peaceful and happy.

The lions could not harm Daniel because of the harmony of his will with the universal Will. The lions represent the destructive elements in the human mind. They represent wars, disappointments, rivalries, jealousies, envy, passions, and so forth, in different horrible guises. Our ego is the lion of lions, and if this is conquered, then these external lions—the different egos around us—are conquered also, and wherever we go, with anyone, whether foolish or wise, good or bad, we now have peace.

To learn the lesson of how to live is more important than any psychic or occult learning. Every day we think we have learned the lesson, but if we had the world would have become a heaven for us by now. We may seek the higher knowledge or the higher things, but the very smallest thing, the control of all the creatures of the mind, which seems as nothing compared with the higher knowledge, once learned and acted upon is greater than all. This is a great step; yet how difficult to gain this, how reasonless it seems! But when we pause to think of the difference between ourselves and animals, we see the greatness in this simple thing of yielding the will. If there is one animal in a place and another one comes to it, the first one wants to bite or bark, or even drive him out of his sight. A dog will do that even though he has finished his dinner and does not want to eat the food that has attracted the hungry dog to the place.

There is an Eastern parable of a dog going to a certain town. His journey was a very long one, taking two or three days as a rule, and yet he arrived before sunset of the same day. The dogs of that town were all very surprised to see him so soon. "Yes, it was a very long journey," the dog said, "but I attribute my speed to the kindness and help of my fellow dogs. Since I left home, whenever I felt tired and tried to stop a moment to rest, four or five would run up and bark at me and want to bite me. So I had to run on without staying to rest in that place, or to search for food. And so it went on at every place I came to, until in the end I have arrived here at my destination.''

This illustrates the animal nature. Man's selfishness shows itself in wanting to get the better of his fellow man. If we developed humanity we should do differently. We should be satisfied with a slice of bread if there were another in need, but as it is, it happens that even when we are fed ourselves, we do not wish anyone else to share the food. The human heart can only be really satisfied by knowing that the other person is happy. True pleasure lies in the sharing of joy with another. From the day that we realize this we begin to act as human beings; hitherto we have not done so, even though we have human forms.

Sages have always repented of all things that make them animal. It is human beings that repent; the animals are pleased with everything that they do. The Bible says, ''Repent, for the kingdom of God is at hand.'' This has to be done all day long. Once one has realized it, the kingdom of God is at hand. The sinner can become righteous at any moment if he makes up his mind; the difficulty is to make it up. The next thing is to carry it out. Revolutions and harmony, war and peace, are all parts of a whole being. But contentment and perfect resignation open up a harmonious feeling and bring the divine will into harmony with our own. Our blessing now becomes a divine blessing, our words divine words, our atmosphere a divine atmosphere, although we seem to be limited beings; for our will becomes absorbed into the whole, and so our will becomes the will of God.

The Attainment of Power

The possession of power brings with it the desire to attain more. We can attain everything that we desire if we only know how. No one attains a higher position unless he follows some hidden trend. The tendency to arrive at some perfection is that which causes one to attain a greater perfection. Even if he attains wealth, a man is tending towards perfection. Napoleon attained something hidden which was great and wonderful, if we could only understand it. So a merchant may perhaps have begun by selling empty bottles, and ultimately becomes wealthy enough to be able to found colleges, libraries, hospitals, and so forth, which proves that there was an inclination to a certain perfection. Even though the ideal may not be so high, the very inclination to attain power is a great force.

There is a spiritual, psychic, occult, telepathic power. How are we to attain to that? The soul feels, "I am a king, but in this mortal casket I have become a pauper," or as Rumi expresses it, "I was created free, but in this flesh I am in captivity and have become weak." From an almighty state of being we have become helpless beings. When we become conscious of spirit, we become conscious of a mighty power hidden, and our spirit is then the expression of the Almighty Power.

The power is in unity, but is lost in variety. Thus, for instance, if we hold a thing in our hand, we can hold it with strength, because all five fingers have united to hold the object. But if we try to lift it by one finger, this one finger may drop it, even though the finger belongs to the same hand. In all aspects of life unity is power. All religions show that power is in unity. This is the secret of philosophy.

There are two aspects of unity: first, the unity of variety; second, unity realizing itself. One is earthly, the other is heavenly. One cannot serve two masters. Unity is the only source of happiness. Unity in realization is far greater than unity in variety.

"When two hearts unite, they can break even mountains." As two fuse in love, the more does intuition grow, the more does one understand whether the other is happy, or pleased, or displeased, whatever distance may separate them. This is nothing but just the unity of the one person with the other. It is clairvoyance. The mother knows the condition of her son at the battle front. She can see him in her dreams. Hearts which are united in love perceive the state of mind of the loved ones. They do not have to study mysticism or concentration, for they have natural concentration. The mother does not pretend to meditate; love teaches her more meditation than a person who pretends to study it can attain. One cannot, however, hold an object in mind when the heart has nothing to do with the object. Pebbles are not made to eat, and therefore one cannot eat them. The mind is never satisfied with either an object or a being which it does not desire; therefore it is no use to concentrate specially on what the heart does not desire. The heart which does not desire needs no special concentration.

Nothing gives greater power of confidence than love. If one loves a person, one has confidence in that person. Hence the mother is as a god to her child. The hen is the most timid of birds until she has chickens; at that time she is under the spell of love, and would not hesitate to fight even an elephant if he were endangering her brood. This shows the power of love. Can any charm or amulet be more powerful than this? The one with a loving heart will travel furthest.

Power can be attained artificially, by magic, or by the different laws of the power of sound, of words, or of concentration. Such power can make a person ill, can make a person run away from the country, can make two hearts separate; many wonders can be performed by the power of concentration.

We do not exist only as body; we exist as heart, as soul. If the heart is kept dead all our life, and we give the body all the things it wants, soft cushions and comforts, is this all we need? The heart is still hungering. The heart wants to see that it is living. The heart longs to be alive. It has been created to love, and it is not loved; it wants to melt. But though it wants all the love and kindness to come to it, it withholds giving when the time comes for it to give. We accept love when love is offered to us, but when the time comes to give, we do not give. But can love really be given? Is love trade? Until this is known, it is impossible to understand love.

To love is to possess a heart, but not as a demon possesses a human being. When a person "comes alive," this means that he has become the possessor of a heart. Whose heart? Heart is that factor of our being, of our thinking, which feels within itself a longing to express love; it is an awakening of love and to a feeling of love. This is the factor which produces thought; this is the factor which produces feeling; in this lies the creative power. All the power which one can possibly wish to attain throughout life is reached by this means.

How can power develop in the absence of unity? Suppose everyone had magnetic power. They would make all the money they could from their clients. Would it be just for some to possess the power of making money, and for others to be perpetually their victims? No, and that is why mysticism was kept hidden for the protection of these others. Those who are not worthy of the hidden knowledge would use their power for selfish purposes, for themselves and for those who belong to them. If ordinary people had this power, one could not even compare them with the devil. Rishis, saints, and sages have experienced the selfishness of man. They know it would be bad for the world if this hidden knowledge were revealed. And who deserves to be illuminated with this knowledge? He alone deserves it who develops his soul in the thought of unity; and he alone receives it.

The progressive steps of enlightenment in the use of power are shown when a man transfers his ambitions first to his family and then from his family to his city, from his city to his nation, from his nation to the whole world, and from the whole world to the whole universe. When the joy of every person he sees is his joy, when the pain of every person is his pain, then he becomes a conqueror and attains power.

Life in This World

Every soul at times asks itself, "Why am I here?" This question arises according to the development of one's intelligence. A man may say, "I am here to eat, drink, and to make merry," but this even the animals do; therefore what more has he accomplished by being human? Another might affirm that the attainment of power and position is important, but he must know that both of these are transitory. Power of any kind has its fall as well as its rise. All things we possess are taken from others, and others in their turn await with outstretched hands to seize them.

A man may say, "We are here to gain honor." In this case someone has to be humbled in order to give him the honor he seeks; but he in his turn may have to be humbled by a still more ardent seeker of honor. We may think that being loved is all-important, but we should know that the beauty in ourselves which makes another love us is transient. Furthermore the beauty we possess may pale in comparison with the beauty of another. When we seek the love of another we are not only dependent upon their love, but are ourselves devoid of love. If we think that it is desirable to love someone who deserves our love, we are mistaken, for we are always liable to be disappointed in the object of our love, who may perhaps never prove to be our ideal. One is led to suppose and believe that virtue is the only thing that matters in life, but it will be found that the greatest number of sufferers from moral hallucination are to be met with among the self-righteous.

Then the only purpose of our life here on earth, if there be any, is the successful attainment of life's demands. It may seem strange at first sight that all which life demands should be allowable and worthwhile attaining; but on a closer study of life we see that the demands of our external self are the only ones we know, and we are ignorant of the demands of the true self, our inner life. For instance, we know that we want good food and nice clothes, comfort of living and every convenience for moving about, honor, possessions, and all necessary means for the satisfaction of our vanity, all of which for the moment appear to us as our life's only demands; but neither they nor their joy remains with us constantly. We then come to think that what we had was but a little and that perhaps more would satisfy us, and still more would suffice our need; but this is not so. Even if the whole universe were within our grasp it would be impossible fully to satisfy our life's demands. This shows that our true life has quite different demands from those with which we are familiar. It does not want the joy experienced by this individual self only; it desires joy from all around. It does not wish for a momentary peace, but for one that is everlasting. It does not desire to love a beloved held in the arms of mortality. It needs a beloved to be always before it. It does not want to be loved only for today and perhaps not tomorrow. It wishes to float in the ocean of love.

It is therefore that the Sufi seeks God as his love, lover and beloved, his treasure, his possession, his honor, his joy, his peace; and this attainment in its perfection alone fulfills all demands of life both here and hereafter. *And God is within.*

Then again it may be said, there is a purpose above each purpose, and there is again a purpose under each purpose; and yet beyond and beneath all purposes there is no purpose. The creation is, because it is.

Life is a journey from one pole to another, and the perfection of the conscious life is the final destiny of the imperfect life. In other words, every aspect of life in this world of variety gradually evolves from imperfection to perfection; and if life's evolution were not so in its nature, there would be no difference between life and death, for life on the surface is nothing but the phenomena of contrast. This, then, is another way of expressing what is the purpose of life.

One may try to see from the point of view of another as well as from one's own, and so give freedom of thought to everybody because one demands it oneself; one may try to appreciate what is good in another, and overlook what one considers bad; if somebody behaves selfishly towards one, one may take it naturally, because it is human nature to be selfish, and so one is not disappointed; but if one appears oneself to be selfish, one should take oneself to task and try to improve. There is not anything one should not be ready to tolerate, and there is nobody whom one should not forgive. Never doubt those whom you trust; never hate those whom you love; never cast down those whom you once raise in your estimation. Wish to make friends with everyone you meet; make an effort to gain the friendship of those you find difficult; become indifferent to them only if you cannot succeed in your effort. Never wish to break the friendship once made.

If anyone causes harm, one should try to think it is because one has deserved it in some way, or else it is that the one who harms knows no better. Remember that every soul that raises its head in life gets much opposition from the world. It has been so with all the prophets, saints and sages, so one cannot expect to be exempt. In this is the law of nature, and also God's plan working and preparing something desirable. No one is either higher or lower than oneself. In all sources that fulfill one's need, one may see one source, God, the only source; and in admiring and in bowing before and in loving anyone, one may consider one is doing it to God. In sorrow one may look to God, and in joy one may thank Him. One does not bemoan the past, nor worry about the future; one tries only to make the best of today. One should know no failure, for even in a fall there is a steppingstone to rise; but to the Sufi the rise and fall matter little. One does not repent for what one has done, since one thinks, says, and does what one means. One does not fear the consequences of performing one's wish in life, for what will be, will be.

Every being has a definite vocation, and his vocation is the light which illuminates his life. The man who disregards his vocation is a lamp unlit. He who sincerely seeks his real purpose in life is himself sought by that purpose. As he concentrates on that search a light begins to clear his confusion, call it revelation, call it inspiration, call it what you will. It is mistrust that misleads. Sincerity leads straight to the goal.

Each one has his circle of influence, large or small; within his sphere so many souls and minds are involved; with his rise, they rise; with his fall, they fall. The size of a man's sphere corresponds with the extent of his sympathy, or we may say, with the size of his heart. His sympathy holds his sphere together. As his heart grows, his sphere grows; as his sympathy is withdrawn or lessened, so his sphere breaks up and scatters. If he harms those who live and move within his sphere, those dependent upon him or upon his affection, he of necessity harms himself. His house or his palace or his cottage, his satisfaction or his disgust in his environment, are the creation of his own thought. Acting upon his thoughts, and also part of his own thoughts, are the thoughts of those near to him; others depress him and destroy him, or they encourage and support him, in proportion as he repels those

around him by his coldness, or attracts them by his sympathy.
Each individual composes the music of his own life. If he injures
another, he brings disharmony. When his sphere is disturbed, he
is disturbed himself, and there is a discord in the melody of his
life. If he can quicken the feeling of another to joy or to gratitude,
by that much he adds to his own life; he becomes himself by that
much more alive. Whether conscious of it or not, his thought is
affected for the better by the joy or gratitude of another, and his
power and vitality increase thereby, and the music of his life
grows more in harmony.

There are two classes of people in the world: the spectators of
life and the students of life. The former class may be compared to
those people who go to the theater and see acted either comedy
or tragedy, and are moved by it to laughter or tears. The latter
may be compared to those who go up in an airplane and view at a
glance a whole city where hitherto they had only seen one street
at a time. The students of life understand the reason of the comedy
and tragedy, while the spectators of life get only a passing
impression of them.

About this the Qur'an says, "We have removed from you your
veil, so your sight shall be keen." When this happens the spectator of life becomes the student of life. We sometimes ask
ourselves, "What is the purpose of life? Is it to eat, drink, and to
make merry?" Surely not. The animals do this, and man is a
higher creation than the animals. Is life's purpose then to become
an angelic being? This likewise cannot be the case, for the
angels were created before man, and are near to God, and
continually praise Him.

Man must be created therefore for something other than either
the animals or the angels; for if man by reason of his piety became like an angel, he would not have fulfilled the purpose for
which he was created. Man is created that he may awaken within

himself humanity, sympathy, brotherhood, love, and kindness for his fellow man.

He may think that he is kind and sympathetic, but in thinking so he makes the greatest possible mistake, for kindness is comparative. This may be illustrated by a story that is told in India of an Afghan soldier, who was once travelling with a Brahmin. The Brahmin, who was a mild and harmless man, careful not to injure the smallest of God's creation, was repeating to himself the word *Daya*, which means 'kindness.' The Afghan, who was a warrior, and understood only the rough side of life, asked him what the word meant. The Brahmin explained that the word was the same as *Rahm* in his language. "Ah," he exclaimed, "I understand very well now what it means. I remember I was kind once in my life, for on the field of battle I saw a wounded man writhing in agony, and I was touched, and I put my dagger through him and ended his suffering."

The claim to be kind and sympathetic is like a drop of water saying, "I am water," but which on seeing the ocean realizes its nothingness. In the same way, when man has looked on perfection, he realizes his shortcomings. It is then that the veil is raised from before his eyes and his sight becomes keen. He then asks himself, "What can I do that I may awaken this love and sympathy in my heart?"

The Sufi begins by realizing that he is dead and blind, and he understands that all goodness as well as all that is bad comes from within. Riches and power may vanish because they are outside of us, but only that which is within can we call our own. In order to awaken love and sympathy in our hearts, sacrifices must be made. We must forget our own troubles in order to sympathize with the troubles of others.

To relieve the hunger of others we must forget our own hunger. Everybody is working for selfish ends, not caring about others, and this alone has brought about the misery in the world today. When the world is evolving from imperfection towards perfection, it needs all love and sympathy; great tenderness and watchfulness is required of each one of us. The heart of every man, both good and bad, is the abode of God, and care should be taken never to wound anybody by word or act. We are only here in this world for a short time; many have been here before, and have passed on, and it is for us to see that we leave behind an impression of good.

The Ideal Life

When speaking on the subject of ideal life, the words of the Prophet of Islam may be quoted, where he says, "Every soul has its own religion"; which means that every soul has a certain direction which it has chosen, a goal to attain to during life. This goal is a certain ideal which depends on the soul's evolution.

For instance a young man in a family understands that he has the responsibility for his mother and father, who are old. It is a duty, and not only a duty but a virtue on his part, that he should devote all that he earns, and give every service that he can render them in their old age. His idea of virtue is that if he can be helpful to his aged parents with money or with service, he will devote both to them, and he considers that to be a virtue. That is the ideal thing for him to do, so he does it. Perhaps he does not perceive anything beyond it, but what he does perceive is virtue in his eyes. And that is why he wishes to do it, and in it lies his satisfaction.

Another person is in business, as the agent of a firm. He thinks, "I am paid by my firm, and the head of my firm is so kind that it is my first duty to prove myself faithful to my firm." He labors with enthusiasm and great zeal from morning to evening, seeing a great virtue in serving well, although he does not pretend to religion or spirituality. But he considers his service as his virtue, and as long as he considers that he is doing his duty, he is following his religion.

Religion in the East is not made into a thing apart from one's life, as in the West where business, profession, and other things on the one side of life, and going to church one day in the week on the other side, together constitute religion, with a prayer before going to rest. But strictly speaking, life is religion. When one has that ideal before one with whatever occupation one is concerned, business, industry, domestic life, or whatever it is, one carries it out, trying to be worthy of it, that is religion.

In the Hindu language, the same word *Dharma* means both duty and religion; both are expressed by one word. "This is your Dharma" means: "This is your faith." How beautiful the thought is! Whatever kind of duty it is, so long as you have an ideal before you and are performing that duty, you are walking in the path of religion.

We, with our narrowness of faith or belief, accuse others of belonging to another religion, another chapel or church. We say, "This temple is better, that faith is better." The whole world has kept on fighting and devastating itself just because it cannot understand that each form of religion is peculiar to itself. Therefore the ideal life is in following one's own ideal; it is not in checking other people's ideals. If a certain thing is one's ideal, that does not mean that another person will agree that it is best to offer prayers ten times a day. He may be doing better by following his religion in his shop than by going to a mosque and offering up a prayer twenty times a day. Perhaps somebody with that ideal cannot see that the other person's way is an ideal also. Leave everyone to follow his own ideal.

Does the ideal remain the same all the time? No, the ideal grows and improves as man grows and improves with the years. Perhaps at some time in his life a man thinks that it would be ideal to have a beautiful house, a beautiful estate, good clothes, and all manner of comforts. From that moment this is the path he ought to pursue. But then he arrives at another ideal. He comes to think, "My surroundings are not important if the people in the town are not happy nor in good surroundings." From that time he cares less for his own house and his beautiful things, and goes into the town every day and seeks to improve the health and happiness of others. He thinks, "The poor in the town should be looked after." This is his new ideal. Before he evolved his new ideal he was only enjoying his beautiful home; he was living up to a lower ideal.

And then later on he may come to say, "Never mind about my town; I think of my whole country." The whole nation comes in for consideration: what is beneficial to it, and what are the things that should be improved. His fortune may not be very great; perhaps his town is not so beautiful as that of someone who is thinking only about his own town; but he is thinking about the whole nation, and so his ideal is still greater. It does not matter to him in which town he lives; his life is in the whole country, in the whole nation. He becomes the spirit of the whole nation. That is his ideal.

Is the man the same, whatever his appearance? We see now that it is all a matter of his ideal whether a man differs from his neighbor, whether he is heavenly or earthly, as high as the Devas, the heavenly beings, or as low as the demons. His ideal makes him as high as the one, or as low as the lowest demons. The greatness of man lies in the greatness of his ideal.

That which makes us esteem those whom we esteem is their ideal. That which raises man from earth to heaven is his ideal; and that which pulls man down from the heavens to the earth is also his ideal. When he does not live up to his ideal he falls to earth; and when he raises his ideal he goes from earth to heaven. He can rise to any height, according to the stature of his ideal.

One person thinks, "Oh, it does not matter; if I have a good dinner, never mind what others have"; another thinks, "It is no pleasure to me to have had a good dinner, since my family still starve; it gives me much more happiness if I have only a frugal dinner, as long as my family are well satisfied." This raises him higher than the person who thinks only of his own happiness. A third person thinks, "It does not matter how I live, so long as I have brought some happiness to the people of my town, or village; that would be worthwhile." His ideal is greater still.

The trust that is sent by heaven is the ideal given to man. That is his charge in life, his responsibility in life. To take care of this and prove worthy of this responsibility and position that has been given to us, that is what should prove to be our ideal, our religion, our Dharma. In the Gospel the 'talent' represents the same ideal; at first it is small, but it expands as we go through life.

This explains the fact that the sin and virtue of two people cannot be the same. For instance there may be two students, and one is sent to a university and is studying for an examination. There are only two months left, but he happens to see an exciting play advertised. He thinks he would like to see this play, and yet there is so short a time for study. "But then it is only one evening, and I can soon make that up; I will go just this once, and it will make no difference," he says. He disregards the importance of the ideal he had: that of passing his examination. He has changed his ideal by thinking that the examination does not matter. So he goes this once, but next day he sees another play advertised, and again gives in to his pleasure; and again and again. His fondness for the theater grows, and the evenings go by, and the time comes when he is no longer ready for his examination. So he fails. Seeing the play was a sin, not because it was a sinful action, but because he failed to keep to his ideal. He was meant to study to pass his examination.

Again, there is another student. He is trying to become a good playwright, or orator, or actor. He sees the same advertisement. He goes to the play and enjoys it very much. Every play he attends adds to his experience and increases his knowledge. The same action has become a virtue, for by going to the theater and giving his thought to the plays he has helped to accomplish his ideal. Therefore it all depends on our ideal whether the same action be a sin or a virtue. We have to follow and prove ourselves worthy of that ideal, and the further we go the more our ideal develops. However small it was at the beginning, we are always progressing as long as we follow it and wish to prove ourselves worthy of it; but when we stray from our ideal we lose the track. And if there is anything wrong or evil in the world, it is this: leaving the track of the ideal that we have set before ourselves.

A person may say that a religious ideal is the true ideal, or a moral, spiritual, or a practical life. Many people say it is much better to be in the world, to live in the world; others say it is better to live away from the wicked world, to get away and live in the forests, the jungles, or the caves. They say, "This is the only way to live." Others say, "Just make merry, eat, drink, and enjoy life." But others again say, "The good life is in the service of man; as much service as we can give, as much kindness, as much love, that is the ideal."

If we ask a hundred people, we will hear of a hundred ideals. Everyone thinks that he who follows his ideal is the best person, and whoever follows another ideal is wicked. Sufis, mystics, ascetics, in spite of all their high ideals, have been killed, beheaded, and tortured by different religious authorities, because these religious authorities had a different ideal, and were convinced that their own ideal was right and the other wrong. They said, "My Church is the only Church which exists, the only one which can teach you the real truth." Is it not true that every Church or every faith in which there is a willingness for others to join, thinks that its ideal and its belief is the best to follow? That is man's foolishness. He wishes everyone to follow the same ideal as his. He does not know that the prophets whom the whole world may follow often could not get their brother or their wife or their children to follow them!

If we read the history of Abraham, Moses, or Muhammad, we see what happened. It was difficult for their own people to follow them, however many other followers they may have had, because every soul has its own peculiar ideal, and it wants to go on towards it.

True preaching would be asking everyone to develop his own ideal, however wrong it might appear to the outsider at the moment. Let each one develop his faculty of doing right in his own judgment. One will see that in time he will develop the real thing, because in him is the light of God and it will never misguide him.

Once I was with a sage whom many people went to see. He pleased them all, and he was not fond of disputing or discussing, because to a sage there is nothing to discuss. Discussion is for those who say, "What I say is right, and what you say is wrong." A sage never says such a thing; hence there is no discussion. But the world is always fighting and discussing and disputing.

Many would come and try to dispute with him, but he did his best to avoid dispute. I was very fond of listening to his way of dealing with inquirers. My friends wanted to discuss what the ideal life is. He said, "Whatever you think it is." But my friends were not satisfied with this; they wanted a discussion. They answered, "Do you think this worldly life, with so many respon-sibilities, with strife from morning to evening, can be the ideal life?" He said, "Yes." They asked, "Do you not think that the life you lead, retirement and seclusion, is the ideal life?" He answered, "Yes." They said, "But how can we give up our present life, our responsibilities to our children, our occupations, and all these things that take up so much time; how can we leave that life in order to follow your ideal life?" He said, "Do not leave it." They went on, "But if we do not leave it, how can we get on in the spiritual life?" Then the sage asked, "What do you mean by the spiritual life?" "We mean by spiritual life a life like yours," they answered. He said, "If you think my life is a spiritual life, be like me; if you think your life is a spiritual life, keep to it. It is not possible to say which life is best. If you think your worldly strife brings you happiness, just keep to it; if you think my life gives you happiness, give up your own. Whatever makes you happy and makes you think you are doing right, do it from that moment, and see what the result is. If it gives you happiness, if you are satisfied while doing it, while reaping its effect, then it is all right. Go on with it, and you will always be blessed."

Therefore when the question of the ideal life arises, no one on earth can tell us that this or that particular way is the ideal. The one who presumes to know this says absurd things. He only tells us what he thinks the ideal; it is not necessarily the ideal for us. Whatever we think best, we should follow it; for then we are on the right path, in whatever direction it may lead, whether to heaven or to earth; both will lead to the same goal if pursued to the end.

The Journey to the Goal

The word journey may be applied to life. As life has two aspects, it may either be called a journey or a goal.

Why should life be called a journey? Because there is change in nature and change of experience. One goes from one experience to another. The whole of the external life is nothing but a succession of experiences, one after the other, night and day. That is why it is called a journey.

Yet there is a part of life from which this life of changes has sprung; the life which is everlasting, which is eternal, the life to which all things return; and that life is the goal. Therefore life is not only a journey, it is a goal. The goal is the stable part of life, the source of life; the manifested life called creation is the journey.

In this way we see there are really two journeys. There is the journey from the goal to the life in the world, and there is the journey from the life in the world to the goal. And both journeys are natural. As it is natural to go forth from the eternal goal, so it is necessary to go from the changing life to the life which is unchangeable.

Which is the most desirable thing in life, to seek for the goal or to dwell in this changing life? The answer is that every person's desire is according to his evolution. That for which he is ready is desirable for him. Milk is a desirable food for the infant, other

foods for the grown-up person. Every stage in life has its own
appropiate and desirable things. The desire to attain to a goal
must be there before reaching it; when he does not feel the desire,
it is not necessary for a man to seek it.

All things are worthwhile when we seek after them; then only
do we appreciate their value; then only are we happy to have them.
We do not need the things we do not know and do not desire. We
need them when we know them and desire them.

The law of nature is that this external life develops gradually,
stage by stage, through rock, through vegetable, through animals, through man. Its depth is intelligence, which is named
'ilm by the mystic. The joy of the whole life is the fullness of
intelligence, and intelligence comes to its fullness in the human
kingdom. It is there that life and the primitive intelligence have
their eyes opened to see and understand and think. "God slept in
the mineral kingdom, dreamed in the vegetable, woke in the
animal, and became self-conscious in the human." But in the
human stage we find that not everyone has the same capability of
thinking and understanding and knowing. It is his thinking
qualitiy that distinguishes man; that is why the real man is the
thinker, he who is capable of thinking. The more thoughtful, the
more awakened the mind, the more can be found in man the
fullness of that attribute for which the whole world was created.

When he begins to think, the question arises why all this was
created. And the answer is that all this gradual development is
towards one single development, that of human life; and in human
life towards the development of mind. Throughout the whole
universe that which has really developed is the mind, which begins
to know the use of all things and all forms, their secrets and the
way in which all things and all forms are controlled.

Another question comes to the thinking mind, after realizing
the secret of all things and all forms, and after knowing the way

in which all forms and all things are utilized, and that is, "Is this enough? Is there not something else that man desires?" Then he will find that there are four different desires: the desire to know, desire to love and be loved, the desire for joy, the desire for peace.

After the toil of the day there is a desire to rest and be away from people. Then there is the desire to get a certain amount of pleasure or joy in things one feels delighted in, such as going to museums and theaters. Another finds comfort and happiness in loving and being loved. The scholarly mind which wishes to know and understand things has happiness and joy when it understands them. If any of these four desires is absent, one is unhappy.

The world is engaged in four different kinds of occupations. To one person some of them may be repellent and undesirable, while to another they seem desireable. Everyone has his own occupation in which he seems to be happy, but that of another seems to him useless, foolish or undesirable. In Sanskrit these occupations are called *Kama, Artha, Dharma,* and *Moksha.* The occupation of Kama is love, affection, attachment, or infatuation, to such an extent that nothing else matters in life, neither money nor position, nothing. Kama is the thing he wants; it is his one occupation.

Artha is the occupation is which a person pursues money; he wishes to be rich, to have property, to make trade prosper. Love does not appeal to him. He calls the lover crazy, foolish, out of his mind. He believes that everybody will like him if he has money, and that it is crazy to pursue love!

Dharma is the occupation of pursuing duty. Such a person says, "These things are not right. The right thing is to do one's duty." Perhaps he is interested in his family, in family duty to mother, father, wife, or children, saying, "This is my virtue;" or in the people, the nation, the poor, or the rich. Whatever he considers his duty he gives his life to. He may be a soldier, a teacher, or a merchant; but he feels justified according to the way he does his duty. The person who is after money thinks he is a fool. The lover thinks he is a fool too. For him the first thing is to convert people to his Church, to do something good for his nation, city, or village.

The fourth occupation, Moksha, is different again. This means to work for paradise, for heaven, for heavenly peace. What is the use of bothering about one's duty? The whole aim is heaven; that is the happiness to look for. All things will change, all will pass— wealth, earthly love—they are all changeable. But paradise, the happiness one can get in the hereafter after all the suffering here, that is the unchangeable. A man who thinks thus is pious. He suffers all his life; he goes through all kinds of pain; he is seeking for that paradise. The lover may say, "How foolish; my paradise is on earth. My beloved is my love. What a foolish person to sacrifice all this, and who knows what will come hereafter?" But the other says, "I can create my own paradise with my wealth."

These four paths are diverse, and everyone considers his own the best and wisest. The Sufi looks on all with tolerance, and knows that there is a path for everyone. The path of the lover is for him, the path of the one seeking for wealth is for him, the seeker after paradise is following his path; it is all a journey. It is simply that there are four different routes by which the journey is made. The Sufi sees the same goal at the end of each; the lover has to meet the seeker after wealth, and both have to meet the one who has done his duty. Therefore at the end of their journey there is a place where they can meet. What does it matter if one does not go by a certain path? Let each choose the way that belongs to his own temperament and tendency. Therefore the Sufi does not worry. He gives no preference to one or to the other. He sees the journey of life being made along one or other of these roads. The saying of Buddha, "Forgive all," comes true. Forgiveness does not come by learning, it comes by understanding that a person should be allowed to travel along that path which is suited to his temperament. As long as he is journeying with open eyes, let him journey.

The great thing is that one should journey with one single desire. There should be the single desire: whether to love a beloved, to collect wealth, or to do some good for the world of humanity, or to attain paradise; there should be the desire to journey to the goal. So many do not know which is the goal or what it is. One thinks wealth is the goal, another paradise, another the beloved. They do not see that there is a still further goal. They are naturally prompted by the desire to get to the goal, and yet are not conscious of the further goal.

As it is said in the Bible, "Seek ye first the kingdom of God, and all things shall be added unto you." The real desire is for that kingdom of perfection, the goal of everything; but how can a person desire that of which he does not realize the meaning? Desire comes by knowing the thing to be desired. If we do not know what the goal is like, how can we be attracted to it?

Rumi, the great Persian poet, speaking about this, says, "Every soul is a captive on earth." And this captivity is in the limited physical body, which man calls his individuality or personality; while the nature of the soul is peace and joy and freedom. In this captivity it lacks these things. That is why the soul begins to feel it, wants this or that: paradise, duty, a beloved, wealth. Reason may suggest, "This is it," and the soul goes after it, but having acquired it, it begins to feel, "No, this is not the thing that I wanted."

All this shows that there is a constant desire of the soul to find its own nature; and until it finds it, it is always looking for something, though what it does not know. Is it not true of every individual in this world that, whatever may be his desire, as long as he has not attained it he is unhappy, and eager and anxious to achieve it? He is longing and suffering and doing all he can to attain it; but when he has succeeded, he does not feel happy. At once a new desire arises; if he has a thousand he wants a million; if he has done one duty there is another, and after that another. So it is with love affairs; so it is with paradise. He will never feel contented and satisfied, because fundamentally it is not the desire that he is really concerned with. Though he crosses the boundary wall of the desire, he finds himself again with a new desire. And this itself proves the fact that there is only one fundamental desire underlying all others: the desire for spiritual perfection.

One is not capable of setting out on the journey to the eternal goal unless the four desires and occupations have been surmounted. In the first place the motive limits one to certain lines of accomplishmemt; and it does not allow one to accomplish anything beyond the scope of that particular motive. As long as a person has the desire to attain to something with a particular motive, he cannot go further. That is why the sages have said, "Rise above the earthly motives. Accomplish all you wish to accomplish in life, whatever be the motive, and then that itself will lead you to a stage from which you can rise above them, and above the earthly desires of the body." They have never said, "Stop, and go into the jungle, and see life from our own point of view." Everybody's path is for himself. Let everyone achieve the fulfillment of his own desires so as to be able to rise above them to the eternal goal.

There are four different paths recognized as leading to the attainment of that goal. The Yogis call them *Hatha Yoga, Raja Yoga, Mantra Yoga, Bhakti Yoga.*

Hatha Yoga is the path of abstinence. This is a form of self-control, acheived by practicing different postures, sitting quietly and trying to slow down the circulation or follow a certain rhythm, or quieting the nerves by a certain kind of breathing. This is all a process of mastery of the body and mind. Sufis call this mastery *Vilayat.*

It is practice rather than study that helps in controlling the nerves of the body, the rhythm of the circulation, the mechanism of the body. The adepts are able to stop every pulsation of the body at will, for a few seconds at a time. There have been experiments made by doctors verifying this power. However surprising it may seem for the external pulse to be controlled in this way, what would it seem like if we could see still more deeply into the life of the adept! The control of mind is so much greater; words can never explain it; one must experience it oneself. The control of the self means the control of everything.

What does it mean when we see a person fail time after time, or another person succeed time after time? It is just a matter of holding the reins of our affairs in our hands. When there is no rein there is failure. Failure means that there has been lack of self-control, whether it is a failure in affairs or in health. Illness always comes when a person has lost the control of self. It is because this is the main theme of metaphysics that Hatha Yoga has been considered of the greatest value. All the miracles and all the wonders that have ever been known in this world have been done by those who have been able to control themselves by abstinence, and therefore to control life. However much were said upon this subject, it would still not express it. To begin with a person is puzzled by it, and he wonders whether he should believe it or not. That is why in the East the adepts never speak of their experiences in the spiritual life. They only tell their disciples to lead it and practice for years. "That will make it clear to you," they say.

The other path on the spiritual journey is that of Raja Yoga. This is the path of life, going through all life's experiences and accepting its responsibilities. On this path there are four stages.

Brahmacharya-shrama is that path where a person works with the intellect. He wishes to know about things, reason about them, and understand them. It is the intellectual attainment of knowledge.

Gruhastha-shrama is the attainment of knowledge through the experience of the responsibilities of life, of home, children, servants, neighbors, friends, and enemies; the experience of living among them, doing one's duty to them, loving them, being kind to them, and taking upon one's shoulders every kind of responsibility; the experiences of welcoming the neighbor, the friend, with a smile even when in distress and despair, or in any difficulty. This itself becomes a lesson.

Wanaprastha-shrama is the service of the world, of humanity. This means considering not only one's family as one's responsibility, but also one's townsfolk, one's race, the world at large.

Sannyasa-shrama is retirement, love of solitude, silence, contemplation, and resignation in regard to all the things of this world.

By these four stages of development perfection is gradually attained.

Mantra Yoga, strictly speaking a system of Yoga based on the repetition of and meditation on sacred words, aims at the attainment of perfection by means of wisdom, understanding life, and seeing through it. The best word to use for such a person is 'seer.' He sees into life, into the depth of life, through a person, through an affair, through a thing. He sees not only the outside, the surface, but by means of concentration he sees through things as with a torch that illuminates whatever is seen. This seeing is called *Jnana*. The journey through life is made by that means.

In Mantra Yoga a person comes in touch with the mysticism of sound when he begins to see and understand; he begins to see that he gains power by sound, that in every vowel, word, composition, a certain effect or element is hidden, because life and the whole of manifestation is the outcome of what may be called vibrations. The scientist today says that life is motion, but the mystic has said so for thousands of years. At the same time he has worked with what the Hindus call *Nada Brahma*: sound-God or vibration-God. He has worked with life according to the law of vibrations, and has seen what great power vibration has. The whole of Mantra Yoga is based on this law of sound or vibrations. But this is a very big subject.

Bhakti Yoga is the most important yoga, especially for those who have the quality of love and kindness, because all the beauty that there is in life is after all what we call love. From it all the virtues spring. The whole beauty of life is in it, and it is as the English song says, "The light of a whole life dies, when love is done." Life's light is love; and when the heart is empty of love, a man is living and yet not living; from a spiritual point of view he is dead. When the heart is asleep, he is as though dead in this life, for one can only love through the heart. But love does not mean give and take. That is only a trade; it is selfishness. To give sixpence and receive a shilling is not love. Love is when one loves for the sake of love, when one cannot help but love, cannot do anything but love. Then one is not forced to love; there is no virtue in that. One does not love because another does. It is simply there; it cannot be helped. It is the only thing that makes a person alive. If a person loves one and hates another, what can he know of love? Can you love one person fully if at the same time you cannot bestow a kind glance on some other person? Can you say you love one person fully when you cannot bear him to be loved by someone else as well? Can you hate a person when love is sprinkled like water in your heart? Love is like the water of the Ganges; it is itself a purification. As the Bible says, "God is love." When love is awakened in the heart, God is awakened there. When a man has journeyed, he reaches the goal as soon as his heart has reached love.

The Sufi says, "The Ka'aba, the divine place, paradise, is the heart of the human being." That is why he has respect for every heart. Every heart is his Ka'aba, his shrine. The human heart is the place toward which he bows, for in this heart is God.

The Purpose of Life

Accomplishment of the Inner Purpose

The first thing that a seeker after truth must realize is the purpose of life. No sooner does a soul begin to feel sober from the intoxication of life, than the first thing it asks itself is, "What is the purpose of my life?" Each soul has its own purpose, but in the end all purposes resolve into one purpose, and it is that purpose which is sought by the mystic. For all souls, by the right and the wrong path, either sooner or later, will arrive at that purpose, a purpose which must be accomplished, a purpose for which the whole creation has been intended; but the difference between the seeking soul and the soul who blindly works towards that purpose is like that between the material and the maker of it. The clay works towards the purpose of forming a vessel and so does the potter; but it is the potter's joy and privilege to feel the happiness of the accomplishment of the purpose, not the clay's. And so it is with the beings who are unconsciously striving towards that purpose and the souls who are consciously striving towards it, both in the end coming towards the same accomplishment; the difference is in the consciousness.

The first step on the spiritual path is when a soul realizes its outer purpose in life. For it is not every soul in the world which even realizes its outer mission in life. And the soul who does not realize it, may go on, perhaps, for its whole life and may not realize it even to the end of its life, but the one who cares to realize it, must sooner or later realize it. For the answer to his question is continually being heard in his own heart. As Sa'adi says, "Every soul is created for a certain purpose and the light of that purpose has been kindled in that soul." If there is already a flame lit even before the person was born on earth, it remains for the person to find out for himself the purpose of his life, although everything outside himself also points to that purpose.

One may ask, "What is the best way for a person to understand his life's purpose?" If one follows the bent of one's own mind, if one follows the track to which one is attracted, if one follows one's inner inclination, which is not satisfied with anything else, one feels, "There is something waiting for me (which one does not know at the time) which will bring me satisfaction." Besides, if one is intuitive and mystical, it is easier still, because then one is continually told what is the purpose of one's life. For nature has such a perfection of wisdom. One sees that the insects are given the sense to make their little houses and to protect themselves and to make a store of their food. The bees, who have the gift of making honey, are taught how to make honey. So nature has taught every soul to seek its purpose. It has made every soul for that purpose, and it is continually calling that soul to see that purpose. If the soul does not hear the call and sleeps, it is not the fault of nature, which is continually calling. Therefore, if I were to say in a few words how to find one's purpose, I would say: by waking from sleep.

One might ask, "Would the outer purpose lead to the inner purpose of life?" Certainly it would. Everything a person does, spiritual or material, is only a stepping-stone for him to arrive at the inner purpose, if he can only take it to be so. If he is mistaken, the mistake is in himself; he is working towards the inner purpose just the same. For all is created to work as one scheme, and therefore each individual is acting towards the accomplishment of the divine purpose. If there is a difference, the difference is of that particular individual.

There are five aspects which give one the tendency towards the accomplishment of the inner purpose: desire to live, desire to know, desire for power, desire for happiness and desire for peace. These five things work consciously or unconsciously in the profound depth of every soul. Working within one, they prompt one either to do right or to do wrong, and yet these five aspects belong to the one purpose in the accomplishment of which the purpose of the whole creation is fulfilled. When the desire to live brings one in touch with one's real life, a life which is not subject to death, then the purpose of that desire is accomplished; when one has been able to perceive fully the knowledge of one's own being, in which is to be found divine knowledge and the mystery of the whole manifestation, then the purpose of knowledge is attained; when one is able to get in touch with the Almighty Power, then the desire for power is achieved; when one has been able to find one's happiness in one's own heart, independent of all things outside, the purpose of the desire for happiness is fulfilled; when one is able to rise above all conditions and influences which disturb the peace of the soul and has found one's peace in the midst of the crowd and away from the world, in him the desire for peace is satisfied. It is not in one or the other of these five desires that there is the accomplishment of the purpose; it is in the fulfillment of these five desires that one purpose is accomplished, the purpose for which every soul was born on earth.

The Desire to Live

The desire to live is not only seen among human beings but it is also seen continually working through the most insignificant little creatures creeping on earth and living in the ground. When one sees how even the smallest insect wishes to avoid any pursuit after it and how it seeks shelter against any attempt made to touch it, fearing that its life may be taken away from it, that shows that even the smallest creature in the world, in whom man cannot find a trace of mind, has a desire to live. It is this desire that, developing in the lower creation in many and varied aspects, shows in fear, in the tendency to seek shelter, in the intelligent way of looking round as the hare does in the fields, as the deer that is continually careful to protect itself from other animals. This desire developed in man shows still greater phenomena of intelligence. War and peace are brought about with the desire of living; the cause behind war is the desire to live; the cause of peace is also the desire to live. There is not one normal soul living on earth who has not the desire to live. Yes, a person most distressed, in a mood of unhappiness, will say at the moment, "I would rather not live; I seek death." But it is not the normal condition. One may say, "Why is death not a desirable thing, since it is only a getting rid of the dense body?" But can we not turn the dense body into a light body? Even matter can turn into spirit. If the divine blood begins to circulate through the veins of a person, this body is no longer a heavy body; it becomes as light as vapor. It is heavy when the weight of the earth has fallen upon it, but when the weight of the earth is taken away from it, it is lighter than the air.

"But," one may say, "is not death an increase of life?" It is another phase of life. The body is a complete instrument; why should we not make the best of it? Why must one hasten death, if one can be here and do something worthwhile? Sometimes one longs for death because one does not know what one is to do here; one is not yet acquainted with the purpose of life; it is that which makes one long for death. Every moment in life has its mission; every moment in life is an opportunity. Why should this opportunity be lost? Why not use every moment of one's life towards the accomplishment of that purpose for which we are here? It is the question of bestirring ourselves to make the best use of every moment of life. That itself will give such a happiness to a person that he will not wish to go. Even if the angels of death came and were dragging him towards death, he would say, "Let me stay here a while longer; let me finish something which I would like to finish."

That must be the attitude. When a person is in his normal condition of mind, his one desire, his innermost desire, is to live. What does it show? It shows that man has acquired all other desires after coming on earth, but this desire to live he has brought with him on earth. It is only by not understanding the meaning of this desire, its nature and character, its secret, that he submits to its being broken by what is called death, by mortality.

If the desire to live is his innermost desire, if it is a divine substance in him, then there is the answer to this desire also; there is a possibility of the fulfillment of this desire. But when one does not dive deep into the secrets of life, without the knowledge of life and death one becomes subject to disappointment, and that disappointment is death. One may say, "If the desire to live is natural, would it not be better to live and prolong the youthfulness of body; and how can that be done?" There are three aspects the Hindus have personified, as Brahma, Vishnu, and Maheish,[1] the Creator-God, the Sustainer-God, and the Destroyer God. In retaining youth there comes the conflict between the two Gods, the Creator-God and the Destroyer-God, because the Destroyer-God is destroying, while the Creator-God is creating. If the Creator-God in you is stronger, then he will win a victory over the Destroyer-God. Nevertheless, there is nothing which is void of beauty in this world. If the soul has received the divine blessing, it will enjoy every aspect of life. Infancy is interesting, childhood has a beauty, youth has its spirit, age has its knowledge and dignity, its wisdom and beauty. There is no note on the piano which has not its particular action, which has not its particular part in the symphony of nature. Whether it is the seventh octave lower or the seventh octave higher, whether it is sharp or flat or natural, whatever key it is, as soon as the harmonious hand has touched it, it creates harmony, it makes of it a symphony. And so we are all as notes before that divine Musician, and when His blessing hand touches, whatever be one's life's condition, whether child or youthful or old or young, the beauty will manifest and add to life's symphony.

The mistake is that man wishes to live through the mortal part of his being; that is what brings disappointment. For he knows only that part of his being which is mortal, and he identifies himself with his mortal being. Hardly one among thousands realizes that life lives and death dies. That which lives cannot die; what dies will not live; it is only a phenomenon of life that makes even that which is not living, for the moment, a kind of illusion of life. When we study the dead body, the greatest study we can

[1] One of the names of Shiva.

make, we see that no sooner has life left it than the whole charm of the body has gone. Why is there not that attraction which has always been there? Why is the body void of all beauty, magnetism and attraction? Why do those who loved that person retire from his dead body, wish to remove it? What has gone from it; what is dead in it? The part which is subject to death is dead; the life which lived in it is still alive. This body was only covering a life; now that life has left. But the living being is not dead; it is that mortal cover which was covering that life that is dead. Is it not, then, the absence of this knowledge which gives a person fear of death?

What is death after all? There is the saying of the Prophet that the illuminated souls never fear death. Death is the last thing they fear. And yet one does not fear anything more than for one's life. One could sacrifice anything in the world—wealth, rank, power or possession—if one could live. If living is an innate desire, then it is most necessary to find the process, the way to get in touch with that real part of ourselves which may be called our being, our self, and thus to become free from what is called mortality. It is the ignorant one who knows only the ground floor of his house; by going to the first floor of his house, he thinks that he is dead; he does not know that he has only left the ground floor and is going to the first floor. Why does this ignorance exist? Because he never tried to go to the first floor. The ground floor is quite enough for him; the first floor does not exist for him, though it is a floor in his own house.

Is immortality to be gained, to be acquired? No, it is to be discovered. One has only to make one's vision keener, in other words, to explore one's self; but that is the last thing one does. People are most pleased to explore the tomb of Tutankhamen in Egypt, in order to find mysteries, regardless of the mystery hidden in their own heart. Tell them about any mystery existing outside themselves: they are delighted to explore it. But when you tell them to see in themselves, they think it is too simple; they think, "I know myself. I am a mortal being. I don't want to die, but death awaits me." Difficulties they make; complexities they raise by their own complex intelligence. They do not like the straight way; they like the zigzag way; they enjoy puzzles. Even if there is a door before them, they say, "No, I do not look for it." If a door opens before them, they do not wish to go out by that door; they prefer to be in the puzzle. It is a greater joy not to be able to find the door for a long time. One who is thus enjoying the puzzle is horrified when he sees the way out. The saying of the Prophet is, "Die before death." What does it mean? It does not mean, "Commit suicide." It only means, "Study the condition of death." One need not die; play it; one should play death and find out what it is. The whole mystical cult is that play, playing death. That play becomes the means by which to understand the mystery hidden behind life.

Man constitutes in himself spirit and matter. What is matter? Crystallized spirit. The original substance. Spirit may be likened to running water; matter, to ice. But if there is water and ice, the water will run, the ice will stay where it is. It does not mean that ice will not return to its original condition; it will, but its time has not yet come. Therefore the water will proceed first, and the ice will stay where it is; the substance stays where it is, but the life, the spirit, passes away. What is necessary, first, for a person, is to make the spirit independent of the mortal covering, even if it be for a moment. By that the fear of death naturally vanishes, because then one begins to see the condition after death here on earth. It is this physical cover which has imprisoned, so to speak, the soul in it; and the soul finds itself in prison and it cannot see itself. What it can see is the cover. Rumi explains it most beautifully in a poem which he has written on sleep, because it is in sleep

that the soul naturally becomes independent of this mortal garb.
He says:

> Every night Thou freest our spirits from the body
> And its snare, making them pure as rased tablets.
> Every night spirits are released from this cage,
> And set free, neither lording it nor lorded over.
> At night prisoners are unaware of their prison;
> At night kings are unaware of their majesty.
> Then there is no thought or care for loss or gain;
> No regard to such a one or such a one.

And the continual longing of the soul is for freedom from this
imprisonment. Rumi begins his book, the Masnavi, with lamenta-
tion of the soul to free itself. But is it to free the soul by actual
death, by a suicide? No! No mystics have done it; it is not meant.
It is by playing death that one arrives at the knowledge of life and
death, and it is the secret of life which will make the soul free.
The different planes of existence, which are hidden behind the
cover of this physical body, then begin to manifest to the person
who plays death. All different ways of concentration, of meditation, which are prescribed by the teacher to the pupil, are all that
process of playing. In themselves they are nothing; they are a
play. What is important is what one finds out as an outcome of
that play, what one discovers in the end. Of course, the play begins
with self-negation. And a person who likes to say twenty times in
the day, "I," does not like to say, "I am not, Thou art." But he
does not know that this claim of "I" is the root of all his trouble.
It is this claim that makes him feel hurt by every little insult, by
every little disturbance. The amount of pain that this illusion gives
him is so great that it is just as well he got rid of it. But that is the
last thing he would do. He would give up his last penny, but not the

thought of "I." He would hold it; it is the dearest thing. That is the whole difficulty and the only hindrance on the spiritual path.

Very often people ask, "How long has one to go on on the spiritual path?" There is no limit to the length of this path, and yet if one is ready, it does not need a long time. It is a moment and one is there. How true it is, what the wise of past ages said to their followers, "Do not go directly into the temple; first walk fifty times around it!" The meaning was, "First get a little tired, then enter." Then you value it. One values something for which one makes an effort; if it comes without effort, it is nothing to one. If a government should ask a tax for the air one breathes, people would protest against it. Yet they do not know that there is no comparison between the air and the money they possess. The value of the one is incomparably greater than of the other. And yet the most valuable things are attained with least effort. But one does not realize their importance. One would rather have something which is attained with a great effort and in the end may prove to be nothing.

It is very simple to think, "Why should every being have that innate desire to live, if continual life is impossible?" For there is no desire in the world which not its answer. The answer to every desire is somewhere; the fulfillment of every desire must come one day. Therefore, without doubt this desire of living must be fulfilled. And the fulfillment of this desire is in getting above the illusion which is caused by ignorance of the secret of life.

The Desire to Know

The desire for knowledge can be traced in all living beings, in the lower creation as well as in mankind. If one notices the movements of the birds and animals in the forest, one sees that besides seeking for their food, playing with their mates, protecting themselves from their enemy, they are also interested in every sensation that comes to them through their five senses. Sound, color, touch, scent, every sensation, has an effect upon them. One can trace in the animals the natural desire to know something, and it is this desire which in human evolution can be recognized as curiosity. From childhood this tendency seems predominant, and the more a child shows this tendency, the more promising the child is, because that shows that the soul part of the child is so much more to the fore. Among grown-up persons, what strikes us most in their personality is that brilliance of intelligence, apart from all their goodness and virtue. If this is such an important thing in life, it must achieve a most important result. And what is that achievement? It is the knowledge of the ultimate truth, which fulfills the purpose of life.

A curious soul begins by trying to know everything that it sees, that it comes in contact with. What it wants to know first is the name of an object, what it is called, what it is for, what it is, what it is used for, how to use it, how it is made, how to make the best of a thing, how to profit by it to the utmost. This knowledge is what we call learning. The different divisions of learning, called by different names, are the classification of this knowledge which one gains by study of the outside world. But life is so short and the field of this knowledge is so vast, that a person may go on and on studying. He may perhaps study one branch of knowledge, and he may find that even one life is not sufficient to be fully acquainted with that one particular branch of knowledge. And there is another person: he is not satisfied with only touching one branch of knowledge; he wants to touch many branches of knowledge. He may become acquainted, to a certain degree, with different aspects of knowledge. It may perhaps make him, if he reaches somewhere, what may be called an all-round man. Yet that is not the thing which will fulfill the purpose of his life. Farabi, the great Arabian scientist in ancient times, claimed that he knew many sides of knowledge; but when it came to showing his equipment in the knowledge of music, he proved to be lacking in the essential part, which was not the theory of music but the practice of music.

But knowledge can be divided into two aspects: one aspect is the knowledge which we call learning; the other aspect is knowing. Learning comes from the reason: "It is so, because of this or that"; that is knowledge. But there is a knowing which cannot be explained by "because"; it can only be said that it is so; it cannot be anything else. The knowledge with its "because" attached is contradicted a thousand times over. One scientist, one inventor, one learned person has one argument; another comes and he says, "This is not what I think; I have found out the truth about it, which the one who looked before did not perceive rightly." It has always been and will always be so with the outer knowledge. But with that knowing which is the central knowledge there has never been a difference and there will never be. The saints, sages, seers, mystics, prophets of all ages, in whatever part of the world they were born, when they have touched this realm of knowing, have all agreed on this same one thing. It is therefore that they called it Truth. It was not because this was the conception of one person, or the expression of another person, or the doctrine of a certain people, or the teaching of a certain religion. No, it was the knowledge of every knowing soul. And every soul, whether in the past, present, or future, whenever it arrives at the stage when it knows, will realize the same thing. Therefore it is in that knowledge that there is to be found the fulfillment of the purpose of one's coming on the earth.

And now one may ask, "What is that knowledge? How can one attain to it?" The first condition is to separate this outer knowledge from the inner knowing. False and true, the two things cannot go together. It is separating the real from the unreal. The knowledge gained from the outer world is the knowledge of the cover of all things, not of the spirit of all things. Therefore that knowledge cannot be essential knowledge. It is not the knowledge of the spirit of all things; it is the knowledge of the cover of all things which we study and call learning, and to it we give the greatest importance. One may say, "What is one to do when the call of the intellectual reason for knowledge and learning is such that it threatens one's faith in the possibility of knowledge by the self?" The answer is to go on, in that case, with the intellectual knowledge till one feels satisfied with it or tired of it. For one must not seek after food if one is not hungry. The food which is sought in absence of hunger will prove to be a poison. Great as it is, the knowledge of self, if there is not that natural desire raging like fire, does not manifest.

One might ask, "Then why should we not try to get to the bottom of all outside things; shall we not by this way reach the same knowledge?" That is not possible. The easiest way and the possible way is to attain to the knowledge of the self. It is the after-effect of this attainment that will give one keen sight into outside things, into the spirit of outward things. The question is about oneself, the knowledge of self, what that knowledge is. Do we know ourselves? None of us, for one moment, will think that we do not know ourselves. That is the difficulty. Everyone says, "I know myself better than I know anybody else. What is there to be learned in myself? Is it the anatomy of the body?"

Yes, the first thing is to understand the construction of the body; that is the first lesson. By the study of this, one will find that there are five different aspects which constitute our physical body. The mystics, for convenience, call them earth, water, fire, air, ether. But these must not be compared with the scientific terms; it is only for the convenience of a mystic. Then one will see the different senses, the organs of the senses: each sense represents one of these elements. And coming to the natural tendencies and needs of life, every action one does has a relation to one of these five elements. This study of the mechanism will make a person understand that something which he always called *himself* is nothing but a mechanism, a mechanism made of five elements, the elements which are borrowed from the outer world. And he will find that his mind, which experiences through all organs of the senses, still remains aloof as a spectator who conceives and perceives the outside world through the mediumship of this mechanism which he calls his body. This knowledge will waken a deep thinker to the fact that he is not his body; although, consciously or unconsciously, there is perhaps one among a million persons who clearly realizes, "My body is my instrument; I am not my body." The one who has come to realize, "My body is my instrument," is the controller of this prison; he is the engineer of this machinery.

And then there comes the next stage of knowing oneself, and that is to explore what one calls the mind. By a minute study of the mind one will find that the different qualities such as reason, memory, thought, feeling, and the ego, all these five things constitute mind. One will find that there is a surface to this and there is a depth to it. Its depth is the heart; its surface is mind. Each quality of mind represents one of these five elements. This again takes us to the thought that even the mind, which is above the physical body, is a mechanism. And the more one is acquainted with the mechanism, the more one is able to manage it to its best advantage; and it is the ignorance of the secret of this mechanism that keeps man unaware of his own domain. This knowledge makes one think, "I am neither my body nor am I my mind; I am the engineer who has these two possessions, these two machineries, to work with to the best advantage of life." Then one begins to ask, "What am I?" For to a certain degree even the mind is a mechanism which is borrowed from the outer sphere, as the body is a mechanism which has been borrowed from the physical plane, which has been gathered together and constructed. Therefore, neither mind nor body is the self. One thinks, "It is myself," only because one cannot see oneself. And so one says of everything one sees, "This is myself." The self becomes acquainted with everything but itself. So that mind which the self has used has become a kind of cover upon the light which fulfills the purpose of life.

When this is intellectually realized, although it does not fulfill the purpose, it begins one's journey in the search of truth. This must be realized by the process of meditation, the process by which the self can separate itself from body and afterwards from mind. For the self, deluded all through life, is not ready to understand, is not prepared to understand truth. It rejects truth; it fights truth. It is like the story, told in my *Divan*, that a lion once saw a lion cub wandering through the wilderness with the sheep. The lion was very surprised. Instead of running after the sheep, he ran after this lion cub. And the little lion was trembling and very frightened. The father lion said, "Come, my son, with me; you are a lion." "No," said the cub. "I tremble, I tremble, I am afraid of you. You are different from my playmates. I want to run with them, play with them; I want to be with them." "Come, my son, with me," said the lion, "you are a little lion." "No," said the cub, "no, I am not a lion. You are a lion; I am afraid of you." The lion said, "I will not let you go; you must come with me." The lion took him to the shore of the lake and said, "Now look in it and see with your own eyes if you are a lion or if you are a sheep." This explains what initiation means and what the initiator teaches to his disciple as meditation. Once the image is reflected in the lake of the heart, self-knowledge comes by itself.

The Desire for Power

It is the desire for all one wishes to achieve that gives one the desire for power. One desires power in order to hold something, to make something, to attain something, to work out something, to attract something, to use something, to rule something, to assimilate something. If it is a natural desire, there is an answer to this. For there cannot be a desire to which there is no answer; the answer to the desire is in knowing that desire fully. Whatever power is gained by outside efforts in life, however great it may seem for the moment, it proves fatal when it comes to be examined. Even such great powers as the nations which existed just before the war,[1] took no time to fall to pieces. There was an army, there was a navy, there was property, a state. An empire such as the Empire of Russia, how long it took to build it! But it did not take one moment for it to break up. If the outer power, in spite of its great appearance for the moment, proves fatal in the end, then there must be some power hidden somewhere, a power which may be called worthwhile; and that power is hidden in man.

A person in the intoxication of outer power that he possesses overlooks the cultivation or the development of inner power, and, depending upon the power that does not belong to him, one day

[1] The First World War

becomes the victim of the very power that he holds. Because, when the outer power becomes greater and the inner smaller, the greater power eats up the inner power. So it is that the heroes, the kings, the emperors, the persons with great power of arms, wealth or outer influence, have become victims to the very power upon which they always depended. So one thinks, "If the outer power is not to be depended upon, then where is that power to be found upon which one can depend?" And that power is to be found in oneself. What power is it? In the terms of the Sufis that power is called *Iman,* conviction. And how is that power built? That power is built by what the Sufis call *Yaqin,* which means belief. It is belief that culminates in conviction. The one who has no inclination to believe will never arrive at a conviction.

But now there is a question. Is even a power developed in one's personality not a limited power? True, it is a limited power. But by following that teaching which Christ has given in the words, "Seek ye first the kingdom of God and all things shall be added unto you," that power is gained which is unlimited power. If not, there is no meaning in calling God "Almighty." The benefit of this word "Almighty" is in its realization. This teaches us in the first place that all might is one might. Although outwardly we see different powers, one greater than the other, either in harmony or in conflict, limited powers working for or against one another, yet by inward realization one finds that there is but one power. In support of this the Qur'an says that nothing is powerful except it shows the same one power, the power of the All-powerful. In other words, in the limited aspect which we see, and in its absolute being, there is only one power. Therefore, there is no might to stand against that power we call Almighty Power, there is no power to work against it; all aspects of strength and power are from it, and in it, and will be assimilated by it in the end.

As long as man is striving for power, as everyone is striving in some way or other, without the knowledge of that all-sufficient power, there will always be a disappointment. For he will always find limitation. His ideal will always go forward and he will find himself short of power. It is only by getting in touch with the Almighty Power that he will begin to realize the All-powerful and the phenomena of the Almighty.

Now the question is, "How can one get in touch with that Almighty Power?" As long as one's little personality stands before one, as long as one cannot get rid of it, as long as one's person and all that is connected with it interests one, one will always find limitations. That Power is touched only by one way, and that is the way of self-effacement, which in the Bible is called self-denial. People interpret it otherwise. Self-denial, they say, means to deny oneself all the happiness and pleasures of this earth. If it were to deny the happiness and pleasure of this earth, then why was this earth made? Only to deny? If it was made to deny, it was very cruel. For the continual seeking of man is for happiness. Self-denying is to deny this little personality that creeps into everything, to efface this false ego which prompts one to feel one's little power in this thing or that thing; to deny the idea of one's own being, the being which one knows to be oneself, and to affirm God in that place; to deny self and affirm God. That is the perfect humility. When a person shows politeness by saying, "I am only a humble little creature," perhaps he is hiding in his words. It is his vanity, and therefore that humility is of no use. When one completely denies oneself, there are no words to speak. What can one say? Praise and blame become the same to one; there is nothing to be said. And how is this to be attained? It is to be attained not only by prayer or by worship or by believing in God; it is to be attained by forgetting oneself in God. Belief in God is the first step; by belief in God is attained losing oneself in God. If one is able to do it, one has attained a power which is beyond human comprehension. The process of attaining this is called *Fana* by the Sufis. Fana is not necessarily a destruction in God. Fana results in what may be called a resurrection in God, which is symbolized by the picture of Christ. The Christ on the cross is narrative of Fana; it means, "I am not." And the idea of resurrection explains the next stage, which is *Baqa,* and which means, "Thou art," and this means rising towards All-might. The divine spirit is to be recognized in that rising towards All-might. Fana is not attained by torturing oneself, by tormenting oneself, by giving oneself a great many troubles, as many ascetics do. For even after torturing themselves, they will not come to that realization if they were not meant to. It is by denying one's little self, the false self which covers one's real self in which the essence of divine Being is to be found.

The Desire for Happiness

Happiness, which is sought after by every soul, has its secret in the knowledge of the self. Man seeks for happiness, not because happiness is his sustenance, but because happiness is his own being. Therefore, in seeking for happiness, man is seeking for himself. What gives man inclination to seek for happiness is the feeling of having lost something which he had always owned, which belonged to him, which was his own self. The absence of happiness, which a soul has experienced from the day it has come on earth and which has increased every day more and more, makes man forget that his own being is happiness. He thinks happiness is something which is acquired. As man thinks that happiness is something which is acquired, he continually strives in every direction to attain to it. In the end, after all his striving, he finds that the real happiness does not lie in what he calls pleasures. Pleasures may be a shadow of happiness; there is an illusion of happiness, because all the illusion which stands beside reality is more interesting for the average man than reality itself.

A happiness which is momentary, a happiness which depends upon something outside of oneself, is called pleasure. Very often we confuse, in our everyday language, the distinction between pleasure and happiness. A pastime, an amusement, merriment, gaiety that take one's thoughts away from the responsibilities and worries and limitations of life and give one a moment's consolation—one begins by thinking that these are the ways of happiness. But as one cannot hold them, and as one often finds that, seeking for what may be called a pleasure, the loss is greater than the gain, then one begins to look for something that will really be the means of happiness. It is this, very often, that wakens a soul to look for the mystery of religion, for the sense in philosophy, for the secret of mysticism, in case he can find some happiness there. But even all these things only help one to find happiness; they are not happiness themselves. It is the soul which is happiness itself, not all outer things which man seeks after and which he thinks will give him happiness. The very fact that man is continually craving for happiness shows that the real element, which may be called man's real being, is not what has formed his body and what has composed his mind, but what he is in himself.

The mind and body are vehicles. Through the mind and body man experiences life more fully, more clearly; but they are not happiness in themselves, nor does what is experienced through them give the real happiness. What he experiences through them is just pleasure, an illusion of happiness for a time. It is not only that the pleasures cost more than they are worth, but very often in the path of pleasure, when a person is seeking after happiness, as he goes further, he creates more and more unhappiness for himself. Very often it happens. Every way he turns, everything he does, every plan he carries out, thinking that this will give him happiness, only produces a greater trouble, because he is seeking after happiness in a wrong direction.

A person might ask, "Is, then, the secret of happiness in the way of the ascetics, in tormenting, in torturing oneself as they have done for ages?" Even that does not give happiness; it is only a distraction from the worldly pleasures which produce illusion.

The ascetic shuts himself up in order to have an opportunity of taking another direction. But very often it so happens that the one who lives an ascetic life is himself unaware of what he is doing and what it is intended for. And therefore even if he lives his whole life as an ascetic, he cannot derive a full benefit from it. His loss is then greater than his gain. For even asceticism is not a happiness; it is only a means of self-discipline; it is a drill in order to fight against temptations which draw one continually in life and which hinder one's path to happiness. Not understanding this, a person may go on living an ascetic life but can never be benefited by it, like a soldier who has drilled all his life and never fought. Many have understood self-denial as the way to happiness, and they interpret self-denial in the form of asceticism, to deny oneself all pleasures which are momentary. There is another point from which to look at it: the creation is not intended to be renounced. We read in the Qur'an that God has made all that is in the heavens and on the earth subservient to man. Wherefore, all that is beautiful and pleasing, all that gives joy and pleasure, is not to be renounced. The secret of all this is that what is made for man, man may hold but he must not be held by it.

When man renounces the path of happiness, real happiness, in order to pursue pleasures, it is then that he does wrong. If in the pursuit of happiness which is the ultimate happiness, he goes on through life, then for him to be an ascetic and deny himself all pleasures is not necessary. There is a story told of Solomon, that he had a vision that God revealed Himself to him and said, "Ask what I shall give thee." Solomon said, "Give me an understanding heart, wisdom and knowledge." And God said to him, "Because thou hast asked this thing and hast not asked long life for thyself, neither hast thou asked riches for thyself, but hast asked for thyself understanding, behold, I have done according to thy word; I have given thee a wise and an understanding heart. And I have also given thee that which thou hast not asked, both riches and honor, and I will lengthen thy days.'' This shows that the true way is not the renouncing of things, but it is making the best use of them, making the right use of them; it is not going away from life, but being among the crowd, being in the midst of life, and yet not being attached to it. One might say that it would be a cruel thing to be detached from anybody who wants our love and kindness and sympathy. You can attach yourself to the whole world if you will not be of the world. If one keeps one's thoughts centered upon the idea of the real happiness which is attained by the realization of the self, and if one does not allow anything to hinder that, then in the end one arrives at that happiness which is the purpose of the coming on earth of every soul.

Peace

The secret behind the whole manifestation is vibration, vibration which may be termed movement. It is the differences of vibration which, when divided by lines, form planes of existence, each plane being different in the rhythm of these vibrations. When we take life as a whole we can draw one line, the beginning and the end, or spirit and matter, or God and man. And we shall find that the rhythm which begins the line is fine and without disturbance, and the rhythm which is felt at the end of this line is gross and disturbing. And these two rhythms may be named the life of sensation and the life of peace.

These are two opposite things. The life of sensation gives a momentary joy; the life which is the first aspect of life gives peace and culminates in the everlasting peace. The joy, however great, is rising and falling; it must have its reaction. Besides, it depends upon sensation; and what does sensation depend upon? Sensation depends upon the outer life; there must be something besides you to cause the sensation. But peace is independently felt within oneself; it is not dependent upon the outer sensation. It is something that belongs to one, something that is one's own self. If one were to ask someone who lives continually in a kind of excitement of worldly pleasures, whom Providence has granted all pleasures imaginable, "What do you wish besides all this that you experience?'' he will say, ''To be left alone.'' When madness comes, when he is out of balance, he will crave for sensation, but when that passion has gone, what he is longing for in reality is peace. Therefore there is no pleasure in the world, however great, no experience, however interesting, that can give one that satisfaction which peace alone can give. A sovereign may be happy sitting on the throne with his crown, with many attendants before him, but he is only satisfied when he is alone by himself. All else seems to him nothing, it has no value; the most precious thing for him is that moment when he is by himself.

I have once seen the Nizam,[1] a great ruler, in all his grandeur, enjoying the royal splendor around him, and then again I saw the same sovereign sitting alone on a little carpet; and it was at that time that he was himself. It is the same thing with everyone. Delicious dishes, sweet fragrance, music, all other pleasures of line and color, beauty in all its aspects, which seem to answer one's life's demands, fail in the end when compared with that satisfaction which a soul experiences in itself, which it feels its own property, its own belonging; something that one need not seek outside oneself, that one can find within oneself, and something which is incomparably greater and more valuable than anything else in the world; something which cannot be bought nor sold, something which cannot be robbed by anyone, and something which is more sacred and holy than religion or prayer. For all prayer and devotion is to attain to this peace.

A man good and kind, a person most learned and qualified, strong and powerful, with all these attributes, cannot be spiritual if his soul has not attained that rhythm which is a natural rhythm of its being, a rhythm in which alone exists life's satisfaction. Peace is not a knowledge, peace is not a power, peace is not a happiness, but peace is all these; and, besides, peace is productive

[1] H.E.H. Mahbub Ali Khan, 6th Nizam of Hyderabad.

of happiness, peace inspires one with knowledge of the seen and unseen, and in peace is to be found the divine Presence. It is not the excited one who conquers in this continual battle of life; it is the peaceful one who tolerates all, who forgives all, who understands all, who assimilates all things. The one who lacks peace, with all his possessions, the property of this earth or quality of mind, is poor even with both. He has not got that wealth which may be called divine and without which man's life is useless. For true life is in peace, a life which will not be robbed by death. The secret of mysticism, the mystery of philosophy, all is to be attained after the attainment of peace. You cannot refuse to recognize the divine in a person who is a person of peace. It is not the talkative, it is not the argumentative one, who proves to be wise. He may have intellect, worldly wisdom, and yet may not have pure intelligence, which is real wisdom. True wisdom is to be found in the peaceful, for peacefulness is the sign of wisdom. It is the peaceful one who is observant; it is peace that gives him the power to observe keenly. It is the peaceful one, therefore, who can conceive, for peace helps him to conceive. It is the peaceful who can contemplate; one who has no peace cannot contemplate properly. Therefore all things pertaining to spiritual progress in life depend upon peace.

And now the question is, what makes one lack peace? The answer is, love of sensation. A person who is always seeking to experience life in movement, in activity, in whatever form, wants more and more of that experience. In the end he becomes dependent upon the life which is outside, and so he loses in the end his peace, the peace which is his real self. When a person says about someone, "That person has lost his soul," the soul is not lost; the soul has lost its peace. Absorption in the outer life, every moment of the day and night, thinking and worrying and working and fighting, struggling along, in the end robs one of one's soul. Even if one gains as the price of that fighting something which is outside oneself, someone who is a greater fighter still will snatch it from our grasp one day.

One might ask if it is not our necessity in life that keeps us absorbed in the outer life and does not give us a moment to experience peace. In answer to this I must say: suppose the outer life has taken ten hours of the day, you still have two hours; if sleep has taken ten hours of the night, you still have two hours to spare. To attain peace, what one has to do is to seek that rhythm which is in the depth of our being. It is just like the sea: the surface of the sea is ever-moving; the depth of the sea is still. And so it is with our life. If our life is thrown into the sea of activity, it is on the surface; we still live in the profound depths, in that peace. But the thing is to become conscious of that peace which can be found within ourselves. It is this which can bring us the answer to all our problems. If not, when we want to solve one problem, there is another difficult problem coming. There is no end to our problems; there is no end to the difficulties of the outer life. And if we get excited over them, we shall never be able to solve them. Some think, "We might wait; perhaps the conditions will become better; we shall see then what to do." But when will the conditions become better? They will become still worse! Whether the conditions become better or worse, the first thing is to seek the kingdom of God within ourselves, in which there is our peace. As soon as we have found that, we have found our support, we have found our self. And in spite of all the activity and movement on the surface we shall be able to keep that peace undisturbed if only we hold it fast by becoming conscious of it.

The Sense of Duty

In the language of the Hindus duty is called *Dharma*, which means religion. The more one studies the nature and character of what we call duty, the more one begins to see that it is in the spirit of duty that the soul of religion is to be found. If duty was not so sacred as to play such an important part in one's life, a form of religion would be nothing to a thoughtful soul. It was, therefore, wise on the part of the ancient people who called religion duty, or duty religion. For religion is not in performing a ceremony or a ritual; the true religion is the feeling or the sense of duty. Duty is not necessarily the purpose of life, but it is as the lighthouse in the port, which shows one, "Here is the landing place, here you arrive, here is your destination." It may not be the final destination, but still in duty one finds a road which leads one to the purpose of life.

It seems that, though the knowledge of duty is acquired after a child has come into the world, yet the child has also brought with him into the world the sense of duty. And according to the sense of duty which the child shows, he gives promise of a good future. A person may be most learned, capable, qualified, powerful, influential, and yet if he has no sense of duty, you cannot rely upon him. As soon as you find out that there is a living sense of duty in a person, you at once feel confidence; you feel you can depend upon that person. And this feeling that you get is greater than any other impression a person could make upon you; in this is all virtue and strength and power and blessing. You value a friend whom you can trust; you value a relation in whom you can have confidence. Therefore, all the qualifications that man possesses seem to be on the surface, but beneath them there is one spirit which keeps them alive and makes them really valuable, and that spirit is the sense of duty. Those who have won the confidence of the whole (and there have been few in the history of the world who have won the trust of a multitude), those have proved to be really great; and it was accomplished by developing the sense of duty.

Now there are five different aspects in considering the question of duty. One aspect is to think of our duty towards the younger generation: towards children, our own children and those of others. To those who are younger in years we have a certain duty. To our friends, our acquaintances who have not yet evolved enough to see things as we do, there is also our duty. And if once one were conscious of this, one would find many things in life which require one's attention, and if they are overlooked one has really neglected one's duty. Whatever be our position in life, rich or poor, we still have a kingdom, and that kingdom is our self. We can help and serve in thought and deed, in word or in action needed at a certain moment. By every attention given to this question, by everything done in this respect, however material it might seem outwardly, a religious action is performed.

Another aspect of duty is the duty to our fellow-creatures; to one's co-workers, to the friends and acquaintances with whom one comes in contact in everyday life, with whom one does not have the feeling of older or younger, or any difference. We have a duty towards them. In the first place, to study the psychology of their nature; if we have to teach them, not to teach them as a teacher;

if we help them, not to help them as a benefactor; whatever help we give them, to do it in such a way that even we ourselves do not know about it. That is the best way of serving. For even to do good is most difficult if we do not know how to do it. If we are able to win the affection of our fellow men and to do some little service unassumingly, without the thought of appreciation or return, we have certainly performed a religious action.

The third aspect of duty is towards those advanced in years. To have sympathy for them, to have respect for their age, for the experience they have gained; even if they have not that qualification or learning which we have, it does not matter. Perhaps they know something more which we do not know. We cannot learn all things; we cannot know all things. There are things that experience teaches; there are things that age brings to them. If in a person, however intelligent and capable, that sentiment for age, that respect for his elder brother, that consideration for those who are advanced in years, his mother, father, brother or sister, teacher or friend, has not yet been born, he has not yet known religion. For in this is the foundation of religion.

It is said that a child of the Prophet one day called a slave by his name and the Prophet heard it. The first thing he said was, "My child, call him Uncle; he is advanced in age." Besides, there is a psychological action and reaction; those who have reached the ripened condition of life have arrived at a stage when their good will for the younger ones comes as a treasure, a living treasure. Sometimes the intoxication of life, one's absorption in worldly activities, that ever-growing energy which one experiences in youth, one's power and position and knowledge and capability, make one overlook this. But if an opportunity is lost, it is lost; it will never come again. We are all in this world travellers, and those near to us or those whom we see, they are the ones we meet on our journey. And therefore it is an opportunity of thinking of our duty towards them. Neither shall we be with them always, nor will they be with us. Life is a dream into which we are thrown, a dream which is ever-changing. Therefore an opportunity lost of considering our little obligations in our everyday life which form part of our duty, is like forgetting our religion.

The fourth aspect of duty is our duty to the state, to the nation, and to all those personalities whom we find therein, above or below: a king, a president, a commander, an officer, a secretary, clerk, porter, or servant; a spiritual source of upliftment, such as a church, a spiritual center and personalities connected with it, priest or clergyman; one's counsellor or teacher. Towards all these we have a duty, and in observing this alone we accomplish Dharma, our duty.

And the fifth aspect of our duty is to God, our Creator, Sustainer, and the Forgiver of our shortcomings. One might say, "We have not desired to come here; why were we sent here?" But it is said in a moment of disturbance of mind. If the mind is still, if a person shows good sense he will say, "Even if there were nothing else given to me in life, to be allowed to live under the sun is the greatest privilege." One says, "I toil and I earn money, and that is my living which I make. Who is to be given credit for it?" But it is not the money we eat; what we eat is not made in the bank. It is made by the sun and the moon and the stars and the earth and water, by nature which is living before us. If we had not air to breathe, we should die in a moment. These gifts of nature which are before us, how can we be thankful enough for them? Besides, as a person develops spiritually he will see that it is not only his body that needs food, but also his mind, his heart, his soul; a food that this mechanical world cannot provide. It is the food that God alone can give, and it is therefore that we call God the Sustainer. Furthermore, at a time when there was neither strength in us nor sense enough to earn our livelihood, at that time our food was created. When one thinks of this, and when one realizes that every little creature, a germ or worm that no one ever notices, also receives its sustenance, then one begins to see that there is a Sustainer; and that Sustainer we find in God, and towards Him we have a duty.

In spite of the justice and injustice we see on the surface of this world, a keen insight into one's own life will teach that there is no comparison between our faults and our good actions. The good actions, in comparison to our faults, are so few that if we were judged we should not have one mark to our credit. It does not mean that justice is absent there. It only means, what is behind law? Love. And what is love? God. And how do we see God's love, in what form? In many forms; but the most beautiful form of the love of God is His compassion, His divine forgiveness. Considering these things, we realize that we have a duty towards God.

It is these five different aspects of duty that, when we consider them and when we begin to live them, begin to give us the sense of a religious life. Religious life does not mean living in a religious place or in a cemetery or in a church, or in a religion that is all outward. The true religion is living and being conscious of the sense of duty that we have towards man and towards God. Someone may say, "How is it that a person who lives a life of duty, is often void of love, beauty, and poetry?" I do not think that duty has anything to do with depriving a person of love, harmony, and beauty. On the other hand, when the real spirit of duty wakens in a person, it is that which begins poetry. If there is a beautiful poem to be found, if there is anyone who has experienced love, harmony, and beauty, it is that person who understands the sense of duty. For instance, a new-born child: he has come from heaven, he is as happy as the angels, he is beautiful in infancy, he is an expression of harmony, and he is love himself; and yet he does not know love, harmony, and beauty. Why?

Because he does not yet know duty. But the moment the spirit of duty is wakened in a person poetry begins; and when poetry is begun, then love, harmony and beauty manifest to his view fully.

But one might ask, "Duty is responsibility; how can we be delivered from this great load of responsibility?" In two ways: he is already delivered of this load of responsibility who has no sense of responsibility. He does not want to take it up as his responsibility. He is quite happy; he does not mind what anybody thinks of him; he does not mind whom he hurts nor whom he harms; he minds his own business quite happily. He is delivered already. And if there is another deliverance, it is attained by living the life of duty; it is by going through it. For going through it will raise a person higher and higher, till he rises above it, and he will be most thankful that he has gone through the path of duty, the sacred path of Dharma; for by this finally he has been able to arrive at a stage of realization in which alone is to be found the purpose of life.

Life on Earth

Man has not been born on the earth to eat and drink and sleep, as all the lower creatures do, but he has been born on earth to learn how to use this fertile earth to its best advantage, how to appreciate the treasures this earth holds, and how to use them rightly. And it is thus that man becomes connected with the earth. The soul comes from heaven and its connection with the earth has in it a secret which leads towards the purpose of life. It is easy for a person to say, "We come from heaven and we are bound for heaven, and while dwelling for some days on this earth what is there that belongs to us? Besides, is it not all sinful, all that belongs to the earth? It is better to escape from it and leave all this which in the end is worthless." This is true, but it is not natural. The natural thing is to be able to appreciate all that is created on the earth. We appreciate it by valuing it. The beauty of the mineral kingdom which one sees in the jewels and gems, each one better than the other, is not something to be overlooked; to see that through a stone the divine light shines, making that stone incomparably greater than the pebbles on the road; to see what a wonderful phenomenon it is that even in a stone God shows His beauty.

The perfection of flowers, the sweetness of fruits, the delicate flavors of different objects of the earth do not seem to have been created for no purpose. In gold, in silver, in metal, in all objects we see in the world, there seems to be a certain purpose to be accomplished here. And the one who is afraid of it, afraid that it will take hold of him, runs away. And what does he do? He loses both, heaven and earth. He has left heaven already; he is leaving the earth. The one who holds it is buried under it. It grows on him and swallows him; that is another aspect of the earth and its law. But the one who understands the purpose of the earth and of its treasures uses them to the best advantage not only for himself but for his fellow men. That is the person who lives in this world fulfilling the purpose of his life.

Do we only see spiritual persons among those who are sitting in the caves of the Himalayas? Do we not see wonderful personalities in the midst of the world? Very often people say that a person who has struggled along all through his life with business and industry and worldly things has become hardened. But I think that the one who has really gained victory over the earth, who really has made a success which can be called a success, has learned something from it. It is not everyone who becomes successful in earthly affairs; it is one among many. And the one who comes to the top has had his difficulties, has had his problems; his endurance, his patience have been tested. He has gone through a sacrifice. He has understood human nature, standing in the midst of the crowd. If he has not read one book of philosophy, if he has not meditated one day, still he has arrived at a plane, at an understanding, where he knows something worth knowing. I considered myself most privileged at times when I had conversations with businessmen, with people who were always busy with the things of the earth and who had really reached the top; and I have simply marvelled to think that instead of hardening them it has softened their nature to some extent, it has given them a sense which can come by spiritual understanding, which is a religious sense; it has developed a fairness in them. By having gone through this world of injustice and having seen what one sees in the business world, they have come to a point of honesty where one begins to see life from a different point of view. And besides that, if anyone ever comes forward and says, "For a philanthropic person, for the good of humanity, I give so many millions for education, for the hospitals," it is they who do it. And I would very much wonder if a recluse who has always kept himself away from money, if he had the charge of many millions, would like to part with any. The point is, whether a person is earthly or heavenly, to be true to the purpose of life is the first moral we have to learn. For even an earthly purpose, however material it may seem, will prove in the end to be a stepping-stone even if one had nothing but that ideal before one.

No doubt all things pertaining to the earth have their influence upon a person. It hardens one, it makes one's heart cold and takes away that tender sentiment that one has towards one's dear ones, towards those whom one loves and on whom one depends, towards one's fellow men. It makes one more and more greedy, and greed makes one unjust. Man becomes covetous, and his cup of desire is never filled; he is never satisfied. The more that comes, the less there seems to be there. Nevertheless, if one does not go through this experience, which is man's test, and one travels by another way, then one has given up a great experience, an experience which really makes the soul noble. A person whom you would otherwise not have understood for ten years, you can understand in one day as soon as there is a question of money. It at once brings out what is hidden in that person.

This shows that it is a great test, a test through which one should go, and one should experience a path which is a part of one's destiny. Therefore the religious or spiritual man, even if he looks with contempt at a person engaged in the things of the earth, should know that it is his path, and a path which is his religion. If he proves to be honest in his business dealings, if he keeps his heart open to those dear and near to him, those to whom he has his obligations, if he keeps the flame of his love of mankind lit in his heart through it all, in the end he will arrive at a stage where he is greater than a saint, because he has kept alive the flame of saintliness through a continually blowing wind.

We must not always try to get away from difficulties, for in the end we shall not manage to get away from them. Life on earth is difficult, and with the evolution of the earth it will be even more difficult; every day it will become more difficult. We can picture the world as a human being, a human being making his life from infancy to age. In infancy, however dependent the infant is, yet he is a sovereign, quite happy in the arms of the mother, in the care of the father; nothing to worry him, nothing to trouble him; there is no attachment, no enmity, he is as happy as the angels in heaven. And so was the beginning of the world, the beginning of the human race especially. The Hindus have called it the Golden Age. And then comes youth, youth with its spring and delicacy and with its responsibility. Youth has its own trials, its own experiences, its own fears. This unsettled condition of the earth was called by the Hindus the Silver Age, which means the age with all the treasures, the springtime of youth. But then as life goes forward, the world comes to the stage of what may be called middle age, the age of cares, of worries, of anxieties, of responsibilities. The Hindus have named it the Copper Age. As life advances, so it has much to bear. A fruitful tree, with the weight of fruits, becomes bent, and so it is with progress. With every step forward there are obligations and responsibilities.

Nevertheless, we must not look forward to difficulties. There is one thing that saves us, and that is hopefulness. And this about which I have spoken is the metaphysical part. What I am speaking about now is the psychological attitude we ought to have. Always hope for the best, and we certainly shall have the best. What we can do is to make ourselves strong enough to go through life on earth; and it is only by this strength of conviction that by whatever path we journey, we shall arrive at the spiritual goal; and whatever be our life, professional, industrial, commercial, it does not matter, we shall live religion, Nature's religion, turning our life into a religion, making of our life a religion. And so even with every earthly success, we shall be taking steps towards spiritual attainment.

The Enjoyment of Beauty

There are two different temperaments that we generally see in the world. One says, "I will not hear music on Sunday, it is a religious day. The liking for colors is emotional. Do not look at pictures; it excites." To enjoy any perfume, to like fragrance, he thinks is sensual. And then there is another temperament that feels the vibrations of the colors, that enjoys delicious food, that admires the straight line and the curve, that is touched and moved by music, that feels exalted by the beauty of nature. And what difference do we find in these two temperaments? The difference is that one is living and the other lacks life. One is living because he is responsive to all aspects of beauty, whether the beauty appeals to his eyes or ears, or to his sense of taste or touch. The other one is incapable of enjoying it.

Man in his innermost being is seeking for happiness, for beauty, for harmony; and yet, by not responding to the beauty and harmony which is before him, he wastes his life, which is an opportunity for him to experience and to enjoy. What self-denial is it to deny the divine beauty which is before us? If we deny ourselves the divine beauty which surrounds us, then the beauty which is within will not unfold itself. Because the condition is that the soul is born with its eyes open outwardly, it does not see the life within. The only way of wakening to the life within, which is most beautiful, is first to respond to the beauty outside. This world with all its unlimited beauty, nature with its sublimity, personalities with divine immanence, if we ignore all this then why have we come, and what have we accomplished here? The person who ignores it turns his back on something which he is continually seeking for. He is his own enemy. By this way he cannot be spiritual, he cannot be religious; by denying himself all that is beautiful around him he cannot be exalted. For if beauty within was the only purpose of life, God would not have created man and sent him on earth.

Besides this, it is the vision of the beauty on the earth which awakens the vision of the beauty which is in the spirit. Some say that it is sensuous and that it deprives one of spiritual illumination. It would, if a person were to be wholly absorbed in it and were to live only in it, and did not think that there was something else besides. Because the beauty which is outside no doubt has a transitory character, it is passing and therefore it is not dependable. For the one who depends upon this beauty and has become absorbed in it and by doing so has turned his back on that beauty which is everlasting, for that person this is certainly wrong. But at the same time, no soul has ever arrived at beholding the vision of the spiritual beauty which is to be found within, without being awakened to the beauty which is external.

One might think that a child who dies very young cannot come to that spirituality through the beauty of life. I will say that the child is sometimes more responsive to beauty than a grown-up person, because a grown-up person has developed in himself a pessimistic attitude, a prejudice; and by that prejudice he is incapable of seeing that beauty which a little child can see and appreciate. For instance, when we look at a person we make a barrier of our preconceived idea before we look at him. A child, an angel on earth, looks at him as it would look at its best friend.

It has no enmity, no preconceived idea about anyone, and therefore the child is open to beauty. A child does not know that the fire burns; the child only knows that the fire is beautiful. And therefore the child is so blessed that every moment of its life it lives in a complete vision of beauty. And so long as that state lasts a soul is in the Garden of Eden; it is exiled from that day when the soul has touched the earthly human nature. Someone may say, "If within the soul there was not the capability of appreciating beauty, how would it be able to perceive the external beauty first?" The soul has, born in itself, a natural craving for beauty. It is a lack in the person if he does not seek it rightly. Is there any person who is not a lover of beauty, who is not capable of appreciating it? He denies himself that beauty which he could have admired freely.

One may ask, "Is the quality of appreciating beauty more spiritual than the craving for knowledge?" I would say in answer, where does knowledge come from? Knowledge comes by observation; observation comes by love of beauty. The first thing is that the flower attracts one's attention, and then one begins to find out where the flower comes from, what is its nature and character, what benefit it is, how to rear this plant. The first thing is that one is attracted by its beauty; the next thing is, one wants to find out its nature. From this comes all knowledge.

There is a kind of artificial learning, not a natural learning, which may be called time-saving. Someone says, "Now people have learned in their lives and they have discovered things for us and written about them in books, and I must learn that by reading the book." But he does not know that he has not learned what that person who has written the book has learned. For instance, someone who has read the books of Luther Burbank, if he has read fifty books on horticulture, has not learned what Luther Burbank had learned. For he had more experiments for himself; he had been in the garden; his joy was such that he could not explain. No doubt another person will benefit by what he has given, but another person cannot enjoy what he has enjoyed, unless he pursues the same course.

In my explanation, spiritual means living. A spiritual person who is awakened to the beauty of poetry, who is quick to admire the subtlety of the poetry, who is appreciative of the beauty of melody, of harmony, who can enjoy art and be exalted by the beauty of nature, who lives as a living being, not as one dead, it is that person who may be called spiritual. And you will always find the tendency of spiritual personalities is to be interested in every person in their lives. That is the sign that they are living. A person who is shut up in himself closes himself; he has made four walls around himself. That can be his grave; he is buried in it. The person who is living, naturally sees all; and, as he sees all, he sympathizes with all, he responds to all, he appreciates all in everybody; and in this way he wakens in himself the sublime vision of the immanence of God.

Desire and Perfection

There is a continual desire working in every soul to see things perfect according to one's own conception of perfection; and as one goes on with this desire, observing, analyzing and examining things and beings, one becomes disappointed and disheartened, and besides one becomes impressed with the lack one sees in conditions, in persons, in beings. No doubt there is one thing that keeps one alive, and that is hope; if it is not right today, tomorrow it will become right; if it is not perfect just now, after some time it will be perfect. And so on this hope one lives, and if one has given up this hope then life ends. If one is disappointed in one person, one thinks that in another person one can find all that one expects; if under one condition one is disappointed, one hopes for another condition which will bring about the fruitfulness of one's expectations. The teachers and the prophets have pointed upward. That symbolically teaches us that it is in looking forward to something more hopeful that one lives, and that is the secret of happiness and peace. But once a person develops one idea that there is nothing to look forward to in life, he has finished living.

You will see around you that those who live and those who help others to live are the ones who look forward in life with hope and courage. It is they whom one can call living beings. But there are others who do not live, for they do not look forward to the life before them; they have lost hope. In order to be saved, they will cling to the hopeful, but if the hopeful also had a limited hope then they would sink with them. Such souls are as dead. Those who lack hope and courage in life lack a sort of energy of spirit. The standard of health as the physician understands it today is an energetic, robust body, but the standard of real health is the health of the spirit; not only the body is living, but the spirit is living. The one who is open to appreciate all, to feel encouraged to do all that comes in his way; who feels joyful, hopeful, ready to accomplish his duty, ready to suffer pain that comes to him; ready to take up responsibility, ready to answer the demands as a soldier on the battlefield—this one shows the spirit hidden within the body. If that condition is lacking, then a person is lacking perfect health and must be helped to gain that energy.

Hopelessness can be overcome by faith—in the first place by faith in God, at the same time knowing that the soul draws its power from the divine source. Every thought, every impulse, every wish, every desire comes from there, and in its accomplishment there is the law of perfection. And in that way a person feels hopeful. But when one thinks, "What shall I do? what am I to do? how am I to do it? I have not got the means; I have not got the resources; I have not got the inspiration to do it"; when one is pessimistic about things, one destroys the roots of one's desires, because by denying one casts away that which could otherwise have been attained. For in recognizing the divine Father in God, one becomes conscious of one's divine heritage, and that there is no lack in the divine Spirit, and therefore there is no lack in life. It is only a matter of time. If one builds one's hope in God, there is an assured fulfillment of it.

It is very interesting to study the lives of the great in the world. We find that some great people have almost arrived at the fulfillment of their undertakings and just before they had reached the goal they have lost it; and there have been some great people who have attained the ultimate success in whatever they have undertaken. You will always find that the souls of the former kind are the ones who were gifted with great power and yet lacked faith, while the others were gifted with the same power, and that power was supported by faith. A person may have all the power there is, all the wisdom and inspiration, but if there is one thing lacking, which is faith, he may attain to ninety-nine degrees of success and yet may miss that very one whose loss in the end takes away all that was gained previously. There is a saying in English, "all's well that ends well," as the Eastern people say in their prayers, "make our end good"; for if there be a difficulty just now we do not mind, because there will be success, the real success, in its completion.

It is in this outlook that we can find the secret of the idea of Paradise, the paradise which has been spoken of by the elevated souls of all times, and in all scriptures you will find a reference to paradise is a hope in the hereafter, a hope in the future. When someone finds that there is no justice to be found in life, or beauty is lacking, or wisdom is not to be found anywhere, and goodness is rare, then he begins to think that justice must exist somewhere; all beauty, wisdom, goodness must be found somewhere, and that is in paradise. He thinks, "It exists somewhere. I shall find it one day; if not in this life, I shall find it in the hereafter; but there is a day when the fulfillment of my hope, my desire, will come." This person lives; and this person lives to see his desire fulfilled. For in reality the lack that one finds in a person, in a thing, in an affair, in a condition, will not always remain. For all will be perfect, all must be perfect; it is a matter of time. And it is towards that perfection that we are all striving, and the whole universe is working towards the same goal. It is in that perfection that the thinkers and the great ones of all times have seen their paradise, because through man it is God who desires. Therefore it is not the desire of man, it is the desire of God, and has its fulfillment.

Life on the physical plane is limited, but the power of desire is unlimited. If desire finds a difficulty in fulfillment on the physical plane, yet it retains its power just the same; and the desire is powerful enough to accomplish its work, rising above or freed from this physical plane of limitations. It is therefore that a hope in paradise has been given by the great ones. In the Bible it is said in the Lord's Prayer, "Thy Will be done on earth as it is in Heaven," which means that there is a difficulty even for the Will of God to be done on earth, because of limitations. Therefore there is a difficulty for the fulfillment of every person's wish, even though in the wish of every person there is the wish of God. Though there is a difficulty in the physical world, because this is the world of limitations, yet the desire knows no limitations. But desire becomes beaten up, enfeebled, worn out, by continually facing the limitations of this physical plane. If hope sustains and faith cherishes it, there is no desire, either smaller or greater, which will not be fulfilled one day, if not on earth, in heaven. It is that fulfillment of desire which may be called paradise.

"Heaven is the vision of fulfilled desire, and hell the shadow of a soul on fire." Someone went to Ali and asked him, "You tell us about the hereafter and the granting of desire there. What if it be not true? Then all our efforts on this earth would be wasted." "Nothing will be wasted," said Ali. "If it were not fulfilled, then you and I would have the same experience. But if it be true that there is a paradise, then you will be the loser and I shall gain, for I have prepared for it and you have scoffed at the idea."

But those who wait for a paradise in the hereafter, or for all things to come true in the hereafter, may look at it differently: that the power of desire is so great that one must not allow it to wait for the hereafter. If there is something that can be accomplished today, we need not wait for it to be accomplished tomorrow. For life is an opportunity, and desire has the greatest power, and perfection is the promise of the soul. We seek perfection, because perfection is the ultimate aim and the goal of creation. The source of all things is perfect; our source is perfect, our goal is perfect; and therefore every atom of the universe is working towards perfection, and sooner or later it must arrive at perfection consciously. If it were not so, you would not have read in the Bible, "Be ye perfect as your Father in heaven is perfect."

Rising Above Limitation

A person who is conscientious in his duty, who attaches great importance to his ideal, is apt to say to the person who is engaged in money-making, "*You* are striving for earth's treasures, *I* am performing what I consider my duty." The person who is making his way towards heaven, who is holding paradise in his expectations, is inclined to say to the pleasure-seeker, "*You* are absorbed in life's momentary pleasures, *I* am working for the life to come." But the person who is busy money-making can also say to the one who is conscientious of duty and the one possessing a high ideal, "If you had to go through the experience which I have to, you would see in this too something worthwhile." And the seeker after paradise may also be answered by the pleasure-seeking soul, as Omar Khayyan said:

> Oh my Beloved, fill the cup that clears
> Today of past regrets and future fears.
> Tomorrow? Why, tomorrow I may be
> Myself with yesterday's sev'nty-thousand years!

This shows that all these seekers after different things, seekers after wealth, seekers after ideal, seekers after pleasure, and seekers after paradise, must have their own ways; they will at the same time have their own reasons. One may contradict another, although they are all making their way to the goal. Sooner or later, with more or less difficulty, they must arrive at the purpose of life.

One may ask, "Which of these four ways is the best way of arriving at the purpose of life?" That way is best which suits you best. The way of one person is not for another person, although man is always inclined to accuse another person of doing wrong, believing that he himself is doing right. In reality, the purpose is beyond all these four things. Neither in paradise nor in the ideal, neither in pleasures nor in the wealth of this earth is that purpose accomplished. That purpose is accomplished when a person has risen above all these things. It is that person then who will tolerate all, who will understand all, who will assimilate all things, who will not feel disturbed by things which are not in accordance with his own nature or the way which is not his way. He will not look at them with contempt, but he will see that in the depth of every being there is a divine spark, which is trying to raise its flame towards the purpose.

When a person has arrived at this stage, he has risen above the limitations of the world. Then he has become entitled to experience the joy of coming near to the real purpose of life. It is then that in everything that he says or does, he will be accomplishing that purpose. Whether outwardly, to the world, it would seem the right thing or the wrong thing, he is accomplishing his purpose just the same. For instance, I have seen holy souls taking part in a religious procession which was made perhaps by the ordinary people; thousands of people making out of it a kind of fete-day, playing music and dancing before the procession, singing and enjoying themselves; and among them most highly developed souls, who might be called saints, doing the same thing, all following the procession. One might wonder if they needed it. Is it good for their evolution, or by this do they gain any satisfaction? No; and yet it does not hinder their progress. They are what they are; they know what they know. A grown-up person by playing with the children does not become a child. He only adapts himself for the time being to the party of children. Did not Solomon sit on a throne and wear a crown? Did it make him less wise, or did it rob him of spirituality? No, for he was above it. For him the throne or crown was nothing but acting in a play for the time being; it was a pastime. We read that Krishna took part in the battle described in the *Mahabharata*. A self-righteous man would look upon it as a cruel thing and would be ready to condemn Krishna for this. But behind that outward appearance, what was there? There was the highest realization of love, of wisdom, of justice, of goodness; the soul had reached its culmination. An ordinary person, even today, will judge it; he would ask how it could be a great Master who led the army of Arjuna.

We come to understand by this that the further we go the more tolerant we become. Outward things matter little; it is inward realization which counts. However sacred duty may be, however high may be the hope of paradise, however great the happiness one may experience in the pleasures of the earth, however much satisfaction one may find in earthly treasures, the purpose of life is in rising above all things. It is then that the soul will have no discord, no disagreement with others. It is then that that natural attitude of the soul will become tolerant and forgiving. The purpose of life is fulfilled in rising to the greatest heights and in living to the deepest depths of life; in widening one's horizon, in penetrating life in all its spheres; in losing oneself, and in finding oneself in the end. In the accomplishment of the purpose of life the purpose of creation is fulfilled. Therefore in this fulfillment it is not that man attained, but that God Himself has fulfilled His purpose.

The Knowledge of Self

If a Sufi is asked what was the purpose of this creation, he will say that the Knower, the only Knower, wanted to know Himself, and there was only one condition of knowing Himself, and that was to make Himself intelligible to His own Being. For Intelligence itself is a Being, but Intelligence is not known to itself. Intelligence becomes known to itself when there is something intelligible. Therefore the Knower had to manifest Himself, thus becoming an object to be known. And by this knowledge the Knower arrives at perfection. It does not mean that the Knower lacked perfection, for all perfection belonged to the Knower; only He became conscious of His perfection. Therefore it is in the consciousness of perfection that lies the purpose of this whole manifestation.

The Sufis say, "God is Love." That is true, but the Love was not sufficient. The Love had to make an object to love in order to see its own nature, to experience its own character, to fathom its own mystery, to find its own joy. For instance, the seed has in it the leaf and the flower and the fruit; but the fulfillment of the purpose of that seed is that it is put in the ground, that it is watered, that a seedling springs up and is reared by the sun; it brings forth its flowers and fruits. This is the fulfillment of that seed which already contained in itself the fruit and flower. A person who does not see the reason of all this is in the seed state; his mind is in the state of a seed which has not yet germinated, which has not yet produced its seedling, which has not yet experienced the springing of the plant.

No sooner does the soul begin to unfold and experience in life the purpose which is hidden within itself, than it begins to feel the joy of it; it begins to value the privilege of living; it begins to appreciate everything; it begins to marvel at everything. For in every experience, good or bad, it finds a certain joy, and that joy is in the fulfillment of life's purpose. That joy is not only experienced in pleasure but even in pain, not only in success but also in failures; not only in the cheerfulness of the heart but even in the breaking of the heart there is a certain joy hidden. For there is no experience which is worthless; and specially for that soul who is beginning to realize this purpose, there is no moment wasted in life. For under all circumstances and in all experiences that soul is expecting the purpose of life.

This may be understood by a little example. A jinn wanted to amuse himself, but when about to do so, he brought upon himself a problem. For the jinn was powerful, and he said to himself, "Be thou a rock"; and the jinn turned into a rock. But by becoming a rock he began to feel solitary; left in the wilderness he felt the loss of action, loss of movement, lack of freedom and lack of experience. This was a terrible captivity for the jinn. For many years this jinn had to have patience, to change into something else. It did not mean that through the rock he did not realize life. For even the rock is living, even the rock is changing, and yet a rock is a rock; a rock is not a jinn. It was through the patience of thousands of years that the rock began to wear out and crumble into earth. And when, out of that earth, the jinn came out as a plant, he was delighted that he had grown out as a tree. The jinn was so pleased to find that out of a rock he could become a plant, that he could enjoy the air more fully, that he could swing in the wind. He smiled at the sun and bathed happily in the rain. He was pleased to bring forth fruits, to bring forth flowers.

But at the same time his innate desire was not satisfied. It kept him hoping some day to break through this captivity of being rooted in a particular place and of this limitation of movement. For a long, long time the jinn was waiting to come out of this limitation. This was better, yet it was not the experience the jinn desired. But at last the fruit became decayed and part of that fruit turned into a little worm. The jinn was even more delighted to feel that he could move about; that now he was no longer rooted to one place and unable to move. And as this worm breathed and was in the sun, it grew wings and began to fly. The jinn was still more delighted to see that he could do this. From one experience to another he flew through the air and experienced the life of a bird, now sitting upon the trees, now walking on the earth. And as he enjoyed life on the earth more and more, he became a heavy bird. He could not fly; he walked. And this heaviness made him coarse, and he turned into an animal. He was most happy, for then he could oppose all the other animals that wanted to kill birds, because he was no longer a bird.

Through a process of gradual change, the jinn arrived at becoming man. And when a man, the jinn looked around and thought, "This is something that I was destined to be. Because now, as a jinn, I can see all these different bodies that I have taken in order to become more free, in order to become perceptive, sensitive, in order to know things, in order to enjoy things more fully. There could not have been any vehicle more fitting than this." And yet he thought, "Even this is not a fitting vehicle, because when I want to fly I have no wings, and I feel like flying also. I walk on the earth, but I have not the strength of the lion. And now I feel that I belong to heaven, and where it is I don't know." This made the jinn search for what was missing, until in the end he realized, "I was a jinn, just the same, in the rock, in the plant, in the bird, in the animal; but I was captive and my eyes were veiled from my own being. It is by becoming man that I am now beginning to see that I was a jinn. And yet I find in this life of man also a great limitation, for I have not that freedom of expression, that freedom of movement, that life which is dependable, that knowledge which is reality." And then this thought itself took him to his real domain, which was the jinn life; and there he arrived with the air of the conqueror, with the grandeur of the sovereign, with the splendor of a king, with the honor of an emperor, and realizing, "After all, I have enjoyed myself, I have experienced though I have suffered, and I have known Being, and I have become what I am."

The Knower manifested as man in order that He might become known to Himself, and now, what may man do in order to help the Knower to fulfill this purpose? Seek continually an answer to every question that arises in his heart. Of course, there are different types of minds. There is one mind that will puzzle and puzzle over a question, and trouble himself for something which is nothing, and will go out by the same door by which he has come in. That person will trouble himself and will wreck his own spirit, and will never find satisfaction. There is no question which has not its answer somewhere. The answer is nothing but an echo of the question, a full echo. And therefore one must rise above this confused state of mind which prevents one from getting the answer from within or from without to every question that arises in one's heart. In order to become spiritual, one need not perform miracles. The moment one's heart is able to answer every question that rises in one's heart, one is already on the path. Besides, the thing that must be first known, one puts off to the last, and that which must be known at the last moment, one wants to know first. It is this which causes confusion in the lives of many souls.

The words of Christ support this argument: "Seek ye first the kingdom of God, and all these things will be added unto you." This is the very thing one does not want to seek; one wishes to find anything else but this. And where is it to be found? Not in the knowledge of another person. In the knowing of self. If a person goes through his whole life most cleverly judging others, he may go on, but he will find himself to be more foolish at every step; at the end he reaches the fullness of stupidity. But the one who tries, tests, studies and observes himself, his own attitude in life, his own outlook on life, his thought, speech and action, who weighs and measures and teaches himself self-discipline, it is that person who is able to understand another better. How rarely one sees a soul who concerns himself with himself through life, in order to know! Mostly, every soul seems to be busily occupied with the lives of others. And what do they know in the end? Nothing. If there is a kingdom of God to be found anywhere it is within oneself.

And it is, therefore, in the knowledge of self that there lies the fulfillment of life. The knowledge of self means the knowledge of one's body, the knowledge of one's mind, the knowledge of one's spirit; the knowledge of the spirit's relation to the body and the relation of the body to the spirit; the knowledge of one's wants and needs, the knowledge of one's virtues and faults; knowing what we desire and how to attain it, what to pursue and what to renounce. And when one dives deep into this, one finds before one a world of knowledge which never ends. And it is that knowledge which gives one insight into human nature and brings one to the knowledge of the whole of creation. And in the end one attains to the knowledge of the divine Being.

The Fulfillment of Purpose

The purpose of life, in short, is that the only Being makes His oneness intelligible to Himself. He goes through different planes of evolution, or planes through which he arrives at different changes, in order to make clear to Himself His oneness. And as long as this purpose is not accomplished, the one and only Being has not reached His ultimate satisfaction, in which lies His divine perfection. One may ask, "Is man the only organ through which God realizes His oneness?" God realizes His oneness through His own nature. Since God is one, He always realizes His oneness through all things; through man He realizes His oneness in its fullness. For instance in the tree there are many leaves; although each leaf is different from the other leaf, yet the difference is not great. Then, coming to worms and germs and birds and animals, they are different one from another, and yet the difference is not so distinct as in man. And when one thinks of the great variety of the numberless human forms, and it seems that there is not one form exactly like another, this by itself gives us a living proof of the oneness of God. In order to show this, Asaf Nizam made a very beautiful verse: "You look at me with contempt. Yes, granted; I am contemptible. But will you show me such another contemptible creature?" Which means: even the worst person is incomparable; there is none like him. It is a great phenomenon, the proof of oneness, the proof of unity, that in the creation of God there is no competition, no one competes with the Creator. In other words, it would be unworthy if the only Being felt, "There is another like Me, even in the world of variety." He retains His pride even in the world of variety: "No one is like Me." Even in the worst guise He stands alone without comparison. One may ask, "Before man appeared on earth, did God realize His oneness?" But who can say how many times man appeared on the earth and disappeared from the earth? What we know is only one history of the planet. But how many planets exist? In how many millions of years have how many creations been created and how many withdrawn? All one can say is this: one cannot speak of God's past, present, and future; one can only give an idea which is the central idea of all aspects of truth; that it is the only Being who existed, who exists and who will exist; and all that we see are His phenomena.

There is a story that can explain the mystery of life's purpose. A fairy had a great desire to amuse herself, and she descended on the earth. And there children had made a little doll's house. She wanted to enter this doll's house, but it was difficult for her to enter into the space where only a doll can go. "Very well," she said, "I am going to try a different way. I will send one finger by this way, and another finger by another way, and each part by different ways." And she separated into different bits, and each bit of herself went through the different parts of the doll's house. And when one part met the other part, at once they rubbed against one another and that was very unpleasant. And there was a fight among the different parts: "Why are you coming my way? this was my way; why do you come my way?" Each part of the fairy's being interested itself in something, in some part of that doll's house. When that moment of interest passed, a certain part of her being wanted to go out of the doll's house. But then there were other parts of the being which were not willing to let it go. They were holding it: "You stay here; you cannot go out." Some parts of her being wanted to push out another part, but there was no way of putting it out. So it was a kind of chaos all through, one part not knowing that the other part belonged to the same fairy, and yet one part being attracted unconsciously to another part because they were parts of the same body. In the end the heart of the fairy moved about also. This heart soothed every other part, saying, "You have come from me. I wish to console, I wish to serve you. If you are troubled, I wish to take away your trouble. If you are in need of a service, I wish to render it you. If you lack anything, I wish to bring it for you. I know how much you are troubled in this doll's house." But some said, "We are not troubled at all; we are enjoying ourselves. If we are troubled, it is by the wish to remain here. Those who are troubled are others, not we." The heart said, "Well, I shall look at you, and I shall enjoy myself too. I shall sympathize with those who are troubled, I shall help those who are enjoying themselves." This was the one part of the fairy's being which was conscious of its atoms scattered all around. But the atoms were hardly conscious of it, although since they belonged to the same body, they were attracted to the heart, knowingly or unknowingly, consciously or unconsciously. Such was the power of the heart. It was just like the power of the sun, that turns the responsive flower into a sunflower. And so the power of the heart of the fairy turned every part of its being that responded into a heart. And as the heart was light and life itself, the doll's house could no longer hold the heart. The heart was experiencing the joy of the doll's house, but was at the same time able to fly away. The heart was delighted to find all its atoms belonging to its body, and it worked through all and through every part of its organs; so, in time, it turned every part of its organs into a heart also, by which this phenomenon was fulfilled.

God is love. If God is love, love is most sacred, and to utter this word without meaning is a vain repetition. The lips of a person to whom it means something are closed; he can say little. For love is a revelation in itself; no study is necessary, no meditation is needed, no piety is required. If love is pure, if the spark of love has begun to glow, then there is no need to go somewhere to gain spirituality; then spirituality is within. One must keep blowing the spark till it turns into a perpetual fire. The fire worshippers of old did not worship a fire which went out; they worshipped a perpetual fire. Where is that perpetual fire to be found? In one's own heart. The spark that one finds glowing for a moment and that then becomes dim, does not belong to heaven, for in heaven all things are lasting; it must belong to some other place. Love has become a word from the dictionary, a word which is used a thousand times in the day, which means nothing. To the one who knows what it means, love means patience, love means endurance, love means tolerance, love means sacrifice, love means service. All things such as gentleness, humility, modesty, graciousness, kindness, all are the different manifestations of love. It is the same to say, "God is all and all is God," as to say, "Love is all and all is love." And it is to find it, to feel it, to experience its warmth, and to see in the world the light of love, and to keep its glow, and to hold love's flame high as a sacred torch to guide one in one's life's journey; it is in this that the purpose of life is fulfilled. According to the common standard of life, a man with common sense is counted to be a right and a fit person. But, by a mystical standard, that person alone can begin to be right who is beginning to feel sympathy with his fellow man. For by the study of philosophy and mysticism, by the practices of concentration and meditation, to what do we attain? To a capability that enables us to serve our fellow men better.

Truth is simple. But for the very reason that it is simple, people will not take it; because our life on earth is such that for everything we value, we have to pay a great price and one wonders, if truth is the most precious of all things, then how can truth be attained simply? It is this illusion that makes everyone deny simple truth and seek for complexity. Tell people about something that makes their heads whirl round and round and round. Even if they do not understand it, they are most pleased to think, "It is something substantial; it is something solid; for it is an idea we cannot understand; it must be something lofty." But something which every soul knows, proving what is divine in every soul, for which it cannot help but know, that appears to be too cheap, for the soul already knows it. There are two things: knowing and being. It is easy to *know* truth, but most difficult to *be* truth. It is not in *knowing* truth that life's purpose is accomplished; life's purpose is accomplished in *being* truth.

Index